R. D. Laing & Anti-Psychiatry

R. D. Laing
& Anti-Psychiatry

Edited by
ROBERT BOYERS

PERENNIAL LIBRARY
Harper & Row, Publishers
New York, Evanston, San Francisco, London

First PERENNIAL LIBRARY edition published 1971.

STANDARD BOOK NUMBER: 06–0802294

Library of Congress Catalog Number: 74–168940

CONTENTS

PREFACE

BECAUSE OF ITS considerable intrinsic merit and also because of the extraordinary reception it has been given in the last few years, the work of R. D. Laing and the people around him surely deserves to be looked at in some detail. It is not altogether clear, of course just what sort of people one would ideally like to have examining so varied an output as Laing's, and there is good reason to wonder how he would himself want to be studied and located. He is, to be sure, a psychiatrist who first made his reputation by writing about his experience in treating psychotic, more specifically schizophrenic, patients, but his audience is hardly a professional one, and many who applaud his psychiatric researches can be said to know very little indeed either about mental illness or the history of psychoanalysis. Finally, one must suppose, it is as a culture critic, a new species of the psychiatrist as prophet, that Laing would be known, for he has chosen in his most recent writings to combine the examination of severe mental disorders with a more general assault on the foundations of western civilization. This is a project that has attracted a large following among philosophers, sociologists, literary people, religionists, practically any group interested in the history of ideas and the dimensions of contemporary culture, with the possible exception of Laing's own colleagues in the psychiatric profession. The range of contributors to this special issue of SALMA-GUNDI reflects this breadth of interest, I should say, though most of our authors, not just the psychiatrists among them, address Laing and his colleagues in a searching and critical way that "true believers" may not fully appreciate.

What follows, then, is a collection of materials that represents, I think, a good deal of the serious writing that has been addressed to Laing and the views with which he is usually identified. Some of the pieces have been selected because they sum up an articulate if not altogether legitimate view held by people of a particular persuasion. Others are included because they are broadly suggestive, if not always applicable to the precise questions we were concerned to address. At least one selection indicates the variety of mis-uses to which Laing can be put, even by those who are convinced of his importance. And the others, I think, establish a context for Laing and his work, attempt to set him in perspective, to establish his relationship to contemporary philosophy and psychiatry. It is a mixed bag, to be sure, but readable throughout, at the very least a useful starting point from which future inquiries can proceed.

I owe special thanks to Robert Orrill of Skidmore College, who has worked with me on this volume, and without whose help and advice it would not be as strong as we think it is.

ROBERT BOYERS
Saratoga Springs, N.Y.
March, 1971

R. D. Laing & Anti-Psychiatry

R. D. Laing: Self, Symptom and Society

BY PETER SEDGWICK

ANY SURVEY OF R. D. Laing's intellectual history must at present labor under certain special handicaps which we have tried to overcome without much hope of securing complete success. In the first place, Laing has performed much of his work in collaboration with others. In several of his published titles he appears as a coauthor with one or more other investigators, and some of his most important activity has been conducted side by side with two other existential psychiatrists, David Cooper and Aaron Esterson. While Laing of course must bear responsibility for work produced under his name, it is possible that special em-

Abbreviations in references to certain of Laing's works run as follows:
PE *The Politics of Experience and The Bird of Paradise*, Penguin edition, London, 1967.
NLR 'Series and Nexus in the Family', *New Left Review*, 15, May–June 1962.
DL 'The Obvious,' in *The Dialectics of Liberation* (ed. D. Cooper), Penguin, London, 1967.
FSC 'The Study of Family and Social Contexts in Relation to the Origin of Schizophrenia', in *The Origins of Schizophrenia* (ed. J. Romano), Amsterdam, 1967.

phases which may be detected in some of his joint works may be due to drafting provided by other collaborators. In the case of Esterson and Cooper particularly, it would be wrong to assume an identity of their views with Laing's, particularly in the works which they have written without his collaboration. Yet some mutual feedback and facilitation among these three writers has taken place at some stage in their psychoanalytic careers: Cooper's book *Psychiatry and Anti-Psychiatry* (1967) draws in part on a research project he conducted with Laing and Esterson; Esterson's *The Leaves of Spring* (1971) develops the research he conducted with Laing in *Sanity, Madness and the Family* (1964). Neither of Laing's existentialist colleagues has yet developed a sustained independent body of theory and research: they are neither merely his mouthpieces nor definitely his rivals. Our analysis will focus principally on the work of Laing himself.

The second difficulty arises from the relative dearth of biographical and autobiographical material dealing with Laing's theoretical development. There are few references in his own writing to the processes of his intellectual formation, and so far only one short biographical account of Laing's psychiatric pilgrimage has been published: an uncritical magazine article by an American admirer of his thought, which is informative without being at all searching on the stages that have led up to his present position.[1] The following outline has therefore been compiled, in the main, from the simple biographical and bibliographical data

[1] James Gordon, 'Who Is Mad? Who Is Sane?', *The Atlantic Monthly*, January, 1971, pp. 50–66.

provided on the dust-jackets and introductory pages of Laing's books, from the writings themselves, and from a very few ancillary published sources. The account is therefore open to correction either in general tendency or in partial detail, as further interview or other biographical material on Laing's development becomes available in the future.

Ronald Laing was born in 1927 in Glasgow, into a poor family: he attended state schools at both the primary and secondary stage, and from grammar school went on to read medicine at Glasgow University. Graduating in 1951, he acquired his first experience in psychiatric work in the British Army from 1951–53 (during what would have been his compulsory period of national military service). He worked in psychiatric medicine in Glasgow during the years 1953–6, in both a city mental hospital and the university's teaching department. During this period in Glasgow, he was accumulating observations on the behavior of chronic schizophrenics, and he apparently found that straightforward humane attention towards these neglected patients produced encouraging results. There is no record at present of any specific therapy, aimed at 'working through' schizophrenic difficulties, evolved by Laing at this stage, but the case-studies of *The Divided Self* are largely drawn from this Scottish sample.

In 1957 Laing moved to a post at the Tavistock Clinic in London, and completed his draft of *The Divided Self* in that year. For some time—it must have been over a considerable interval—he had been reading deeply in the literature of Freudian and neo-Freudian analysis, as well as among existentialist writers of both a psychiatric and a literary persuasion.

His use of the latter, in *The Divided Self*, is most unusual for a writer born and nurtured within Britain:
Laing was able to extract fertile insights into psychotic
and allied states of mind not only from clinicians of
the European phenomenological school (Binswanger,
Minkowski, Boss) but from philosophers and artists
(Sartre, Beckett, Tillich, Heidegger and even Hegel)
who dealt in non-pathological, indeed fundamental
situations of human existence. These concepts, in
partial conjunction with those of Freudian psychoanalysis, were applied to the knotted thought-processes
and behaviour of an obscure group of severely disturbed mental patients, who had been hitherto regarded as inaccessible to rational comprehension. One
of the most difficult of philosophies was brought to
bear on one of the most baffling of mental conditions,
in a manner which, somewhat surprisingly, helped to
clarify both. Existential philosophy, with its reputation of introverted cloudiness and speculative in-
discipline, was here set working in a concrete, practical and socially urgent context (the understanding
of the mentally ill); conversely, a major form of
psychosis was elucidated as a mental system possessing
lawful shape and sequence, comprehensible in existential terms as the outcome of rational strategies
adopted by the patient in the face of an ambiguous
and threatening personal environment. The clinical
descriptions in *The Divided Self* are set in a vivid,
clear style, often with an unobtrusive poetic skill, as
with the portrayal of the patient Peter's imaginary
smell ("the sooty, gritty, musty smell of a railway
waiting-room") or the images of desolation (like 'the
ghost of the weed garden' or 'the black sun') which

haunt the remnants of personality inside the young hebephrenic Julie.

As we begin *The Divided Self*, Laing informs us that he personally as a psychiatrist finds great difficulty in detecting the 'signs and symptoms' of illness in psychotic patients, since their behaviour actually appears to him as meaningful and appropriate rather than as odd or irrelevant: he then provides us with a stunning demonstration of what it means to understand patients as human beings rather than to classify them as instances of a disease. He gives a long quotation from the nineteenth-century psychiatrist Emil Kraepelin, who reports a spate of excited talk produced, in front of an audience of students, by a young catatonic patient in response to the doctor's questions. Laing is able to show very convincingly that through the adoption of only a slightly more sophisticated vantage-point on the patient's behaviour (i.e., by assuming that he is capable of discreetly ridiculing his interrogator), almost all of the young man's utterances, which have struck Kraepelin as the inconsequential ramblings of an organic disease-process, can be seen as comprehensible responses to the immediate situation he is in. What is particularly noteworthy about Laing's use of this example is the fact that Kraepelin's interpretation (or rather, non-interpretation) of his patient's behavior has been on record for decades in several countries as a classical casenote of psychiatry without anybody, apart from Laing in 1960, trying to re-value it.

The final chapter of *The Divided Self*, a thirty-page discussion of a single schizophrenic patient named Julie, introduces what will be a characteristic theme of Laing's theorising: an extended analysis of the patient's family background. Julie's relatives have developed a sequence of definitions about her which runs, throughout her lifetime, roughly as follows: as an infant, Julie was a 'good' girl; later, particularly in adolescence, she became a 'bad' girl negative and rejecting towards her parents; finally, in her present condition, her behaviour has overstepped even the bounds of 'badness' and she is 'mad', mentally ill, a patient. This sequence forms, in a number of ways, a prototype of the analysis of schizophrenia that will be developed by Laing in future works, where the Good-Bad-Mad progression will be seen as the usual pattern for the 'election' of an individual into the role of madness by other members of his insidiously demanding family.

However, this first book of Laing's can be distinguished from his later work on at least three counts. There is not a hint of mysticism in it, not the faintest implication that there is any further world of being beyond that described by natural and social science (phenomenology being included in the latter). There are no intimations of an innermost substance or grounding of all things and appearances, lying perhaps in some core of inner personal reality beyond the probings of the clinician. Laing has in fact been at deliberate pains, in his borrowings from the more opaque existentialist writers, to de-mystify their categories. The floating, abstracted concepts of Being and Not-Being, the whiff of dread before death and the hints of the supernatural, characteristic of Kierkegaard and Heidegger, are replaced by transparent, empirical usages. 'Ontological insecurity', which is said to lie at the heart of serious mental illness, simply means a profound personal uncertainty about the boundaries between the self and the world, which can be contrasted with the differentiation of ego-boundaries that takes place in normal child development. 'Being-in-the-world' means social interaction between persons, and Kierkegaard's 'Sickness Unto Death' is not the loneliness of the soul before God but the despair of the psychotic. Laing is, in short, naturalising the mystical elements of Continental existentialist thought.

In the case of a non-mystical existentialist like Sartre, he does not, of course, de-mystify: instead, he de-moralises, in the literal sense of removing a moral implication. Sartre's category of 'bad faith' is a description of the morally reprehensible evasions and excuses which the inauthentic individual uses to conceal the fact that he is free to choose his own life. Laing also uses the 'bad faith' concept, but only as the starting point of a morally neutral (because clinical) discussion of the 'false-self' system of inner personal defences erected by schizoid and hysteric patients.

The second cardinal feature of *The Divided Self* follows from this. Since there is no super-reality beyond the here and now of actual people, psychotic patients are not seen as the mystics or prophets of this super-sensory world. They are not, as in the later Laing, pioneers in the exciting endeavor of exploring "inner space". The only inner space that is ever even hinted at in the text amounts simply to the set of private coordinates which map out the fantasies of the psychotic. Material and interpersonal reality is the only one that we have got: consequently it forms the only standard against which the schizophrenic's expe-

rience can be tested. By this criterion, the schizophrenic has failed. He has fallen short of normal,
healthy sensory and emotional achievement: we are
left in no doubt, in fact, that he is in a thoroughly
bad way. Laing's reluctance to use the term 'disease'
(because of the implication that a 'disease' may have
discrete and impersonal 'symptoms') does not imply
any refusal to admit the disturbance, disorder and
profound alienation of the psychotic state.

Thirdly, this disturbed state is an attribute, at
least in large part, of the individual who presents himself as the patient. The condition called 'schizophrenia' by doctors is, in Laing's terms, still very
much like a *syndrome*, i.e., a set of characteristics
attributable to an individual, cohering typically and
meaningfully with one another and demarcating this
person from other conditions which are given different
names (such as 'hysteria' or 'normal development').
These defining, co-existing characteristics are not impersonal or subpersonal attributes of the individual,
isolated bits of his behavior like a high temperature or
a twitching leg. They are, on the contrary, deeply
personal in quality, occurring at the highest level of
integration of his behaviour, and related to his whole
fundamental orientation towards the world he perceives and moves in. All the same, 'schizophrenia'
is still a pattern of responses manifested by individual
persons: it has not vanished, as it does in the Laing
of five years hence, into the criss-cross of distorted
and distorting signals that typifies Laing's description
of the patient's family in which no individual is 'ill'
or 'schizophrenic' at all. Even the patient Julie of
the last chapter of *The Divided Self* (with all its detail of the family cross-press at work upon the patient)

is presented unmistakably as a disoriented individual operating with a complex repertoire of psychotic mental gambits. Her 'existence', and the modes in which she construes it, form the basic material of the narrative. By contrast, the schizophrenic girls of *Sanity, Madness and the Family* (1964) have no existence separable from that of their relatives: it is not they, but their families as a whole (though it is not always clear whether the girls themselves are included) who bear the basic attributes of the syndrome.

Laing has himself recognized this important shift in his thinking, and has even apologised for his earlier concentration on the individual patient. In the preface to the Pelican edition of *The Divided Self*, he has written that while the book did entail an understanding of the social context of the patient, 'especially the power situation within the family, today I feel that, *even in focusing upon and attempting to delineate a certain type of schizoid existence, I was already partially falling into the trap I was seeking to avoid.*' (Italics added.) If 'schizophrenia' is not a name which refers to any kind of a personal condition, then any attempt to describe it, even in very sensitive terms, must be a 'trap'. However, Laing has not gone on to explain how far he still regards as valid the mode of analysis practised in *The Divided Self*; it is doubtful how much of the early Laing could be reconciled with the radical scrutiny of the later books.

Laing leapt ahead of the theoretical framework of his first work very soon after it was published. In 1960 Jean-Paul Sartre issued the 750-page Volume One of *Critique de la Raison Dialectique*. The

Critique marked a sharp turn in Sartre's philosophy in that it purported to offer a new foundation for a general science of man, an 'anthropology' in the broadest sense which was intended to expose the basic nature of all thinking about society (including both sociological and historical thought), to outline the structural prerequisites for the formation of all social groups, and to state the laws governing the succession of one form of social organization by another. At this time Laing was settling into a research programme at the Tavistock dealing with interaction inside families (both with and without a schizophrenic member). Laing's research now tended to emphasise the interdependence between a subject's outlook on other people and their perception of him, especially within a closed social group: the main ideas of the *Critique*, with their emphasis on the formation and bonding of groups, lent themselves to assimilation by this theoretical perspective. Laing's next book *The Self and Others* (1961: revised as *Self and Others*, 1969) was a collection of essays partly reaching into his new preoccupation with family communication-patterns, partly developing his earlier analysis of the world-view of the psychotic patient. It owes no debt to Sartre's *Critique*, but in the following year Laing published an article ('Series and Nexus in the Family') [2] which, for its analysis of family interaction, drew on Sartre's newest ideas as well as on the early findings of the Tavistock project.

Laing's work was now becoming closely associated with that of Cooper and Esterson. Cooper had come to London following his medical training in Capetown

---

[2] In NLR (see reference above).

and was working as a doctor in British public mental hospitals, in one of which he was to supervise a research programme of treatment based on Laing's theory of schizophrenia. In the early Sixties he cooperated with Laing on a more literary enterprise, the production of a short book summarising for English readers the gist of Sartre's recent philosophical writing. The fruits of this intense labour of exegesis appeared in 1964 as *Reason and Violence: A Decade of Sartre's Philosophy*; it is a straightforward condensation of Sartre's *Critique* to one-tenth of its original length, so compressed as to be virtually incomprehensible to anyone seeking an introduction to Sartre's thought, and resembling a précis for private study rather than a popularisation for any intellectual audience. (Cooper's chapter in the book on Sartre's *Saint Genet* forms a clear contrast to the rest of the text in its liveliness and clarity.) At any rate, the intellectual collaboration of Laing and Cooper was well under way by the early Sixties, and was soon to result in more creative forms of common writing and therapeutic practice.

Esterson has been a shadowier figure, less associated with public occasions (such as the Dialectics of Liberation conference) than the other two. He had graduated in the same year as Laing from the Glasgow medical school, and then became a British general practitioner, a doctor on an Israeli kibbutz and a hospital psychiatrist back in Britain. In 1958 [3] there was published the report of a research collaboration between Laing and Esterson on the effects of 'collusive pairing' among members of a psychotherapeutic

[3] 'The Collusive Function of Pairing in Analytic Groups', *British Journal of Medical Psychology*, 1958, Vol. 31, pp. 117–23.

group: through the authors' existentially interpre-
tative glosses, the group comes through as an uneasy,
abrasive gathering of seven small-time con-men, but
the report does offer a foretaste of the later Laing-
Esterson work on human ploy and counterploy in
small social settings. Esterson joined Laing as a
research associate in the Tavistock family project,
publishing its main report with him in 1964. Like
Cooper, he has now gone into private practice as a
psychoanalyst, and has published his own book *The
Leaves of Spring: A Study In the Dialectics of Madness*, outlining his own position as an existential therapist.

On Laing's thinking in the Tavistock Clinic programme, influences now converged from two widely
separated quarters: Paris and Palo Alto, California.
Terror and engulfment had defined the schizophrenic's personal desolation in *The Divided Self*; engulfment and terror, exercised overtly or insidiously by
the familiars of the mental victim, were now specified
as crucial agents of human derangement both in
Sartre's essays in psychoanalysis and in the contributions of the Palo Alto school of schizophrenia-research headed by Gregory Bateson. (Research-groups
in the United States led by Theodore Lidz and Lyman
Wynne had come to a similar viewpoint on the origins of schizophrenia, but Bateson's approach must
be credited with some priority in time as well as a
more general influence.)[4] Sartre had produced case-

---

[4] A broad summary of the work of these research-groups,
with a careful separation of their distinct positions, is given
by Elliot G. Mishler and Nancy E. Waxler, 'Family Interaction Processes and Schizophrenia: A Review of Current
Theories', *International Journal of Psychiatry*, 1966, Vol. 22,

studies illustrating his new sensitivity to pathological
social pressures for some years before the *Critique*:
both the Genet of *Saint Genet* and the main character of the play *Altona*, the war-criminal Franz Von
Gerlach, are shown as experimenting with mental
strategies of self-definition in response to the ignomin-
ious labeling which society has affixed on them. Suffocating in a web of competitive, exploiting relationships, Genet and Franz both express and evade their
human responsibilities by performing intense mental
work (involving a criminal and homosexual career
in the former case and a sort of voluntary psychosis
in the latter) on the demeaning and degrading social
categories ('thief' or 'murderer') which they know
to constitute the terms of their appearance in the
eyes of others. The omnipotent unconditioned ego of
the old Sartre is now an 'alter ego': Self and Others
(to crib from Laing's terminology) now mutually
and ferociously impinge in the most critical areas of
personal choice. The parallelism between the vision
of human bestiality given in Franz's death-speech at
the end of *Altona* and the history of the normal social
bond outlined in the *Critique* has often been pointed
out: in both, man is a cruel, malignant species lying in
wait to thwart and destroy man himself. And the
Critique's version of human evolution is basically a
detailing of this social cannibalism, which is an in-
eluctable historical imperative in a world of scarcity,
accompanying all social transitions and transformations so long as individuals are replaceable by one
another in the struggle for scarce resources.

Laing's *New Left Review* article of 1962 makes use

pp. 375–413; reprinted in *Family Processes and Schizophrenia*
(E. G. Mishler and N. E. Waxler, eds.), New York, 1968.

of two of Sartre's basic group-categories, applying
them in the context of family behaviour. The *Critique*
visualizes an initial, minimal stage of group-forma-
tion in which the members share a common goal but
do not depend on each other for its practical achievement: they may, however, fabricate a crude sort of
group-identity through their awareness of one another's behaviour, or by being able to name a single
target as the subject of their separate hostilities. A
bus-queue, a bunch of anti-Semites and the world's
system of stock-exchanges are examples of this type of
group, which Sartre terms a *series*. A deeper and more
solid form of social unity is attained in the *bonded
group*, whose members each take a decision or 'pledge'
before the others to join together in linked activity for
the achievement of the common group-goal: revolutionary cells, football-teams and lynch-mobs are examples of bonded groups. The basis for this fusion
is always *terror*, registered within each individual as
the fear of what the other group-members will do to
him if he secedes or betrays.

Laing describes two family-patterns which cor-
respond to Sartre's identification of human groups.
There is one domestic situation which is essentially a
'series'; the members of such a family lack any personal concern for one another though they may
make a great display of concern for the likely effects
of scandal, thereby showing that the basis for their
group's existence lies in an anticipation of 'what the
neighbours will say' rather than in any shared relationships within the home. Laing also describes
a family-constellation, termed a 'nexus', which like
Sartre's bonded group is held together by fear,
anxiety, enforced guilt, moral blackmail and other

variants of terror. The nexal family is like a criminal
society where mutual protection is only the obverse
of mutual intimidation. Another Sartrean distinction
which Laing now emphasised in his analysis of families is the difference between 'praxis' and 'process'
in the explanation of human action. *Process* refers to
events that appear to have originated from no particular person or persons: they just happen or proceed,
with no identifiable human decision or wish at the
back of them.[5] (Most people perhaps regard everyday politics in this light, as something which just happens to happen, like the weather.) In contrast, *praxis*
is action which can be traced to definite decisions
undertaken out of definite motives by definite people;
social analysis should undertake to show praxis at
work where apparently only process exists. That is,
social events can be rendered *intelligible* (a term of
some importance in the later Sartre and Laing) by
showing that they are the outcome of decisions taken
in a social field by motivated actors; and Laing is is-
suing notice of his purpose to seek intelligibility and
praxis in quite gross and grotesque forms of human
pathology.

Laing had already written, in *The Divided Self*,
about the necessity for understanding in the interpretation and treatment of psychotic behaviour. Even
before his baptism in Sartre's *Critique*, Laing was em-
phasising the potential intelligibility of much that was
apparently crazy. But the type of understanding which

[5] Such at least is Laing's concept of "process": see *Sanity,
Madness and the Family* (1970 edn.) p. 22. Sartre however uses
process to designate a type of group action (as that of workers
on an assembly-line) where the purpose of the group is exterior
to its members: *Critiques de la Raison Dialectique*, 1960, pp.
541–52.

Laing seeks after 1960 is distinct in its concern for
the anchoring of explanation in the *social setting* of
the patient. The psychotic 'symptoms' of the schizophrenics in *The Divided Self* can be rendered intelligible (in a broad, non-Sartrean sense) by viewing
them as expressions of a fragmented or split Self. They
do not have to be converted into forms of 'praxis', i.e.
of human communication within a set of people, in
order to be understood. In his first book, Laing trans-
lates psychotic behaviour into the terms of action,
which may include inner or mental action; subsequently he insists on a translation into the terms of
*re*action, or of action in the flux of others' actions on
the subject.

But the neo-Sartrean framework was only a general
specification of the type of understanding which Laing
had already begun to accept and seek in the clinical
field. The American research-groups who were working on the family backgrounds of their schizophrenic
patients were also situating the 'process' of psychotic
illness within the 'praxis' of communication from parents to their children (even though they did not use
the terminology of Sartre in describing their work).
In his second book *The Self and Others*, Laing drew
heavily on the work of these researchers: their concepts become interwoven with those of Sartre in
later writings by Laing and his collaborators. Here
we will provide only a short composite account of the
hypotheses and findings of the American teams.

The pathology of family communication has become one of the great research enterprises of American science. Hundreds of families have trooped into
the laboratories of academic institutes and hospitals,
there to have their entire verbal output tape-recorded
over many sessions, their gestures and eye-movements

filmed and their biographies unearthed
interdisciplinary panels of doctors, psych
ologists and technicians. The families
select theatre for a period of hours or mo
a kind of real-life TV serial based on ⌐ ⌐sual
domestic interchange, and then depart. They leave
behind them a mass of sound-tracks, videotapes, behavior checklists, completed test-sheets and other re-
velatory material, a huge deposit of past praxis which
is then worked over for months by the bureau of investigators, and in due course delivered to the interested public as a journal article. The cumulative bibli-
ography of the Schizophrenic Family forms a veritable
saga of modern home-life, running in repeated in-
stalments through some half-dozen scholarly channels
over about fifteen past years, and with no end-point
yet in sight. The origin of the series is usually traced
to Bateson's 1956 paper[6] outlining what has become
known as the 'double bind' theory of the origins of
schizophrenia. The expression 'double bind' refers
to a specific pattern of disturbed communication, de-
tectable within pathological families, in which one
member is subjected to a pair of conflicting injunc-
tions or 'binds', both of them highly unsettling or
traumatic; a third injunction, implicit in the situation,
may prevent the threatened party from leaving the
field and so avoiding the conflict. The unfortunate re-
cipient of these messages is lost whatever he does,
and if the ordeal is repeated tends to opt out of
social interaction and to lose confidence in the accuracy of his perceptions of other people.

The 'double bind' mechanism is, however, only one

[6] G. Bateson, D. Jackson, J. Haley and J. Weakland, 'Toward a Theory of Schizophrenia', *Behavioral Science*, 1956,
Vol. 1, pp. 251–64.

. many modes of violence and fraud which have been seen to operate in disturbed families. A double-bind household constitutes, in the very cast-list of its *dramatis personae*, a group whose principal characters, both separately and co-presently, would bode ill for domestic peace, even independently of the discovery of any specific types of intimidation in their language and behaviour. Mr. Doublebind is reported to be a shifty, spineless, passive father, impoverished and rigid in his mental processes and bewildered by tasks involving quite elementary social graces. In the enactment of the family drama, he is constantly upstaged by his spouse, a domineering dragon of a woman who sets unrealizable demands on the life-style of her children and is then insecurely reproachful to them when they fail to live up to her immature stereotypes. The suffocating, spiky embrace of Mrs. Doublebind, her tiresome niggling obsession with conventional manners, her intellectual and emotional dishonesty and her incessant moral blackmail are all repeatedly documented in the literature. The Doublebind children are a dependent, weedy brood, mentally unstimulating and mutually disloyal. If they are ever more than bit-players in the tribal charade, it is through their role in ganging up, in coalition with their unspeakable parents, against the unlucky fall-guy or girl of the house, Charles (or Clarissa) Doublebind. It comes as no surprise to note that Charles/Clarissa, a naive and dithering but basically rather sweet personality, has been driven into a spiralling psychosis through this unholy conspiracy of pressures from his/her nearest and purportedly dearest. The Doublebind menage is a blood-besmirched arena for internecine assaults and insults, a telephone-network of crossed lines, scrambled messages and hung-up receivers. The research agents who have eavesdropped on Doublebind conversations and painstakingly decoded their obscure content have let us know just what has been going on in this grim parlor. The Doublebind family is duly incriminated as a *pathogenic communications system* or *nexus of mystification*. They are convicted in the fact of their disagreement one with another, for such discordances of outlook are to be taken as attempts to *disconfirm, disqualify* and *invalidate* the autonomous personal experience of the other, especially of the victim Charles/Clarissa. Let them not, on the other hand, try to escape the charge by agreeing with one another: the common assent of the Doublebinds is a *collusion*, and any mannerisms of warmth or co-operativeness should be seen as expressions of *pseudo-mutuality*, a false front of domestic solidarity tricked up for the outside world by this collection of competitive, mutually suspicious individuals. Any counter-move by Charles/Clarissa against this onslaught of mystification is met with a successful counter-counter-move which places him/her in an *untenable position*. (No younger Doublebind has ever been found to be in possession of a tenable position: on this the witnesses are unanimous.)

The climax of this vicious campaign against an offspring is reached when the Doublebind family decides to 'elect' Charles/Clarissa as an insane mental patient, thereby expelling him/her from their totalitarian kingdom. The chorus of false attribution and impossible injunction, orchestrated by the monstrous Mrs. Doublebind (who at this stage exercises the wily stratagems of a Goneril or Regan against the combined Lear-Cordelia figure of her child) rises to a crescendo of rejection; at this point orthodox psychiatry affixes the label of 'schizophrenic' upon the family scapegoat, in a degradation-ceremonial of hospital admission which inaugurates a lifetime's career as a mental patient.

In the last sentence of this dramatised account of the theory, the incrimination of psychiatric medicine comes from Laing and his London colleagues: the American researchers have in the main refrained from any radical indictment of psychiatry's own collusions. For the American teams tend to regard 'schizophrenia' still as the name of a behavioral and cognitive disorder attributable to individual patients (though caused by their family circumstance): the notion of 'treating' such a disorder by appropriate medical or psychotherapeutic means is not usually queried in their analysis. Laing, on the other hand, is sceptical about the very existence of a schizophrenic malfunction from which the patient can be said to be suffering: 'schizophrenia' means, if anything, the communication-disorder of the whole family, so that the language of 'diagnosis' and 'treatment' of somebody called 'a schizophrenic' would simply mask the web of familial connexions which is the real truth of the matter.

The framework outlined above, admittedly in the bold strokes of caricature, but not, I believe, with any essential infidelity to these authors' meaning, takes us from the Laing of *The Divided Self* to the stage his work had reached by 1963–4. *The Self and Others* (1961), *Sanity, Madness and the Family* (1964) and the *New Left Review* article of 1962 are the products of this stage, which still refrains from any celebration of a super-sanity achieved by the psychotic in his voyage into inner space. (The first indications of what has been termed Laing's 'psychedelic model' of schizophrenia appear during 1964.) The book *Interpersonal Perception: A Theory and a Method of Research*, written by Laing with two Tavistock team-mates, H. Phillipson and A. Russell Lee, also belongs in the phase under persent review (despite its date of actual publication in 1966) since its focus is on the perception of family members by one another.

In *The Divided Self*, the boundaries of Laing's existential analysis have been drawn around the patient: its typical chapter headings run '*Ontological insecurity*', '*The embodied and unembodied self*', '*The inner self in the schizoid condition*', '*Self-consciousness*' and '*The self and false self in a schizophrenic*'. The space of the patient's self is not of course uninfluenced by other people, but its topography is mapped as that of a relatively closed system. By contrast, *The Self and Others* is nearly always inside relationships involving at least two persons: its second part deals with those stratagems of small-group action which may 'drive the other person crazy', while its first section is a *tour de force* which tries to establish the social, interpersonal content of such apparently private modes of experience as masturbation and psychotic depression. The change in Laing's standpoint for the analysis of schizophrenic behavior becomes quite dramatic. *The Divided Self* had achieved its comprehension of madness by entering the apparently fractured logic of the patient's world-view and supplying the missing terms. When the hebephrenic girl Julie speaks, in her disjointed way, about 'a told bell', 'the occidental sun' and 'Mrs. Taylor', these utterances are rendered meaningful by construing them as puns: Julie is a 'told belle' (a girl told what to do and be); 'accidental son' (because her mother had half-wanted a baby boy); and 'tailor-made by her parents'. But in the 1964 book by Laing and Esterson, interpreting the family-patterns around eleven schizophrenic girls as variations on the theme of Clarissa Doublebind, none of the patients is ever reported at any point as uttering 'schizophrenese'. *There are no word-salads or schizoid puns to be interpreted.* At any rate none are transcribed in the text out of any of nearly two hundred hours of recorded interviews with these patients. The symptoms have become totally dissolved in the flux of social praxis. One girl (Lucie) displays what might be thought to be a rather hesitant speech-style, with an abundance of rambling qualifications to her remarks: but most of us have come across a fair number of interviewees with the same style and no psychotic diagnosis. The parents of these girls are scarcely less confused and 'thought-disordered', in the quoted transcripts, than their disgraced and labelled offspring. The insane patients of *The Divided Self*, with their dislocated body-images, splintered self-systems and depersonalised fantasies, sound as though they need some kind of specialised and continuous attention; Laing does not object to the provision of this attention under medical auspices. But with the eleven women of the 1964 series, one is at a loss to understand why they were ever sent into hospital at all, unless on the assumption that the medical authorities are in collusion with their rejecting families. For we are given no reason to suppose that anything is actually the matter with Maya, Lucie, Claire, Sarah, Ruby, June, Ruth, Jean, Mary or Hazel.

The disappearance of the symptom can be indicated from Laing's changing attitude towards schizophrenic speech. In *The Divided Self* he admits, in effect, that he is unable to understand, or translate for others' benefit, everything that a schizophrenic patient has to say:

A good deal of schizophrenia is simply nonsense, red-herring speech, prolonged filibustering designed to throw dangerous people off the scent, to create boredom and futility in others. (Penguin edition, p. 164.)

Compare this with the conclusion to the preface of the 1970 edition of *Sanity, Madness and the Family*:

Surely, if we are wrong, it would be easy to show it by studying a few families and revealing that schizophrenics really are talking nonsense after all. (Penguin edition, p. 14.)

The pawky sarcasm here comes from a new confidence. Incoherence and confusion will vanish into comprehensibility once the family-context is supplied. It is no longer 'simply nonsense', to be explained as the outcome of a deliberate effort to talk nonsense.

At several points during Laing's argument in this period, one encounters a constant and serious ambiguity over the applicability of his ideas to 'normal' families. It is not even clear whether, within his terms, 'normal' families can be said to exist at all. Part of the uncertainty arises from the way in which Laing takes over some of Sartre's descriptions of the social bond in non-pathological groups, and uses them to explain developments within what must be rather severely disturbed family settings. It will be recalled that Sartre accounts for the more intense kinds of group-affiliation by positing the internalization of violence or 'terror' among the membership. Laing's construct of the 'nexal family' outlines a sim-

ilar process of bonding through terror, but he widens
the category of terror so as to include within it virtually any form of concern felt by one member of a
family over the effect that another member's actions
may have personally on him:[7]

The highest ethic of the nexus, then, is reciprocal
concern. Each person is concerned about what the other
thinks, feels, does.

My security rests on his or her need for me. My need
is for the *other's* need for me. His or her need is that I
need him or her. My need is not simply 'need' to satisfy
biological drives. It is my need to be needed by the
other. My love is a thirst, not to satisfy my love, but a
thirst to be loved. My solitude is not for an other, but
for another to want me . . . And in the same way, my
emptiness is that the other does not require me to fulfill
him or her. And similarly, the other wants to be wanted
by me, longs to be longed for by me. Two alienated loves,
two self-perpetuating solitudes, an inextricable and time-
less misunderstanding—tragic and comic—the soil of
endless recrimination.

In such families it is assumed that to be affected by
the others' actions or feelings is 'natural'.

. . . . If Peter is prepared to make sacrifices for Paul,
so Paul should be prepared to make sacrifices for Peter, or
else he is selfish, ungrateful, callous, ruthless, etc. 'Sacrifice' under these circumstances consists in Peter impover-
ishing himself to do something for Paul. It is the tactic
of *enforced debt*.

One way of putting this is that each person *invests in
the other*.

Now this is Laing's description of the life-style of
families living in a sort of 'family ghetto', involved in

---

[7] The subsequent citations are from NLR.

a 'reciprocal terrorism' as 'gangsters' caught in a mu-
tual-protection racket. In a knowing tone not free
from a certain lofty satire, Laing is attacking those human relationships which have built into them some
anticipation of exchange, or some sense of a limit that
will be violated if the exchange is unreciprocated. The
blindness of these passages is unbelievable. For, of
course, assumptions of a continuing reciprocity, along
with anticipations of a possible limit to the relationship in the event of a non-return of affection or action, are very common indeed outside family ghettoes
and even outside families.[8] The agony of unrequited
sexual passion; the feeling of 'unwantedness' in infirm
parents dependent on their children; the unease
aroused by oblivious guests who overstay their wel-
come; the unpopularity of the non-union worker who
accepts a wage-increase won through the activity of
his organised mates; our disillusionment in fair-
weather friends who are on hand for social pleasant-
ries but absent in times of distress—all these, on
Laing's analysis, are targets just as eligible for criticism as the nexal family. To 'invest in' another being's anticipated response is seen literally capitalistic
and hence disreputable: the 'debt' of a relationship
has to be 'enforced', a deliberate *tactic*. The converse
might be expected to follow: that the sacrifice of one
individual for another ought to continue indefinitely
even if it remains unacknowledged or despised.

But ought we to expect such saintly expenditure of

[8] It has been persuasively suggested that the moral norm of
reciprocity is a universal component of human ethical codes,
and a logical prerequisite of any attribution of either exploita-
tion or stability within a social system: Alvin Gouldner, 'The
Norm of Reciprocity', *American Sociological Review*, 1960,
Vol. 25, pp. 161–78.

infinite pains in our families? Are women liberation-
ists simply wrong to rebel against the endless impoverishment of culture and personality which has been
the housewife's traditional lot? May not parents ever
decide that they have had enough insufferable presumption from their children, or children from their
parents? Would not, in short, a little more terrorism
in the cause of reciprocal concern be a highly desirable outcome in many homes? And is not recrimination ('comic' or 'tragic' as the case may be) sometimes a more progressive state of affairs between two
partners than the submissiveness of one partner? For
it seems inconceivable that new demands for equality
in personal relationships could ever be found without
some expectation of the very reciprocity which is so
frowned on here by Laing.

The mystery of the 'normal' family becomes more
perplexing when we look at the home-lives of the
schizophrenic girls reported in the Laing-Esterson
book. The original perspective of *Sanity, Madness
and the Family*, on its first publication in 1964, appeared to be straightforwardly comparative: it was
subtitled *Volume I: Families of Schizophrenics*, a
formula with the clear implication that a Volume
Two would follow dealing with families untenanted
by a schizophrenic member. Laing did in fact report
that the Tavistock programme was making comparisons with the patterns of communication in non-
schizophrenic, 'normal' families. Both elementary scientific method and common curiosity would dictate
the choice of a comparative framework for this research: in the absence of a control group drawn from
nonschizophrenic households, how could any behaviour of the patients' families be said to explain the

origins of schizophrenia? Yet the descriptions of the
girls' families in the 1964 study contain remarkably
little that might be specifically schizogenic. These
are rigid, demanding parents, setting unrealistic, over-
weening standards which block their children's autonomy; they define the approved behavior-patterns
of their daughters in ways which stifle the girls' self-
images; and their expectations for the family's future
are often contradictory and incoherent. But all this
is true nowadays of many households which display
feuding between generations, suppression of young
personalities—and a complete absence of schizophrenic children. Laing's and Esterson's account of
the Abbotts and the Lawsons is striking not because
it presents unfamiliar material but because we have
seen it (or heard about it) all before. And the theoretical framework outlined in the introduction is
again non-specific to schizophrenia: '. . . we are interested in what might be called the family *nexus*
. . . The relationships of persons in a nexus are char-
acterised by enduring and reciprocal influence on
each other's experience and behaviour.' The concept
of 'nexus' is now used to include not simply the disturbed family but any family at all (or, for that matter, any close and enduring face-to-face group). Laing
seems to have resolved the ambiguity of his earlier description of 'the nexal family' by taking a decision
that *all* families must be nexal.

In the recent re-issue of *Sanity, Madness and the
Family* (Penguin, 1970) the effort to sustain a comparative explanation without resorting to a comparative research-method appears to have been abandoned. For the work is no longer presented as the
first instalment of a series which will deal in turn

with schizophrenic and nonschizophrenic families. The subheading *Volume 1* has been dropped, and it is made clear in the new preface that no comparative data from other kinds of families are ever going to be presented: 'Would a control group help us to answer our question? After much reflection we came to the conclusion that a control group would contribute nothing to an answer to *our* question.'

Laing and Esterson posed the 'question' that was the topic of the investigation as follows: 'are the experience and behaviour that psychiatrists take as symptoms and signs of schizophrenia more socially intelligible than has come to be supposed?' They claim that they are not out to test the hypothesis that certain family interaction-patterns cause schizophrenia (a project that would indeed, they admit, have required a control-group) but simply concerned to show that the patients' experience and behaviour 'are liable to make more sense' when viewed in the family context than outside it. Yet, even if we were to take at its face-value the authors' disclaimer of any interest in a causal investigation, it by no means follows that comparative evidence 'would contribute nothing' to illuminating the problem of social intelligibility in schizophrenic behaviour. Supposing it were found, on examining normal families, that these displayed interaction-patterns of mystification which were precisely similar to those found in households with a schizophrenic member: would not the vision of schizophrenic behaviour as an intelligible reaction to such mystification become rather more uncertainly founded? Or supposing that we were to analyse the family processes surrounding patients with an acknowledged organic diagnosis of mental disorder (epi-

leptics, say, or mongol children) and found that the
reactions of the patient 'made more sense' within the
domestic context than when taken in isolation from
it. We might conclude that there was some general
syndrome of interaction within handicapped families,
affecting schizophrenic and other diagnoses in
roughly parallel ways, where the initial disability and
the parents' reaction to it, the child's reaction to his
parents' reaction and his physiological deficit were
deeply intermingled and confused. This would tend
to tell against a view of schizophrenia which regarded
it as a reactive condition pure and simple, requiring
no organic predisposition in the patient. If the demand for 'intelligibility' in the description of human
action means more than a preoccupation with telling
stories—*any* stories—about the person cast as subject,
we must be careful to check the stories that we tell
about him with the stories that might be told just as
easily about quite different sorts of people. Laing cannot evade the requirements of comparative method
by an appeal to 'intelligibility.'

This lapse is all the stranger because Laing's other
published study from the Tavistock programme (*Interpersonal Perception*, 1966; jointly with H. Phillipson and A. Russell Lee) pays explicit tribute to conventional scientific canons in its use of empirical
control-material and tests for the statistical significance of comparisons. The Interpersonal Perception
Method (or IPM), devised by these three authors on
the basis of a hypothesis by Laing on the supposedly
greater interpersonal insight displayed by schizophrenic patients vis-à-vis their relatives, is validated in
this study by comparing the test-scores of couples
from disturbed marriages with those produced by rel-

atively trouble-free couples. The assumptions of the
book are by and large those of orthodox marital coun-
selling: we do not have here a radical-nihilist critique
of the lie at the heart of human relationships, but a
liberal-reformist statement that some relationships are
discernibly better than others. The better ones,
within the terms of the IPM, are those where the
parties achieve a close matching in their perceptions
(a) of the way in which they are perceived by one another (b) of the fact that their partners perceive
them correctly as perceiving something or somebody.
Disturbed couples, on the other hand, exhibit constant mismatchings or disjunctions between what
each thinks the other perceives or feels. The postu-
lates of the study could hardly be in greater contrast
with the rest of Laing's work. 'Reciprocal concern'
(in the case of the untroubled couples) here hardly
implies terror, but rather an achieved harmony. The
possibility of a mutually benevolent 'nexus' is con-
ceded, and the anticipation of violence as the cause
of social bonding is totally absent from the analysis.

Interpersonal Perception does not, however, represent a break or interlude in the development of
Laing's thought. Despite its rather kindly inconsist-
ency, its uncharacteristic hint of mellowness in the
understanding of intimate relationships, it does follow
through his earlier emphasis on the spiral of interlocking perspectives in the transaction between persons. We have suggested that, as Laing's theory progresses, this vision of interlocking others tends to take
precedence over any attention to those characteristics
of an individual which are not defined in terms of his
immediate peers' perception. The 'vanishing of the
symptom' is only part of the disappearance of the

subject, the displacement of 'the self' from an internally-structured space to a group-directed field. The couples who get tested on the IPM are asked about their judgment of their partners purely in relation to those aspects of behavior which are manifested *within the couple itself:* other characteristics of the person remain unchallenged. The husband and the wife will rate themselves and each other on such statements as 'He finds fault with me'; 'I take her seriously'; 'He is wrapped up in himself'; and so on. It is out of bounds for them to consider whether one or the other of the pair is a depressive, a spendthrift, hysterical, career-minded or even sexless. In the world of the IPM, marital disharmony depends not on whether Mr. Smith is a drunken good-for-nothing but on whether Mrs. Smith thinks that he thinks that she is bitter towards him and on whether he actually does think that she is bitter. In the marital case-history provided as an illustration by the authors, the focus on, so to speak, the outer coils of the onion is remarkable. 'Mrs. Jones' is reported to be very unhappy with her husband, largely through her (unfounded) suspicion that he has slept with another woman. The IPM questionnaire-sheets completed by the Jones couple establish (a) that she does not love him; (b) that he is conscious of the fact that she does not love him. But these (on the face of it, plausible) indicators of marital rupture need not be taken as definitive, since they are drawn only from the first windings of the perceptual spiral. They matter less than the fact that Mr. and Mrs. Jones are in considerable agreement at the higher, more indirect levels of attribution: thus, she correctly perceives him as perceiving her as feeling disappointed in him, and so on. The Jones' per-

spectives on one another may be at odds, but their
meta- and meta-meta-perspectives concur: they may
be out of love, but *they at least know it*. And on the
strength of these disillusioned, bitterly refracted
awarenesses, the authors conclude that the unloved
Mr. Jones and the unloving Mrs. Jones have a hope-
ful marital prognosis, with 'a good capacity to work
with and contain their conflicts.' It needed an awful
lot of statistics to produce that avuncular twinkle.

Up to the mid-Sixties, Laing's conceptual journey
had been from Self to Others: it was soon to concentrate once again on the charting of an individual
rather than a social space. From 1964 onward he became associated with an interpretation of schizophrenic experience which was not entirely original
(Gregory Bateson had a few years earlier hinted at a
similar perspective[9]), but that has since become identified as Laing's personal vantage-point on the field:
schizophrenia was henceforth to be seen not as a psychiatric disability but as one stage in a natural psychic
healing-process, containing the possibility of entry
into a realm of 'hyper-sanity'[10] as well as the destructive potential of an existential death. Psychiatric
medicine offered, at best, a mechanistic bungling
which would frustrate the lawful progression of this
potentially natural process; at worst, it drove its patients insane with its murderous chemistry, surgery
and regimentation. Instead of the 'degradation cere-
monials' performed on patients by doctors and nursing staff (a degradation inherent in the very act of
diagnosis and examination no less than in the imper-

[9] In Bateson's introduction to *Perceval's Narrative: A Patient's Account of his Psychosis*, Stanford, 1961.
    [10] PE, p. 129.

sonal processing of mental hospital admission), what was needed was a sympathetic 'initiation ceremonial, through which the person will be guided with full social sanction and encouragement into inner space and time, by people who have been there and back again.' Schizophrenic experience was, at any rate in some patients, no more than the first step in a two-way voyage which led back again into 'a new ego' and 'an existential rebirth.' [10] Laing's therapeutic community (Kingsley Hall) was founded in 1965 in an attempt to provide a sympathetic setting for the completion of the schizophrenic's cyclical voyage: hospitals, with their formalisation of roles and their traditions of interference, could not be expected to furnish the conditions for successful 'initiation.'

The novelty of these views, measured against not only orthodox psychiatric theory but also against Laing's own previous writings, should be apparent. Their introduction was both sudden and confident: fully-fledged statements of the position appear in lectures and articles presented by Laing in the course of 1964 and 1965, often before a non-medical public. The Institute of Contemporary Arts, the *Psychedelic Review*, the radical journals *Peace News*, *Views* and *New Left Review*, the London weekly *New Society*, and an inconsequent jamboree dignified under the name of 'First International Congress of Social Psychiatry' (which met in chaotic conditions in a large London school) were the first recipients of the new message. Laing also presented his case to the writers and artists who were working with him in the 'sigma' project: Kingsley Hall, and to some extent David

[11] PE, p. 106.

Cooper's schizophrenia-research ward at the Shenley
Hospital outside North London, were in this period
part of the scene frequented by this wing of the cultural Left.[12] (Cooper's research-project, it should be
noted, never seems to have operated within the 'psychic voyage' view of schizophrenia, and his writings
in the area usually refrain from following Laing into
the 'inner space' of the psychotic's hyper-sanity.)
Laing's presentations before medical audiences have
continued in the vein of his pre-1964 theorising: he
does not usually try to tell doctors and psychoanalysts
that their schizophrenic patients are super-sane voyagers into aeonic time, but rather develops (often
with impressive skill and clarity) his classifications of
misleading family-talk and his notations of the psychotic's layered fantasies.

Laing's sharp turn towards the celebration of the
schizophrenic condition was accompanied by two developments in his thought whose conjunction appears as something of a paradox: his language becomes at once both *more socially committed* and
more mystical. The schizophrenic's experience is seen
as an indictment of the conventional world's standards of what is sane or insane; and his incarceration
and punishment in the mental hospital necessitates
a critical appraisal of 'the larger context of the civic
order of society—that is, of the *political* order, of the
ways persons exercise control and power over one
another' [13] In his 1965 preface to the Pelican edition
of *The Divided Self*, Laing insists that his critique

---

[12] For Laing's association with 'sigma', a London-based
avant-garde precursor of the counter-cultural Underground,
see Jeff Nuttall, *Bomb Culture*, London, 1968.
[13] PE, p. 107.

should be taken as a condemnation not simply of the micro-world of the family but also of the larger social order, the civilisation of 'one-dimensional men' which 'represses not only "the instincts", not only sexuality, but any form of transcendence.' 'The statesmen of the world who boast and threaten that they have Doomsday weapons are far more dangerous, and far more estranged from "reality" than many of the people on whom the label "psychotic" is affixed.' [14] Two years later, in his contribution to the 'Dialectics of Liberation' conference in London [15] (which he sponsored with three other psychiatrists) he again juxtaposed the small-scale assaults of modern psychiatry side by side with the huge lunacies and systematic violence perpetrated by the world system of imperialism: one may criticise the parallelism for being too merely a juxtaposition, for failing to integrate the critique of small-scale terror with its larger counterpart. Laing's political pronouncements have been emotionally radical rather than theoretically articulate. All the same, an immediate consequence of his shift after 1964 was (at any rate for some years) an unmistakeable willingness to take account of political and social structures at the national or international level.

The other and apparently contrary move, towards

[14] An informed critic has pointed out that Laing has withdrawn the preface in the recent reissue of *The Divided Self*, and speculates that this may signal 'some theoretical or ideological backtracking'. (Alan Tyson, 'Homage to Catatonia', *New York Review of Books*, February 11, 1971) In an interview this year (1971) Laing has declared that he is 'not an activist in the ordinary sense of the word' and temperamentally not very well suited for radical activism. (Gordon, *op. cit.*, p. 61)
[15] DL, pp. 21–5.

an immersion in mysticism, is even plainer in this period. Jeff Nuttall, the chronicler of project 'sigma',
may display less than verbatim accuracy when he
reports how

Laing enacted a catatonic ceremonial, summarily describing its magical function. 'It's a question', he said, 'of
coming down from the surface of things, down to the
core of all things, to the central sphere of being in which
all things are emanations.' [16]

But there are enough half-hints of the transcendental
beyond in Laing's own work over 1964–7 which go
almost as far in an otherworldly direction.

Orientation means to know where the orient is. For inner space, to know the east, the origin or source of our
experience.
  There is everything to suggest that man experienced
God . . . It seems likely that far more people in our
time neither experience the Presence of God, nor the
Presence of his absence, but the absence of his Presence.
With the greatest precautions, we may trust in a source
that is much deeper than our egos—if we can trust ourselves to have found it, or rather, to have been found by
it. It is obvious that it is hidden, but what it is and
where it is, is not obvious.[17]

  Occasionally we even find an explicit analogy
drawn between the role of the psychoanalyst and that
of the religious celebrant:

  . . . I believe that if we can begin to understand
sanity and madness in existential social terms, we, as
priests and physicians, will be enabled to see more clearly
the extent to which we confront common problems . . .

[16] Nuttall, p. 227.
[17] PE, pp. 136, 117; DL, pp. 32–3.

Among physicians and priests there should be some who are guided, who can educt the person from this world and induct him to the other.[18]

Laing, in short, regards the psychotic's experience of an alien reality as something akin to a mystical apprehension: it is not "the effulgence of a pathological process' but the faithful reflection of another actuality which is concealed from us by the blinkers of our mundane civilisation. The madman can be 'irradiated with light from other worlds', and partakes of 'those experiences of the divine which are the Living Fount of all religion.' [19]

What is the nature of the apprehension achieved by the mystical lunatic? It appears that the psychotic condition may enable one to overcome a deep rift in the human personality, characteristic of 'normal' man in our type of society. Modern civilisation has created a fissure between the 'inner' and the 'outer' layers of existence, between 'me-here' and 'you-there', between 'mind' and 'body'. These divisions of personality are not inevitable or natural, but the outcome of 'an historically-conditioned split'; we can conceive of a point in human existence before this lapse from fusion occurred, an 'original Alpha and Omega of experience and reality' to whose one-ness the mystic and the schizophrenic both manage to return.[20] It is

[18] 'Transcendental Experience in Relation to Religion and Psychosis', *Psychedelic Review*, 6, 1965 (reprinted in modified text in PE, p. 108); PE, p. 114. A similar statement by Laing likening psychosis to a religious state of mind and invoking the interest of priests is his preface to Morag Coate, *Beyond All Reason*, Philadelphia, 1964; this, even though the author of this outstanding memoir of a schizophrenic career repudiates the religious content of her old psychotic fantasies.

[19] PE, p. 114, and *Psychedelic Review, loc. cit.*

[20] PE, pp. 113, 103, 50.

not the psychotic who is 'alienated' or has the 'split personality', in Laing's terms, but the so-called 'normal' person: alienation and splitting are indeed the basic conditions for our repressive normality and its apparatus of anti-human institutions.

The schizophrenic patient, then, is engaged in a lonely voyage back towards the primeval point of one-ness: it appears that he is in some sense re-tracing the steps taken by the whole course of human evolution, and that once he has regressed far enough he will be able (just how or why is not at all clear) to advance back again into the world of common twentieth-century normals. Laing's description of the destination of the backward voyage is picturesque if imprecise: 'in and back and through and beyond into the experience of all mankind, of the primal man, of Adam and perhaps even further into the being of animals, vegetables and minerals;' 'to temporal standstill . . . to aeonic time . . . back into the womb of all things (pre-birth).' The psychotic return is recommended to all who are able: 'we have a long, long way to go back to contact the reality we have all long lost contact with'; and 'This process is one, I believe, that all of us need, in one form or another. This process would be at the very heart of a truly sane society.' [21]

This perspective on psychosis is, of course, unique in psychiatry. There are moments when Laing appears to approach the thought of Carl Jung in his emphasis on religious archetypes, necessary to the integrity of the personality and deeply embedded in the

---

[21] PE, pp. 104, 106, 137; 'What Is Schizophrenia?', *New Left Review*, 28, November-December 1964, p. 68 (reprinted in modified text in PE, p. 107).

collective memory of the human race: as when he speaks of 'the emergence of the 'inner' archetypal mediators of divine power, and through this death a rebirth, and the eventual re-establishment of a new kind of ego-functioning, the ego now being the servant of the divine, no longer its betrayer.' [22] But neither Freud nor Jung, nor any neo-Freudian or neo-Jungian, nor for that matter any other existential analyst has taken the stance that psychosis is a higher form of sanity. Schizophrenia is breakdown, sheer affliction, for virtually all psychiatric schools; only for Laing does it mean also breakthrough and blessing.

Why did the switch in Laing's theory take place, and why in the two directions of social radicalism and personal mysticism? It was not a necessary consequence of any of his previous doctrines. There is nothing in his earlier work which would turn the Tavistock physician into a Left-wing critic, or the canny rational Scot into a psychedelic mystagogue. The move towards social commitment might be explained, perhaps, by the influence of Sartre, especially in Laing's joint work with David Cooper (who appears to be more of a politically engaged person). Jeff Nuttall has included Laing in the manifestations of 'Bomb Culture', the ideological fall-out from the rise and decline of the Campaign for Nuclear Disarmament in Britain; yet the early Sixties were a quiescent phase of politics, a time of impasse for mass-movements and of immobility for radical thinkers. It was an odd time for anybody to move Leftwards, especially if he was also getting into transcendental intuitions at the same time.

[22] PE, p. 119.

And what can explain Laing's sudden discovery of the authentic illuminations that are conferred on fortunate schizophrenics by their delusions? It is not as if he had amassed a heap of fresh evidence pointing to previously un-noticed regularities in the psychotic state. The literature of psychotherapy contains several autobiographical accounts of the re-emergence of personality from madness, and Laing has added little to these beyond the story of the brief psychotic episode ('A Ten-Day Voyage') undergone by an artist friend in 1940 and recorded twenty-four years later.[23] Further accounts of schizophrenic experience, on lines which follow Laing's theory of what should be taking place, are due to be published shortly, but these have come from members of the Kingsley Hall community, which became established only after he had already reached his new conclusions. The autobiographical fragment 'The Bird of Paradise' invites us to believe that Laing has himself made the journey to 'that beginning of beginnings that is nothing at all . . . that Alpha and Omega' which precedes the tawdry dualities of common living.[24] Despite some obvious resemblances between the literature of the LSD-trip and the record of his ecstatic encounter with 'The Bird of Paradise,' Laing has denied that the experience he recounted was induced by LSD: 'It was merely a description of some of the things that make up my own inner life.' [25] One critic has speculated that the inward journey of the 'Bird of Paradise' passage reflects a schizoid episode in Laing's own career of involvement with schizophrenic pa-

[23] PE, pp. 120–37.
[24] PE, p. 156.
[25] Gordon, op. cit., p. 59.

tients[26] but the experience described sounds much too compressed and too articulately mystical to have come from a psychotic personal breakdown. One is left with a coy and cagey impression that Laing *knows something* about the Alpha-and-Omega mystery of the transcendental trip: but if he has freaked out or flipped out, it can never have taken him very far from the world of desk and couch, patients and colleagues and the ordinary human urgencies that stop most of us from launching off into infinite madness.

It is not very likely that a mystical personal episode could have sufficed alone to impel Laing towards his 'psychedelic' theory of schizophrenia: we must regard his adoption of the position as a considered choice. Many people have undergone transient occasions of apparently overpowering intuition into the nature of reality, only to consider these experiences in a very sober and sceptical light once their immediate impact has faded: my own apprehension of the enormous secret of the universe, discovered in the dentist's chair under the influence of nitrous oxide, remains as a vivid memory although it has done little to modify my predominantly materialist philosophy. Both Laings's recent movements, towards social criticism as well as towards a mystique of psychosis, are intelligible only as the systematic development of some elements in his earlier perspective on madness. *The Divided Self* had taken the first step of viewing schizophrenic experience in goal-directed terms: Laing went on to extend the area of meaning in the schizophrenic's world-view, which was to be seen now not

[26] David Holbrook, 'R. D. Laing and the Death Circuit', *Encounter*, August 1968, pp. 41–2.

simply as shot through fitfully with intention but as
a valid vantage-point in its entirety. Psychotic reality
is in essence a competitor, a rival, a challenge to the
reality defined by the normal and the sane. The sane
and the normal eliminate their rival by declaring it to
be madness, a deviation to be visited with legal and
other penalties. Peaceful co-existence between the
normal and the psychotic ideologies is impossible,
and it follows that any person who accepts the psychotic vision as authentic must at once declare war
on the world-view of the normal consensus; at the
very least he must declare a critical suspension of
judgment on the received social values which decree
the limits of sanity and insanity. At times Laing
seems to be saying that one cognitive system is as
good as another, that your 'delusion' is my 'reality'
and nothing can adjudicate between us. At other
times it looks at if the patient is right in perceiving
as he does, and the rest of the world is blind or wil-
fully ignorant. In Laing's celebration of the schizophrenic we sometimes find hints of the traditional
literary figure of the Holy Fool, the crazed seer, the
Cassandra or Poor Tom whose disjointed prophecies
condemn a society ripe for judgment. This is of
course only a limited and rhetorical radicalism: it is
saying 'How dare a crazy world label me as crazy?'
Laing has suggested that there is no pattern which
may be rationally discerned within the world political
system or the nation-state: 'The irrationality of the
whole' is a final one since we lack any context of
ideas which could tease out the reasons behind the
unreason of the system.[27] So Laing no sooner offers
his indictment of our social order than he abdicates

[27] DL, pp. 15–16.

from the task of providing the evidence and the concepts which would make sense of his critique. But then, if his movement towards critical social analysis *was* primarily a consequence of his identification with patients, one would not expect it to develop the intellectual energy of a more committed politics.

The journey into mysticism is no less consequent on Laing's position of solidarity with the schizophrenic. We may see the growth of his ideas as a progressive and serial challenging of the whole catalogue of schizoid 'symptoms' that is customarily presented in psychiatric textbooks. Each manifestation of behaviour that in orthodox medicine is offered as a 'sign' of clinical pathology is taken by Laing to be a comprehensible act which, when aligned against its social context, appears as eminently reasonable and sane. Does the schizophrenic utter a 'word-salad'? Well, it isn't quite as mixed-up and incoherent as *that*: here, here and here it makes rather good sense, with one or two poetic turns of phrase that are pretty striking. Besides, the chap often does start talking stark nonsense every now and then, quite deliberately, just in order to throw the likes of you and me off the scent. Does the patient present 'inappropriate affect,' grimacing when he should keep his face still and reacting coldly in situations demanding a show of emotion? Only according to that mother of his, an unreliable and partisan witness: and besides, who wouldn't grimace at that old tyrant? If the patient hears voices inside his head, it is because he lacks the personal confidence that would enable him to claim ownership of his own thought-processes; if he retreats into the waxy-automaton passivity of the catatonic state, we can understand his withdrawal from a responsibility and an agency he feels to be impossible.

So far, so good: all the symptoms have been validated as meaningful and even worthy forms of behaviour. But what are we to make of the great central syndrome of the dissolution of personality itself, the 'loss of ego-boundaries' characteristic of so many severely handicapped schizophrenics who literally do not know where they themselves leave off, and a reality exterior to themselves begins? Up to his psychedelic phase, Laing accepted the typical medical and psychoanalytic descriptions of these states of being: his existential accounts of 'de-personalization', 'de-realization' and 'boundary-loss' augment rather than contradict the orthodox text of clinical psychiatry. But if the schizophrenic experience was to become completely validated, to enter the realm of health and normalcy rather than of sickness and handicap, ego-loss and de-realization had to become positive virtues, or at least viable alternatives to our common-sense, interpersonally bonded realism. Laing calls this identity-anchored, space-and-time-bound mode of experience, common to most members of society, *egoic experience*. The ego is 'an instrument for living in *this* world': and as such is scarcely an unmixed blessing. Characteristic of the modern age is an over-emphasis on egoic adaptation to exterior realities, a drive to control 'the outer world' at the cost of forgetting 'the inner light' of imagination and phantasy. Laing appears to concur with traditional mystic philosophy in regarding the egoic mode as 'a preliminary illusion, a veil, a film of *maya* . . . a state of sleep, of death, of socially accepted madness, a womb state to which one has to die, from which one has to be born.' [28]

[28] PE, pp. 113, 114, 116.

The alternative to downgrading the 'egoic' (which appears to be a synonym for man's perception of and activity in the world of nature and society) would have been to admit that the loss of the boundary between 'inner' and 'outer', 'ego' and 'world', was a terrible misfortune: and this Laing could not do if he was to pursue his project of out-and-out solidarity with psychotic experience.

I do not believe that Laing's mysticism can run very deep. He himself, after all, must utilise 'the egoic mode' very frequently, in seeing patients, setting up therapy-units, delivering papers to conferences, and so on. If Kingsley Hall and Wimpole St. are just part of the illusory veil, the film of *maya*, it hardly seems worth the effort to get up and go there. Laing's principal activity, as a dedicated professional psychiatrist, is much too extroverted to permit us to suppose that he takes the mystical and the transcendental as the prime clue to reality. Much of his following may be oriented towards the pursuit of inner experience through drugs and meditation, but such devotees are hardly likely to be cut from the same cloth as Laing himself. The drug-using drop-out is not the kind of person who is likely to engage in the arduous work of sustained interaction with catatonics, and the mystic will find it hard to keep one eye on his navel and the other on the analysis of family conversations or the presentation of medical articles in the world of *maya*. Laing's advocacy of mysticism must be seen as part of his rationale for non-intervention in a schizophrenic's delusions; it springs from his insistence that all human experience is potentially valid and potentially intelligible, that none of it should be shunted off into a garbage-heap for incineration by sanitary technicians. The analogy between the psychotic and the psychedelic states, between the mystic's other-worldliness and the schizophrenic's withdrawal, was an inevitable move in his campaign to upgrade the status of the apparently abnormal and insane. It is a crucial move, because if we refuse to follow Laing this far we are left with the position that the schizophrenic is a disabled victim—of precisely what set of circumstances need not be considered here—whose basic perceptions and reactions can only to a limited degree be understood in the terms of 'intelligibility'. The standards of the 'egoic', of technical and interpersonal rationality, are the only ones we can have; he who journeys away from this reality of ours may be following any one of a number of projects (from harmless escapism to religious bigotry) but he cannot be engaged in a 'natural healing process' or in the quest for a primal 'Alpha and Omega' for whose existence there is no evidence in individual or in social history.

It is now six or seven years since Laing made his series of transcendental pronouncements. Although he published a book reprinting many of them in 1967 (*The Politics of Experience*), he has not repeated or developed this theme further. In a BBC radio broadcast on 'Religious Sensibility' during the spring of 1970 [29] he opposes the rationalist and Marxist view that religion is a reflection of social conditions. All the particular expressions of religious belief may be legitimately attacked by rationalist criticism, for these are merely 'images', dramatic expressions which are an imperfect but indispensable attempt to reach after

[29] *The Listener*, April 23, 1970, pp. 536–7.

spiritual truth. 'Spiritual sensibility derives its forms, but not its substance, from the forms of society.' This apologia for religious belief is of the typically chastened and tepid form taken nowadays by intelligent Christians. Yes, I quite agree that all the propositions of the Apostle's Creed are false or meaningless. Yes, the justification of faith in terms of miracles, or the appeal to Scripture, or through any of the traditional theological arguments for God, is absolutely fraudulent. But I am a religious man, I can't justify it logically at all, I just find it irresistible. Laing puts it that he himself 'has been brought up to take religious propositions seriously. Those of us who cannot help ourselves are compelled to continue the impossibly absurd project of keeping these [forms of revelation] alive.' Laing's talk outlines the history of his own religious development: brought up in a Presbyterian household, he remained immersed in Scriptural theology till the age of 18, when he was exposed to the shock of contact with non-believers at his university. He then became an atheist, believing that religion was 'an epiphenomenal superstructure' dependent on particular socio-economic conditions; since then he has moved back to an acceptance of religious belief, though no longer of Christian dogma. On mystical experience he says nothing, though the recollection of successful meditations would have stiffened his argument quite considerably. We are left with the impression that Laing's involvement in the transcendental has cooled (if indeed it was ever more than lukewarm).

The main elements in the development of R. D. Laing's philosophy and psychology have now been sketched. His more recent writings have added noth-

ing to these basic features, although some specialisa-
tion of his earlier interests must be noted. Laing's
latest work continues the search for formal paradigms
of human relationship which he began in the closing
pages of *The Self and Others*: a modified algebra of
sets is invoked to summarise the 'mappings' of relations and attributes within a family or a personality,[30]
and the lay-out of the gnostic, paradoxical verses that
comprise the volume *Knots* attempts to capture some
basic interpersonal stratagems and manoeuvers in
their most elementary form. An extra dimension of
complexity has now entered Laing's analysis of family
background, for he now believes that the nexal web
of mystification may reach back over at least three
generations, so that the patients' grandparents and
great-grandparents, though long since dead, may figure as major actors in the ferocious drama of the psychotic household. Laing describes one young man of
twenty-three, involved in precisely such a multi-gen-
erational paradigm: 'On his father's side: His father
(Peter's grandfather) was identified with *his* mother's
(Peter's great great grandmother's) identification of
herself as her father's (Peter's great great grandfather's) ideal wife', and Peter therefore internalised all
these relations by mapping them on to his own torso,
partitioning his right and left flanks among different
branches of his psychic family-tree. The linkages may
also extend across a number of separate nuclear families as well as backwards into the ancestry of a single
home: Laing has been influenced in this regard by
the Philadelphia psychiatrist Ross Speck, who in or-

---

[30] E.g., in *The Politics of the Family*, Toronto, 1969 (to appear from Pantheon Books, New York, 1971), p. 16; FSC, p.
144.

der to treat a disturbed mother-and-son pair reconvened, for a single therapeutic session, an entire network of no less than 35 persons spanning seven different families and twenty years of pathological relationship with the mother.[31] This new emphasis on cross-generational and cross-family linkages takes us even further away from publicly accessible data: it is bad enough trying to establish firm evidence about the patterns of interaction in a single household uncomplicated by long-removed neighbours or long-deceased relatives. The prospects for effective therapy must be particularly grim if it is to depend on the copresence of so many parties, any one of whom might have a good excuse for not turning up. The vistas of possible causal influence are always endless: even to attempt to draw them out will mean a loss of adequate perspective, and in practical terms a dead-end of infinite regressions.

Such *culs de sac* may, however, be no more than minor tributaries to the main tendencies in Laing's work, which are obviously capable of considerable further development by him and his co-thinkers. The theory and the therapy of mainstream psychiatry are bound to be indebted to Laing, and to similar vanguard trends in social medicine, if only because no other rival approach, whether biochemical or environmental, seems to possess any dynamic or momentum of comparable power. Laing's theories of schizophrenia are powerfully aided, in the public view, by the distinguished cultural and philosophical apparatus in which they repose: his popularity rides with the great timeliness of many of these supporting

[31] FSC, pp. 145, 141.

ideas, which often raise vital issues of a kind traditionally ignored by doctors, natural scientists and even social scientists. Any critique of Laing cannot possibly answer him by brandishing the latest piece of blotting-paper on which the chemical juices of a hospitalised schizophrenic have been analysed. He must be met in terms of the larger questions, of method in the human sciences and of the nature of 'illness' and 'treatment', which he has raised so trenchantly.

The Meta-Journey of R. D. Laing*

BY JAN B. GORDON

They might ignore me immediately
In my moon suit and funeral veil
I am no source of honey
So why should they turn on me?
Tomorrow I will be sweet God, I will set them free.

The box is only temporary.

Sylvia Plath

R. D. LAING IS AN EXPLORER who has initiated a new
mode of "mapping" the frontiers of consciousness.
And every explorer needs some equipment and the
proper conditions for his journey: a space that is
metaphorically or literally filled to such an extent
that the adventurer is urged to strike out on his own;
some utopian imagination which will allow him to
know when he has found a suitable place to conclude

* I wish to thank my colleague, Murray Schwartz, for his
advice and numerous insights offered me in the writing of
this essay. I also acknowledge the permission granted by the
editors of *Modern Poetry Studies* to use material from an essay
of mine, " 'Who is Sylvia?' The Art of Sylvia Plath," which
was originally published there (Volume 1, number 1) in the
autumn of 1969.

the quest; a tradition of other explorers who have
failed to reach the promised land; and finally, some
a priori notion of togetherness with the landscape, an
ontologically sufficient "home" where there was, once
upon a time, no difference between man and his environment, "inner" space and "outer" space. This
fourth condition is described in some detail in *The
Gospel According to Thomas* that is prefixed to
Laing's *The Bird of Paradise*:

When you make the two one, and
when you make the inner as the outer
and the outer as the inner and the above
as the below, and when
you make the male and the female into a single one,
so that the male will not be male and
the female not be female, when you make
eyes in the place of an eye, and a hand
in the place of a hand, and a foot in the place
of a foot, and an image in the place of an image,
then shall you enter into the Kingdom.

This territory, like most Edens, is unfamiliar except
as an act of consciousness, and the double-removal
that obtains when that act of consciousness is mythi-
fied, means, in one sense, that Laing is writing a history of self-consciousness disguised as an account of
man's Fall. The kingdom which existed prior to this
Fall was a realm where *behavior* and *experience* were
identities—every man *did* what he *was*. But the lapse
occurred in its traditional etymological sense, implying a splitting which was not vertical, inducing repression and, ultimately, depth analysis, but horizon-
tal, insofar as it involves projection, displacement,
and introjection.

This separation is a psychic wound that corre-

sponds to the wounds that so many classical kingdoms suffered and which, invariably, prompted some
would-be saviour to go on a quest for the oracle.
Only when the right question was asked was there
hope for the restoration of fertility in some life-re-
newing shower. But the question may well have been
man's real "double-bind," since that which distinguished the questioner was, paradoxically, that which
had caused the plague. For Oedipus, the fact that he
continues to question his "origins" means that he
alone will discover the nature of his "family" arrangement. And it is precisely these "origins" that have
educated him into the self-education that ensues
from asking the first question. We are questioning
ourselves into a disastrous sickness, and the first pages
of *The Divided Self* picture traditional psychoanalysis as one of the causes as well as symptoms of the
disease:

Psychiatry could be, and some psychiatrists are, on the
side of transcendence, of genuine freedom, and of true
human growth. But psychiatry can so easily be a technique of brainwashing, of inducing behaviour that is adjusted, by (preferably) non-injurious torture. In the best
places, where strait-jackets are abolished, doors are un-
locked, leucotomies largely foregone, these can be replaced by more subtle lobotomies and tranquilizers that
place the bars of Bedlam and the locked doors *inside* the
patient. Thus I would wish to emphasize that our "normal" "adjusted" state is too often the abdication of ecstasy, the betrayal of our true potentialities, that many
of us are only too successful in acquiring a false self to
adapt to false realities.

                    ("Preface" to the Pelican Edition, p. 12)

The psychiatrist, as Laing envisions him, is only

heightening our troubles: first, by using a reductive
terminology that de-personalizes the patient into
components like "complex" or "psyche" and secondly,
by a veritable "vocabulary of denigration" that provides the pretense of objectivity while actually dis-
tancing the analyst from the patient's being-in-the-
world. The closer the analyst comes to understanding
the patient's difficulties, the farther he must of necessity remove himself from the patient. This activity
only aids and abets the schizoid tendencies in the culture. The traditional Freudian psychoanalyst is therefore a sort of voyeur whose urge to "objectivity" is
only a mask, or better, a one-way mirror that turns
others to stone à la the myth of Perseus and Medusa
(references to which abound in Laing's work). The
clinical psychiatrist who forever wishes to be more
"scientific" or "objective" confines himself to the
"objectively" observable behaviour of the patient before him in the conviction that he thereby sees neu-
trally. Rather than observing symptoms which we
believe to be expressive of the patient's being-in-the-
world, we must relate his actions to his way of experiencing the situation he is in with "us."

For R. D. Laing, the analyst who looks at a patient's actions as "signs" of some disease is already
imposing his own being-in-the-world onto that of the
patient. The same error would ensue were the doctor
to imagine that he could "explain" his present as a
mechanical resultant of some immutable and inscru-
table past. This is, of course, quite antithetical to traditional psychoanalysis. Freud himself described neurosis as "an abnormal attachment to the past," hence
all of the pressure in Freudian analysis to return to
childhood through dreams or the construction of

some "play." The assumption is that there is some
event or pseudo-event in one's past which provides a
clue for the ensuing behavior. For Freud, behavior
occupies a time continuum, therefore the emphasis
upon the "case history" as a parameter in traditional
analysis. Laing would undoubtedly argue that there
is a twofold antinomy in the very notion of an historical fact. Although an historical fact is what "really
took place," where did anything take place? Each
episode in the patient's "history" resolves itself into
a multitude of individual psychic movements. Each
of these movements is no more and no less than the
translation of unconscious development, hence history is no more "given" than any other set of facts.
Insofar as the "case history" aspires to meaning, it is
doomed to select a region, a period in the patient's
life, a particular kind of patient within a particular
group, and to make that patient stand out, as a dis-
continuous figure, against some continuity that is
barely sufficient to be used as a backdrop. A truly
complete "case history" would cancel itself out.
What makes history possible at all is that a sub-set of
events is found, for a given period, to have approximately the same significance for a contingent of individuals who have not necessarily experienced the
events in the analyst's model. To Laing, as to Sartre,
history is never history, but history-for. History does
not escape the obligation of all knowledge—notably,
that of employing a code to analyze its object, even if
a continuous reality is attributed to that object. Thus
the analyst who studies a "case history" for clues to
the reality of a patient's being-in-the-world is in a terrifying position philosophically: if he claims to reach
the continuous, it is impossible, being condemned to

an infinite regress—the agony of meta-history. To render it possible, events must be quantified and thereafter, temporality ceases to be the priviliged domain of historical knowledge because as soon as it is quantified, each event in the patient's life can be treated as if it were the choice between possible pre-existents.

Laing's argument against Freud set forth in the first two chapters of *The Divided Self* must be viewed therefore in a much larger context. Like so many revolutionaries, his struggle is waged against those forces of history who reconstruct a patient's life from the "evidence" of prior events. When he wrote *The Divided Self*, Laing was only twenty-eight, nearing the end of his formal training. And the object of his scorn is quite clearly those teachers who have trained him in the more traditional skills of post-Freudian analysis. One is scarcely into the book before its author has written an exaggerated caricature of twentieth century psychoanalytic "treatment" which sees the patient as inaccessible. The object of the parody is poor Kraepelin whose summation of a patient's obstinacy was part of a 1905 lecture:

'Although he undoubtedly understood all the questions, he has not given us a single piece of useful information. His talk was . . . only a series of disconnected sentences having no relation whatever to the general situation.'

Laing points out, quite astutely, that the patient's discontinuity results from an attempt, conspicuously or unconsciously, to parody Kraepelin's staccato approach to him: "What is your name?" "Why are you so belligerent toward me?" That is, the patient's responses are part of a psycho-social situation in which the patient's experience of the analyst is built-in to the matter in which he allows himself to be treated. The doctor may see the patient's responses as "signs" of a "disease" or he may, as Laing prefers, see this behaviour as being expressive of his existence. One could press Laing's observations farther by saying that the confusion between the two approaches to the patient would imply that existence itself has become a disease—an equation which analysts share no small responsibility in making.

Of course, Kraepelin's interview is a straw man of the worst sort. Laing's portrait makes him resemble some sixteenth century analyst, or better, the equivalent of a psychiatric medicine-man whose attempt at cure is a parody of some primitive torture. Anyone who has been in analysis recognizes that most psychiatrists ask a minimum of questions, usually confining themselves to the use of certain "cue" words or phrases that are designed to evoke the patient's own verbalization. The court of inquiry which Laing has set forth at the outset of *The Divided Self* is a distorted account of the history of psychiatry which aids in establishing his own role as a revolutionary. That is to say that Laing is using a distorted history to establish his own false-self system, and thereby becomes that which he accuses his tormentors of being. "Our teachers are imprisoning us," would seem to be the cry of the young turk who attempts to establish the new order.

The corollary to this pattern in R. D. Laing's thought is his definition of psychosis.

I suggest, therefore, that sanity or psychosis is tested

by the degree of conjunction or disjunction between two persons where the one is sane by common consent.

The critical test of whether or not a patient is psychotic is a lack of congruity, an incongruity, a clash, between him and me.

The 'psychotic' is the name we have for the other person in a disjunctive relationship of a particular kind. It is only because of this interpersonal disjunction that we start to examine his urine, and look for anomalies in the graphs of the electrical activity of his brain.

                                       (*The Divided Self*, chapter 2)

Eschewing any consideration of the patient's ability to function, R. D. Laing sees the psychotic as determined exclusively by *relationships*. When we make him aware of the discontinuity that exists between his behaviour and those of us whom we regard as normal, we only heighten the discontinuity. The act of separating "him" from "us" is an act of condemnation. Hence, he sees most traditional analysis as a process of verifying a radical disjunction which the analyst himself has had a share in widening. The analyst resembles a computer which is programmed to find an answer, but the answer is part of the program. What we get is a kind of contagion which sweeps over both the doctor and the patient, and from which neither can extricate himself. Hence Laing imagines most analytical sessions as operating no differently than scores of other human relationships; the responses form part of a larger "system" in which all parties conspire to produce a plague of psychic disaster. The infinite regress of this "system" means that we are all imprisoned, and, more importantly, that schizophrenia and paranoia share a complementary field.

What is striking about this vision is that Laing has adopted the epistemology of phenomenological thought and applied it to a more alien realm. It was the phenomenologist, particularly Maurice Merleau-Ponty, who tried to give the *cogito* a different meaning: the act of doubting in which I put in question all possible objects of my experience. This act grasps itself in its own act of operation and thus cannot doubt itself. The very act of doubting obturates doubt. The perceiver grasps himself, not as a constituting subject which is transparent to itself, and which constitutes the totality of every possible object of thought and experience, but as a particular thought, as a thought engaged with certain objects, as a thought in act; and it is in this sense that I am certain of myself. In "The Primacy of Perception" Merleu-Ponty describes this process by which thought is given to itself; he becomes certain that the individual perceiver is not merely thinking this or that, but is simultaneously aware that he is simply thinking. Thus he can get outside the psychological *cogito* without taking himself to be a universal thinker. The perceiver is in one sense a thought which recaptures itself as already possessing an ideal of truth (which it cannot at each moment wholly account for) and which is the horizon of its operations. This thought *feels* itself rather than *sees* itself, searches after clarity rather than possesses it, and always creates truth rather than finds it. The object of perception has become identical with the structure of behaviour, accessible both from within and from without. It could be said that Laing is doing nothing more than extending the implications of the early Gestalt psychologists. Our perceptions never advance until the horizon of meaning they open up becomes, through speech, what in theatrical language would be a *real decor*. The communicative world between patient and analyst is no more a bundle of parallel consciousness than space is made of simultaneous points in themselves. Our traces mix and intermingle in the process making a single wake of public durations. The field of existence is identical with the field of language and eventually, for Laing, at least, with the field of history.

Perceptually, then, Laing is interested in using a methodology by which the "je" becomes a "moi," or, stated more simply, a condition which will enable the "self" to be both a subject and an object simultaneously. And that condition is dangerously close to the schizoid "being/and" world. It is a prerequisite which demands that man never be submitted to the fate of an external nature or history and thereby stripped of his consciousness. In emphasizing the "primacy of experience" Laing means that the experience of perception is our presence at the moment when things, truths, values are constituted for us; that experience itself is a nascent logos; that it teaches us, outside of any dogmatism, the true conditions of objectivity itself. Laing's exploration of the patient's experience is by no means a question of reducing human knowledge to sensation, but of assisting at the birth of this knowledge and thereby of making it as sensible as the sensible. It is an attempt to recover the consciousness of rationality by achieving a truth which quite literally "passeth beyond the understanding." This level of experience is primordial, and Laing truly believes that it reveals to us the permanent data of the problem which culture attempts to resolve. If we have not tied the subject to the determinism of an external nature and have only placed it in the bed of the perceptible, which it transforms without ever quitting it, we run less danger of submitting the subject to some impersonal history. Laing seems to be implying that history is nothing more and nothing less than other people; it is the inter-relationships we establish with them, outside of which the realm of the ideal appears as an alibi. History is identical with the family.

Surely, there are profound practical implications within the philosophical implications of Laing's argument. Once one's life is inherent in the perceived world and the human world, even while it recreates it and contributes to its meaning and making, then morality can never adhere in the maintenance of a private system of values. Principles are innately mystifying unless they are put into practice, unless they vitalize our relationship with others. Thus we can never remain indifferent to that aspect in which our acts appear to others. Just as the perception of a thing opens me up to being, by realizing the paradoxical synthesis of an infinity of perceptual aspects, in the same way the perception of the "other" founds morality by realizing the paradox of an *alter ego*, of a common situation, by placing my private perspectives and my incommunicable solitude in the visual field of another and of all the others. If I convert all of my relations into an environment, then in the very act of perception, my "self" will oscillate between "je" and "moi." Although it may transform the act of perceiving the patient's "world" into an arena, any judgment, and hence morality, is impossible. Laing seems to be implying that a sufficiently common situation invokes the Kantian request that I come to legislate a certain act as moral law in order to determine its rightness or wrongness. But the paradox of the *alter ego* is frightfully close to the schizoid condition that Laing presumes to be mapping. What I am suggesting is a curious tension in existential psychoanalysis; in comparing an empirical with an eidetic psychology, Laing, like Husserl, is establishing a relation like that which exists between sociology and statistics. Statistical or "objective" analysis is necessary to psychoanalysis, but does not coincide with it. We must get into contact with the social phenomenon, and understand it in its own proper frame, in order to invest the statistical facts with a social meaning. But in the process of understanding the social phenomenon (in this case, the patient's being-in-the-world), we must assume his experience. By experience, of course, Laing really does not refer to experience as it is traditionally understood, but rather that process by which we come in contact with the psyche by phenomenological reflection. He is, perhaps willfully, confusing experience and *intentionality*.

It is not only that the analyst must oscillate between subject and object in terms of his phenomenological position. But the typical Laingian patient is torn between a similar desire to reveal himself coupled with the necessity of remaining concealed. A colleague of mine reading through *The Divided Self* found himself almost compelled to underline several paragraphs, which was inevitably followed by his writing the word "voyeurism" in the margin. That seems, to me at least, to be a remarkably appropriate response. The sensitivity censors of the psychoanalyst are always concerned with *access* to the patient's being-in-the-world. Rather than treating the patient, the doctor engages in transforming an essentially private and internal world into a public one by understanding the private spaces. There is the implicit understanding that a patient lives in a "world" that has some internal coherence, and that this metamorphic space does not exist apart from him, nor he apart from it. But the analyst must perform this task without risking the danger of de-individuating the patient's "self" which would only abet any discontinuity. And hence the necessity for what amounts to a continuing alternation between the analyst's presence and his disappearance. The chapter entitled "The Embodied and Unembodied Self" sets forth the feelings of what Laing takes to be a typical schizoid's "world":

The individual's actions are not felt as expressions of his self. His actions, all that David called his 'personality' and which I have proposed to call his false-self system, become dissociated and partly autonomous. The self is not felt to participate in the doings of the false-self or selves and all its or their actions are felt to be increasingly false and futile. The self, on the other hand, shut up with itself, regards itself as the 'true' self and the persona as false. The individual complains of futility, or lack of spontaneity, but he may be cultivating his lack of spontaneity and thus aggravating his sense of futility . . . The self is extremely aware of itself, and observes the false self, usually highly critically.

If one were to substitute Laing's discussion of David's terrifying self-consciousness for the continuing peek-a-boo dance of the analyst advocated in Laing's existential psychoanalysis, they would seem almost identical. In his very attitude toward the patient, Laing is sympathizing. He is coming into contact with the "in-

ner" world of the psychotic by an astute imitation
of the very same self-consciousness which is so threatening to the patient. By making the patient his own
"double," the doctor lives the analysand's existential
life!

There is considerable risk involved in using phenomenological reflection to approximate the "world" of
the schizophrenic. Traditional psychoanalytic training usually involved a period during which the
psychiatrist-to-be was placed in analysis. The analyst
was placed in the posture of the analysand in order
to "work through his own problems" in such a way
as to avoid the evils of "counter-transference." Its
purpose was to enable the prospective psychiatrist
to avoid losing the distinction between "je" and "moi"
that was threatened when projection took place.
Laing would say that such a breakdown of the analyst's ego structure is, contrary to being evil, an absolute necessity. By "mapping," he refers to precisely
this process whereby the particular discontinuity encountered by the patient is a *function of* an operation
whereby elements and relations between elements,
from one set, called the domain, are superimposed
upon elements and relations between elements called
a range:

Projection can then be regarded as a mapping of inside onto outside, and introjection a mapping of outside
into inside. Families are of peculiar significance and interest, because more than any other social set, they are
both domain and range, for projections *to* outside, introjections *from* outside into them; *and* they are the range
for projections onto them *from* the members of the family itself, as they are the domain of introjections onto
individuals in the family. Projections onto the family,

from family members, combined with introjections onto them from outside, are combined to form a product which is in turn further projected and introjected: such projections and introjections are in turn introjected and projected, and so on, endlessly.

(*The Politics of the Family*, chapter 5)

For Laing, then, one's body is of unique significance because it is the range for introjective mappings from all domains: and these introjective sets provide a "pool" for projections in turn to any domain, from which re-introjections and re-reprojections can be carried on almost without end. Words like "sets," "domain," and "function," however, serve to give all away. Laing is establishing an anti-calculus to accompany his anti-psychiatry. And in *Self and Others*, he concludes with a peculiar sequence of integration and differentiation that is, in calculus, a cruel parody of the schizophrenic's difficulties with self-*integration* and the *differentiation* from others. He is providing a notation for the nexification that takes place within certain social sets. For example:

> if $p \rightarrow p$ represents the way the own person sees himself
>
> and if $p \rightarrow O$ represents the way the own person sees the other

and similarly

> if $O \rightarrow O$ represents the way the other person sees himself
>
> and if $O \rightarrow p$ represents the way the other person sees the own person
>
> and if $p \rightarrow (O \rightarrow O)$ is the way the own person views the other's view of himself

and if $p \rightarrow (O \rightarrow p)$ is the way the own
person sees the other's view
of him,

Then,

a social encounter may be represented by p's
idea of o's idea of what he, p, thinks of
himself, p

$$p \rightarrow (O \rightarrow (p \rightarrow p))$$

At each point along the line (and this line is infinite
in terms of the possible variations), each individual
is mistaking his affection for the "other" for his need
to validate himself in the eyes of the "other." Of
course, no real communication is possible but only a
series of meta-communications which protect me from
the exposure of a genuine confrontation. Parenthetical expressions and bracketing multiply as the individuals build fortresses about themselves. A world
where everything is a function of a reciprocity of
mapping is a realm where incredible energy is being
expended upon re-enforcing the parentheses. Every
social meeting is a potential nest of self-consciousness
which the analytic situation parodies by a recreation
of the patient's self-reflection in and through phenomenological reflection. But if the danger in the schizophrenic's behaviour is the mystification of the "self"
into some highly defensive false-self network, then
Laing runs a somewhat parallel danger in his anti-
calculus which reduces human interaction to a set
of symbols, and hence is just as denigrating as the
language of the traditionally trained psychoanalyst.
Mathematics is a most subtle way of transforming the
time-dimension, and hence history, into a topology.
A science of human experience which emphasizes

human relationships is not, simply because of that feature, more humane than a doctor-scientist who treats illness objectively. The mixture of dramatization and mathematics with which Laing concludes *Self and Others* makes every analytic situation resemble a cheap soap opera. Will Jill defend herself against Jack's opinion of what Jill thinks Jack should be? To pun on Laing's thought processes, dramatization, too, has a theory of limits, and unless we observe it, the spaces that the self occupies become just as depersonalized as the interior of Laing's parentheses.[1]

The one feature that most of Laing's patients seem to share is some exquisite vulnerability. His schizoids are invariably more sensitive than the rest of us, simply because they have never compromised by adopting the false-selves necessary to maintain cohesion. Though considerably more heroic, the refusal to engage in the activity of self-mystification does not imply heightened sensitivity, but may, just

[1] This convolution of communicative patterns which depersonalizes the speaker as well as the object of communication may result from the fact that the schizophrenic typically exhibits weakness in three areas of discriminating communicational modes either within the self or between the self and others: he has difficulty in assigning the correct communicational mode to the messages he recieves from other persons; he has difficulty in assigning the correct communicational mode to those messages which he himself utters or emits nonverbally; and he has difficulty in assigning the correct communicational mode to his own thoughts, sensations, and percepts. The peculiarity of the schizophrenic is not that he uses metaphors or false-metaphors, an implication that we would draw from Laing's thought, but that he uses unlabelled metaphors. See the essay by Gregory Bateson et al., "Toward a Theory of Schizophrenia," in *Behavioral Science* (winter, 1956–57), pp. 251–263.

as well, suggest an inability or unwillingness to engage
in imaginative transformations. Because of the fra-
gility of being which Laing equates with ontological
insecurity, the schizoid, as described in his books and
articles, is unusually adept at self-concealment. He
may learn to "frown his approval and applaud his
displeasure" to such an extent that all the world sees
is not him. His actions are not his real self, but a
mask which enables him to function socially. Ultimately, he is unable to locate his "real" self and
hence comes to live the irreal as a defensive substitute.
He becomes wholly equivocal, a potential person, and
finally, nothing at all. If he even temporarily stops
pretending to be what he is not, and steps out as the
person he has come to be, he emerges as a no-thing.
He has no sense of self, and the truth about his existential condition is lived out. What is existentially
true is lived as really true. He claims that he is dead,
but he is really alive. Yet, in terms of the patient's
being-in-the-world, he is quite dead indeed.

The description in the paragraph above is really
a sort of Laingian archetype—the collected attributes
of a typical patient who has sought out professional
help. Like the shopkeeper in the song by Simon and
Garfunkel, his patients' most interesting and observable symptom is that they are always "faking it." A
man has been married to the same woman for ten
years and feels as if he has never really slept with her.
Or a dutiful daughter whose case is detailed in *Sanity,
Madness and the Family* has always been studying in-
tensely only to discover, at some crucial point in her
development, that relentless concentration upon her
studies is the way in which she avoids confronting her
family. Every time she opens a new book, her parents

must regard it as an act of rejection. Crises in his patients always occur at the level of personal confrontation, and hence as a function of one's socialization rather than his biographical development. Part of Laing's argument with history is undoubtedly his scorn of traumatic incidents in one's biography and his lack of interest in origins. Almost never do we have mention of the incident which prompted a patient or prompted his relatives to seek out help. Why, on this particular morning, was this particular act seen as such a disjunction from the past? Laing's neglect of development aspects of schizophrenia is understandable in terms of the dynamics of "mapping"; after all, projections used by explorers have markers denoting direction, but seldom time. As we might expect, Laing's examples never include children, save perhaps in the fictional volume and now best-seller, *Knots*, where a large number of poems are rhymes involving Jack and Jill who exist here, as before, in fairy tales. The reader is left to wonder whether Laing's interest in the family is encouraged by his emphasis upon regression rather than development. The family is the one unit where the interaction is spatial rather than temporal; arrested development would be one way of metaphorically talking about "mapping" since time is never a variable in any of the equations in *The Politics of the Family* or *Self and Others*. Kingsley Hall, the psychic commune in London where Laing and his staff have encouraged interaction, is, in one sense, a family, and since the group dynamics there is rather free-form, there are none of the normal diurnal and nocturnal rhythms which govern most hospitals. One way of talking about the self-multiplication and/or fragmentation

which takes place in the schizophrenic might be to
regard it as an effort of the patient to produce his
"own" family whose members are the various false-
selves which are alternately projected and re-projected and hence represent a kind of artificial defense
against the world in the same way that the primitive
clan provided the defense for the nomad. Politics
hence comes to be a result of the mapping of the
body politic, and the future of the state is a function
of states of being.

Hence, Ronald Laing's popularity among political
activists, particularly those of New Left persuasion, is
more easily understandable. He wages an incessant
argument against history and sees any suggestion of
scientific objectivity as an excuse for psychological
colonialism—a way of superimposing the analyst's
being-in-the-world onto that of the patient and hence
altering the maps unfairly. Since those of us "outside" institutional walls are no more "sane" than
those inside (only more adept at manipulating our
false-selves to provide a better defense and hence
more capable of protecting ourselves), Laing feels
that those with psychic courage are all behind bars.
We might as well turn the inside out and the outside
in, a quite common ploy among revolutionaries. Ad-
ditionally, there is a certain puritan strain in his
thought which sees no compromise possible between
absolute withdrawal and a collusive activity which
produces psychological indebtedness and, finally, dependency. What Laing does not see is that people
who are not in some pathological condition can en-
act and then relinquish their false-self systems and
hence are capable of considerably more psychic mo-
bility than Laing gives them credit for. In an im-

portant sense, his myth of human interaction is very static; there is nothing conditional or provisional about it. Whereas Freud saw compromise as an absolute necessity for the growth of the individual, Laing equates that growth with false growth and a colluding functionalism which leaves us only the choices of withdrawal or persecution. Whereas Piaget would allege that the child's ability to manipulate his sequence of false-selves is one of the ways in which he comes to use symbols (particularly the child's experience of the *stade du miroir*), Laing would deny any growth-value and envisions that experience as only a mode of defending the ego.[2]

Although Laing emphasizes the primacy of experience, it is almost impossible to reconcile his analysis of the experience of schizoid individuals with social theory. For example, in the *Politics of Experience* he claimed that "there is no such 'condition' as 'schizophrenia,' but the label is a social fact, and the social fact is a political event." Yet, on the cover of the book, he argues that "the schizophrenic may be simply someone who has been unable to suppress his normal instincts and conform to an abnormal

---

[2] For an opposite view of the consequences of the ego-split, one should consult the work of Jacques Lacan, particularly the essay, "The Function of Language in Psychoanalysis" in *The Language of the Self*, edited by Anthony Wilden (Baltimore: 1968). The logical consequence of the Lacanian categories of the signifier, and the Symbolic, the Imaginary, and the Real means that metalanguage is an absolute necessity for our constitution of the Other. What Laing would call a "symptom" is really nothing more than a statement in a metalanguage about an object language. He would undoubtedly accuse Laing of concentrating upon only one language level rather than regarding the Other as simply the *rest* of the system in which the subject is involved.

society." Such represents an attempt to shift the emphasis for the burden of schizophrenia from the "inside" to the "outside," and is, by the way, a characteristic of schizophrenia! In *Sanity, Madness and the Family*, Laing argues (in the "Preface to the Second Edition") that "no one should deny us the right to disbelieve in schizophrenia," and further adds that he and his co-author will offer no model of it. Throughout, he attempts to regard schizophrenia as a label and nothing more. Yet, in the ensuing "Introduction" to the same volume, his first sentence is as follows: "For five years now we have been studying the families of schizophrenic patients. This book is our first report on that research." Now, the culture is not labelling, as Laing alleges, but rather Laing himself is. In *The Divided Self* he had made a clear distinction between schizophrenic and the non-schizophrenic:

The individual may experience his own being as real, alive, whole: as different from the rest of the world in ordinary circumstances so clearly that his identity and autonomy are never in question . . . he thus has a firm core of ontological security.

The culture recognizes that person as sane, whereas there are others who are less fortunate:

The individual in the ordinary circumstances of living may feel more unreal than real; in a literal sense, more dead than alive; precariously differentiated from the rest of the world, so that his identity and autonomy are always in question . . .

(*The Divided Self*, chapter 3)

Clearly, again, it is not the culture or "them" that is labelling, but R. D. Laing himself! And that labelling is absolutely necessary in order to treat the schizophrenic. If people do not "get" schizophrenia, but "are" schizophrenic, as the knight of Kingsley Hall suggests, are we not leaving out a third possibility, notably that people "become" schizophrenic?

Laing, of course, could never arrive at such a position, for the conversion to politics takes place too quickly in his thought. Although he believes that the "world" of the schizophrenic is an existential enactment of his ontological situation, he can never believe that society is a natural expression of human needs. Yet, other specialists in schizophrenia, Winnicott, Fairbairn, and Guntrip, see the archetypal experience of man's growth in terms of the individual developing, as integral with his sense of his own identity, the capacity to relate to others. In this picture of human nature, the function of the ego is not adaptation, as it is for Ronald Laing, but *integration*. Symbolism and culture are the primary means by which human beings become human and work on their problems of becoming whole and then "seeing through." Hence, there can be no question about the desirability of an ego dissolution such as that advocated by Laing. For Guntrip schizophrenia is a "dramatic version of basic ego-weakness" which constantly demands fulfillment and validation.[8]

In Winnicott's terms, this ego-weakness is not a product of "society" with the family as the agent of repression, but of a failure of the "ordinary adequate mother." Dissolving, insurrection, and that process of mind-fuck which Laing describes as "driving people out of their wretched minds" is no solution at all. Like so much activist rhetoric, it accomplishes

[8] Harry Guntrip, *Personality Structure and Human Interaction* (London, 1961), p. 114.

the "rip-off" (of our false-selves and hence our false
values) without substituting a new value structure,
which, one suspects, must come from the "inside."
Otherwise, we merely exchange the hell of subjectivity for another, and more tragic underworld. Laing
is, in short, a neo-romantic faced with the problem of
how to thrive without feeling guilty. Rather than
treating it as primarily an internal problem, he emp-
ties the self and locates the evil in *them*:

The direction we have to take is *back* and *in* . . . They
will say we are regressed and withdrawn and out of contact with them . . . they will try to cure us. They may
succeed. But there is still hope that they will fail. . . .
                                  (*The Politics of Experience*)

This regressive journey is a voyage out of dependency
upon anyone or anything and, like the "trips" of
those Alastors and Epipsychidions of romantic poetry,
is finally circuitous. The romantic "figure" endlessly
pursues some image representing Ideal Beauty until
he discovers that any communication with the object
of his aesthetic quest induces her transformation into
a witch whose visage bears a striking resemblance to
his own. The inability to achieve communion with
the "other" converts what would have been a linear
pilgrimage into a circular self-reflexive journey to the
psyche. Perhaps this is one reason why so many com-
panions of questors en route to one or another of
those domed and doomed kingdoms of art in the
nineteenth century seem to be but extensions of the
solitary wanderer. Such "doubling" is nothing more
than the aestheticization of self-consciousness and
comes to be stylistically manifested as the *doppel-
ganger* in stories like *Dr. Jekyll and Mr. Hyde* or *The*

Picture of Dorian Gray. An additional danger occurs when the pilgrim discovers that his quest is internal rather than external which may well account for those ellipses with which so many romantic quest poems break-off. The non-dependent voyageur rapidly approaches the existential condition of the voyeur, and ocular introjection mainfested as a desire to fill up elite space alternates with the fear of being seen, with the terror of implosion.[4] What I am suggesting, stated succinctly, is that there is something in the nature of the particular journey on which Laing asks us to accompany him, that enables us to get in touch with the world of the schizophrenic precisely because it is schizophrenic. It duplicates, even recapitulates, the schizophrenic's journey, but that structural repetition by no means accomplishes anything more than a first step in the analytic procedure.

The dilemma of the schizophrenic's being-in-the-world has a number of characteristics which Laing observes and comments upon. Its orientation is a

---

[4] In fact, the *fin-de-siecle* with all of its emphasis upon "doubles" and reflected images is a kind of metaphoric representation of the collective "illness" which Laing is describing. When the self comes to regard *itself* as an object, all is neutralized within a fortress of desire. The popular image of the hermaphrodite hence becomes a sort of emblem of mystification. And the language of this period in literary history tends to be a highly stylized gossip—a language that enables us to participate passively. Its self-reflexiveness is suggested by a number of features: one can create his own beginnings and endings (hence, like most schizophrenic tongues, it has no time dimension) with gossip; it can be joined and exited at will (hence the gossiper is well-defensed); and it is highly exaggerated and overwrought almost to the extent of being a metalanguage. The structure of the consciousness that engages in it is sodomic, it fills up its own impacted space re-projected as the Other.

primitive oral one, concerned with sustaining life
while remaining terrified at the prospect of absorption.
It loses a sense of physical contact with any reality
outside itself, while the "inner" self, of whose defense such care has been taken, becomes a torture
chamber.[5] The relationship of the self-false-self-system,
since it involves a participation through detachment,
is inevitably guilt-laden. Because the individual has
set up a relationship within his own being that would
normally be extra-personal, there is a certain dread
of onanism, accompanied by a fear that creativity and
creative relationships are wasting away with an ensuing desperate need of constant renewal. Losing the
conditioned, the self loses its identity; having lost
reality, freedom of choice retreats into the distance.
Being already dead, one no longer fears death—hence
the almost constant threat of suicide in the acute
schizophrenic. Death or incarceration within the walls
of some mental institution becomes the ultimate defensive posture since only in that state can one avoid
death to himself and the murder of the other. Love
is no solution since loving someone, for the schizophrenic, is equated with being like the other person
and hence with the implosion that destroys the self.
Self-hatred and masochism is the inevitable result of
a post-romantic narcissism. And Laing's advocacy of
a dissolution of the ego on the part of the analyst,
while it may aid him in understanding the schizophrenic, scarcely provides more than a multiplication

[5] This feature of schizophrenic existence may well account for
the abundance of references to epidermis or sheets or layering
in the poetry of Sylvia Plath. The schizophrenic tends to be
highly sensitive in this area precisely because she may feel that
she is existing without her skin, the barrier between "inside" and
"outside."

of shells which have lost their substance. That is to say that the price of understanding may be joining the "family." What Laing has accomplished is the construction of a system which makes nihilism functional. Unfortunately, the very concept of a "cure" is impossible within his vision of things. Since every supposed therapy is merely one more example of collusion with an abnormal culture, the analyst's role is simply that of "riding shotgun" with the patient on his trip. Although Laing describes the voyage in, he never talks about the return portion of the journey. Just how does he distinguish between a mystification which transforms the self into an "it" and the dissolution of the analyst's self which accomplishes the same thing?

One suspects that Laing himself might answer that the psychoanalyst must become a saint who lives by denial. Yet, saints have a mediating role which Laing would forever renounce, and by no means would he set an example in life. He hears confessions and establishes community, but salvation must never be the goal of the pilgrimage. Nor would he allege that the "new" man must be born from *within*, as would the traditional saint, but rather wants to bring this about by challenging the social structure which in its infinite normality, kills thousands in Viet-Nam. All this is to say that R. D. Laing is a strange sort of saint, puritan saint—which is itself, as much a self-referential paradox as any of the pseudo-statements in *Knots*. The type, it is to be supposed, always emerges at times of schism, historical or ontological. Laing is a saint whose audience in general follows a contour that parallels the popularity of the Beatles and acid-rock: emerging as an experiment from England, entering a kind of underworld drug culture where phrases like "like man" yoke all disparates together in a kind of psychic patchwork; exported (introjected?) to the United States where he becomes popular on university campuses; and finally enters the free classroom (usually English literature or philosophy, but almost never psychology courses), and is finally taken off the bulletin board courses and placed within the regular course syllabus—always the last item to be radicalized. But it is a pattern which approximates that used by political groups to *polarize* the culture. That is, until the polarizer comes apart at the seams at some point during one of the metaphoric trips.

Laing's British citizenship (he is actually Scottish, which perhaps makes his puritanism as well as his saintliness more understandable) is doubtlessly a contributing factor to the nature of his interests and the structure that it assumes. The country itself is a spatial island which has always been vulnerable to implosion. Enclosure, whether it be in the incessant British round-about, the compartmentalized railroad coaches (even in the lower classes), or the semi-detached house, seems almost part of the structure of consciousness in the country. The nation seems to delight in the façade, some outer mask that muffles a disagreeable interior, be it the architectural front of Buckingham Palace or the glistening silver serving dishes that disguise a less than mediocre meal. Of course, the British "gentleman," unruffled at times of distress, is the perfect embodiment of that quite visible veil that separates a private interior from the highly stylized façade.[6] So necessary is this separation

---

[6] See my essay, "An Atlantic Dialogue: Setting as Consciousness" in *Salmagundi* (autumn, 1968), pp. 56–72.

that when the private affairs of men invade the public posture, as in the Christine Keeler affair, governments fall. The one constant in Laing's view of the world is violence, but it is a violence that is never recognizable because it is hidden within some larger, self-perpetuating system. The expense of losing touch with one's mask in Great Britain is that the mask quickly comes to be used defensively rather than offensively. Non-Britishers, like Roy Schafer, whose *Aspects of Internationalization* is concerned with some of the same issues as Laing's *The Divided Self*, approaches schizophrenia from a quite different perspective: the evolution of identifications, the place of fantasy, and shifting levels of consciousness in the processes of internalization. When he talks about violence, it is seldom hidden in the institutional variety but is quite close to the surface. For Laing, the system, like the schizophrenic, has no surface because *it* is all surface.[7]

But, even if they offer no assurance of salvation, saints must offer some redemption from the throes of an older religion. And that debased faith which lurks behind so much of R. D. Laing's thought may well be the famous chapter on "Bad Faith" in Sartre's *Being and Nothingness*. Laing is a disciple of the French extentialist, and wrote, with David Cooper, *Reason and Violence*, an examination of Sartre's

[7] Roy Schafer, *Aspects of Internalization* (New York, 1968), p. 154. Schafer distinguishes between identification and introjection in a manner quite opposite from that of Laing. In introjection, one imagines having what one lacks or may lose; in identification, one becomes what one needs to be. Introjection perpetuates needfulness and ambivalence, and forestalls renunciation, but it continues the struggle with the object in the process of self-development.

works between 1950 and 1960, including the *Critique of Dialectical Reason*. In that book, the authors reiterate Sartre's notion of a *project*, which is an individual's choosing what he wants to accomplish from among the possibilities that exist under present conditions. The subject's project often *depasses* the given conditions, which means that, although the subject may restructure the original situation to meet his needs and desires, he is continually influenced by the original that he is changing. The old is simultaneously surpassed and retained in the new:

The project is both negation and realization: it retains and unveils the depassed which it has negated at the very moment of depassment.

(Laing and Cooper, *Reason and Violence*)

Although man is circumscribed by material conditions, he can act on these to change them. Man is characterized by the depassment of a given situation, above all else, because he is able to "*do* or *undo* . . . what has been done to him." On the ontological level, Sartre's notion of a project which depasses finds its correspondence in Laing's thought with "mapping," which is, after all, merely another form of *projection*.

This intense interest in Sartre might have led Laing to see such projection as an attempt to overcome the dehumanization of the double-bind. In the famous chapter in Part I of Sartre's treatise, *Being and Nothingness*, he gives the example of a woman who has consented to go out with a man for the first time. Again, the context is a romantic quest of sorts that concludes with doubling. Although our young woman well knows the intentions of the man regarding her and recognizes that sooner or later she will have to make a decision regarding his advances, the woman never recognizes the urgency, electing instead to postpone the reckoning. She concerns herself only with what is respectful and discreet in the attitude of her companion. And she restricts her behaviour to what is in the present. Even were he to say something like "I find you so attractive," the woman would probably choose to disarm the phrase of its sexuality. The chances are, as Sartre wisely observes, she attaches to the conversation and the speaker only the *immediate* meanings which she imagines as objective qualities. The qualities of the male become fixed in a permanence like that of *things*; it is no other than the projection in the strict present of those qualities into the temporal flux of her life. She does not lack knowledge, but is, to the contrary, profoundly aware of the desire which she inspires. Yet the desire cruel and naked would always humiliate and horrify her. Simultaneously, she never finds charm in an attitude which would be only respect. Satisfaction is obtainable only from a feeling which is addressed wholly to her personality, i.e., her full freedom. Should the man then grasp her hand, the young woman would be forced into an immediate decision—notably how to defend against disinformed desire. She can neither withdraw her hand (for such is to break the charm of the evening) nor grasp his (for such is to engage herself).

The woman may, Sartre adds, casually sentimentalize about Life in an effort to achieve transcendence over the supposed disappearance of choices. In the process she reduces her "self" to its essential aspect; faced with the prospect of engaging or withdrawing her hand, she elects to merely leave her hand limply in his. The process which she engages in men-

tally might go something like this: I will detach my
hand from the rest of my body in order to make the
hand the not-me. The not-me (which would corre-
spond with Laing's false-self system) protects the
"me" from being hurt. The hand is no longer part of
her, but has become disembodied, creating a schizoid
condition. In the process both partners have colluded
in a dehumanizing journey from the self existing to
the self-existing-as-for-which. In an effort to avoid access to the self, the woman has martyrized her nothingness. What Laing does is to give the dynamics
which I have been discussing a political dimension
by relating it to the way in which the body politic
colludes in the surrender of its freedom. In the process, a romantic journey that began in good faith, concludes in "Bad Faith."

All of this makes love relationships a cruel parody
of romantic love, whenever we encounter it in Laing's
books. If one were to take him seriously, we humans
are more desirous of desire than any object. Hence, a
schema of what happens to "romantic" love would
look something like this:

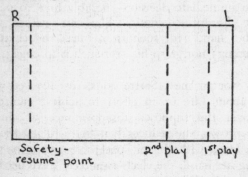

The woman defends the goal line whose coffin-corner flag bears the word, *rejection*, whereas her opponent, the male, defends the *love* goal line. Typically, the man participates passively, which is to say that he puts the ball into play by kicking off after losing the toss of the coin. On the first series, she threatens his goal line and hence his identity, and in order to prevent the loss of one's territory (presumably her crossing the goal line would be accompanied by wedding bells rather than the habitual cannon), he says, "I cannot give you everything until I know more about you," to which she replies, "That is what I have known all along; you really do not love me as an act of commitment." This represents her loss of ten yards back to the line marked "2nd play." She tries again, only to run into his hesitancy a second time, and is thrown for yet another loss. Eventually, the field is going to be shortened and her back is against her own goal line. At the very moment when a safety is imminent, she yells or suggests by gestures that she needs to be rescued. She may even call time out and walk out of his apartment. But of course, he colludes to rescue her, lets down his umbrella, prevent defense, and allows her to complete the bomb which puts her once again in a threatening position to score. Of course, she partially feigns her offense, since she recognizes that the best way to get into scoring position is to sustain a few losses that will prompt a guilt-laden rescue attempt. And he knows that his best chance for scoring occurs when he allows her to get too close to his own end zone, painted with the word, *love*. Hopefully our dream couple can avoid the imprisonment of an ever-shortening field at some point in their relationship by realizing that there are not really two different goal lines, but only one. Then they would recognize how dependent their offense is upon the defense of the "other" and vice-versa and vice-vice-versa. But such would take both teams out of the hall of mirrors in which they are playing the Interaction Bowl. In one sense, such a realization would shorten the field even more; the polarization substitutes one kind of despair for another, though Laing would never see it as a good substitution.

The analyst, for Laing at least, is faced with a similar struggle, and his world has a similar kind of echoing concentricity as its characteristic feature. So many of the lines are dotted, or parenthetical, or comprised of vertical ellipses in the field of the schizophrenic. For Laing, there was a time when man's behavior was one with his experience. He continually speaks of "loss" and a journey-back, in spite of the fact this trip never involves a return to the patient's childhood. But after this fall into self-consciousness, man's behavior became a defense against the other experiencing his experience. The traditional analyst who treats behavior forever treats the defensive line of the patient. And the more he strives to understand and decipher the behavior, the more behavior the schizoid "throws off." He must get inside the fortress, inside all the concentric circles to some presumably genuine self (see figure on following page).

Of course, Laing never entertains the thought that Goffman frequently does, notably that this "real" self, too, may be just as presentational as the series of false-selves. Frequently, it seems that for Goffman, particularly in The Presentation of Self in Everyday Life, the self that Laing imagines as occupying some

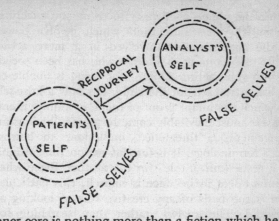

inner core is nothing more than a fiction which he has mystified in reverse. Could what Laing imagines to be *the* self be nothing more than a zero, which in mathematics, enables us to proceed operationally, but has no or little value other than a position occupier?

Winnicott, whose work in schizophrenia is not nearly so nihilistic as that of Laing, sees another way of turning the "inside" to the "outside" which avoids many of the problems posed by Laing's methodology. He sees schizophrenia as a failure of development which arises from an inability of the child "to gather his bits together . . . bits of nursing technique and faces seen and sounds heard and smells smelt are only gradually pieced together into one being to be called mother." [8] As the infant pieces the object together, he also pieces himself together, for upon this self-construction *depends* his reality-sense. But the mother is also torn by other pressures. Our society

[8] D. W. Winnicott, "The Mirror Role of the Mother" in *The Predicament of the Family*, edited by Peter Lomas (London, 1967).

attaches the notion of identity to *doing* and *enacting*, to essentially masculine traits which involve power and the acquisitiveness involved in a more active exercise of *becoming*. A woman who has been social- ized into substituting "doing" for being is unable to establish a true self for the child, but only a false-self with which the infant is out of touch in a quite literal sense. He must inevitably come to regard "her" as an impingement, a threatened implosion, to borrow Laing's terminology. It is for this reason that Winni- cott urges a "mirror-role" for the mother. Since what the infant sees in her face is himself, this particular vision is the basis of any creative way of looking at the world. The analyst, rather than searching for something "lost" on some trip with the patient, must re-enact the primary relationship—he must provide a mirror for the patient to piece himself together in. Only when the patient engages in an act of self-dis- covery can he distinguish the "self" from "the other." And that knowledge of barriers is a prerequisite for the establishment of identity; the one thing he may not need is a companion who accompanies him and then says, "look at what *they* are doing to us." Hence the analyst must act in the mirror-role to "give back what the patient brings"; only by providing identity- dependence can the analyst move through depend- ence and into something else. By holding the mirror up to the patient, the analyst recapitulates the first loss or absence and enables a recovery of images which can be used for putting the self back together rather than fortifying *it*.[9]

[9] This assumes an essentially passive role on the part of the analyst. It further assumes that he must become part of the constitutive "family" of the schizophrenic. Historically, this

Unless the body can be differentiated from others, self-destruction and re-birth are identities, part of the infinite sequence of tautologies which make up the schizophrenic's world. If Winnicott is accurate in his analysis of the schizophrenic situation, then we are really dealing, in part, with a failure of domestication. And indeed the schizophrenic imagination would seem to be oriented according to *proxemics*— the spatial dimension of human occasions. Although most of us are highly self-domesticated animals, the domestication process is only partial in the schizophrenic. When approached too closely, panic sets in, much the same way as it does when we approach an un-domesticated animal in the wilderness. In describing their feelings, such patients refer to anything that happens within their "flight line" as taking place literally *inside themselves,* one of the consequences of being unable to distinguish where self and false-self have any tangency. The schizophrenic, then, is not merely boxed-in in terms of his choices, but has quite literally used up all of his empty spaces. Hence, the coffin or incarceration within some mental institution, contrary to offering release, is the final stage in a journey that began with the eidetic reduction of experience. Early death and imprisonment seem to be the alternatives left to the revolutionary romantic questor who discovers that his journey has not created

would involve a regression of a different order than that advocated by Laing. The history of the psychoanalytic movement is actually being recapitulated. Developmentally, psychology moves from an interest in the oedipal, an essentially three person relationship, to the anal, and finally, to the oral. When the analyst is constituted as an imitation of the mother's being, he is, in an important sense, making every situation a "family affair" in a double sense.

new spaces, but has self-reflexively used them all up:

a finger points to the moon

Put the expression
  a finger points to the moon, in brackets
  (a finger points to the moon)
The statement:
  'A finger points to the moon is in brackets'
is an attempt to say that all that is in the bracket
  (   )
is, as to that which is not in the bracket,
what a finger is to the moon

$$(Knots)^{10}$$

[10] Although space does not permit a critical examination of R. D. Laing's volume of poems, the circular nature of the journey on which we accompany him might be suggested by the fact that the last three "knots" can be read either down the page, or from left to right. Although Laing alleges in his prefatory comment that the web is endless, as a matter of fact, each poem ends when there is no longer a way to distinguish the primary from the secondary-process operations. What had been a sort of epic poem (beginning in ontic *medias res*) is converted to an oracular fable, a mass-saga in which the narrator has been refined out of existence.

Schizophrenia and the Mad Psychotherapist

BY LESLIE H. FARBER

Editor's note: What follows is reprinted from Dr. Farber's extremely important volume, *The Ways of The Will* (Basic Books, 1966; Harper and Row paperback edition, 1968). While it has not been a practice of ours to reprint material, especially when it is more or less available to most readers, we think Dr. Farber's essay useful to an understanding of Laing's work and the peculiar dynamics of his development. Convinced that the essay belonged in any collection of items on Laing, I called Dr. Farber in the summer of 1970 to discuss the idea with him, and he confirmed my original impulse. Dr. Farber had not been thinking of Laing but of a previous generation of analysts when he wrote the essay in 1962, but he agreed that it might be helpful to think of Laing in the terms proposed for the earlier therapists.

We expect, then, that the following essay may provide a suitable frame in which Laing's remarks may be considered. While it does not really serve either to discredit or validate particular insights at which Laing and his associates have arrived (something Dr. Farber never intended it to do, of course), it brings under scrutiny the origins of those insights. Surely when we are dealing with a prophetic figure like Laing, a species of the analyst-as-seer, this is a perspective we need to consider.—ROBERT BOYERS

IN PREVIOUS ESSAYS (see especially chapter 8 of *The Ways of The Will*) I have attempted to describe the peculiar and painful nature of the therapeutic life with schizophrenia—its emptiness, meaninglessness, lack of confirmation—in short, the circumstances that lead to a particular despair on the part of the therapist and that may subsequently evoke in the patient a response of pity for his doctor's plight. I suggested further that such pity might very well lead the patient to assuage the therapist's anguish through therapeutic movements intended to confirm the therapist as therapist. It seemed to me then, as it seems to me now, that despair is more or less intrinsic to the therapeutic life with schizophrenia and that such despair, moreover, if acknowledged rather than disowned, if contended with rather than evaded, *might* (the word is important have a salutary effect on therapy.

My aim in this essay is to examine what happens, especially to the therapist himself, when this despair is *not* acknowledged, not contended with.

By and large, the response of my colleagues to the earlier paper was one of agreement, although several older therapists, some exceptionally capable in their work, were not persuaded by my argument, feeling that my account of the agonies of therapy was both overdrawn and unfaithful to their own experience.

And, while I was working on the paper and was absorbed with schizophrenia and the hazards of ministering to it, I became aware that a number of younger therapists, each with several years' experience treating schizophrenia, were seeking, in one way or another, to take their leave of this area of psychiatry. The reasons they contrived for abandoning their work with schizophrenics were various, but I began gradually to suspect that underlying all their logic and detachment, their talk of the value of varied clinical experience, of opportunities elsewhere, of a yearning for private practice was a vague and brooding, and unspoken, apprehension that their sanity was at stake. In this apprehension, they were often joined by their wives, who also felt vaguely troubled by subtle changes in their husbands. Although they had difficulty describing this alteration, they seemed to have no doubt that it constituted an unhappy development. Even when nagged or beseeched by their husbands for reassurance, these wives were unwilling or unable to consider the changes they observed as part of a decent maturation of character. I am trying as carefully as possible to avoid being clinical. Clinical categorizing here would be as inappropriate to our purposes of describing and understanding as clinical self-scrutiny was inadequate to the perplexing and ominous restlessness these younger therapists found themselves caught up in. Neither they nor their wives worried that they might fall victim to a particular clinical disorder, least of all schizophrenia. If they feared for their sanity, it was in a private, unprofessional way; they wondered to what degree they were becoming what they were not, or—with equal relevance—to what degree they were not becoming what they were.

At any rate, the objections raised by some of my

older friends to my paper on therapeutic despair, as well as the uneasiness and concern of these younger men, have prompted me to reconsider my own experience in this area. For a period of over twenty years that includes working with schizophrenics, as well as those young doctors who spend their days treating schizophrenic patients, I have also had the good fortune to know and to be instructed by several very great therapists, therapists with grave theoretical differences, but sharing nevertheless that power sometimes called "charisma," which the dictionary defines as: "a grace, as a miraculously given power of healing, or of speaking with tongues, or of prophesying, etc., attributed to some of the early Christians." Then, too, I have had a passing acquaintance with those occasional, ragged, even disreputable healers who seem to burst full-blown, apparently with little preparation, into the world of schizophrenia, brandishing their therapeutic powers with a flourish that far exceeds their theoretical accomplishments. Their period of therapeutic vitality is usually comparatively brief, and their subsequent course or fate, disagreeable. In short then, as I looked about me at three different groups of therapists—the young, the old, and the vagabonds —I could not escape concluding, allowing for certain remarkable exceptions, that the hazards are indeed serious for those who choose to devote their professional lives to the treatment of schizophrenia.

I sometimes wonder what impression the hospital world of schizophrenia—for example, a sanitarium devoted exclusively or primarily to schizophrenic patients—might make on someone who happened into it without advance explanation or preparation. His first thought, one he would quickly correct, would be that it was difficult to tell the doctors from the patients. But, as soon as he dismissed this notion—in spite of conceits to the contrary it is not a difficult distinction—I suspect that, as he observed the therapists in ordinary conversation and listened to them in meeting, it might strike him that no word but theatrical or histrionic could do descriptive justice to their extraordinary manner. He would have to conclude that, for reasons mysterious to himself, these therapists had apparently abandoned what must once have been their more usual habits of expression in favor of some more florid and declamatory style—a style that appeared to transcend style, elevating mere form or manner to substance itself.

At this point, let me describe an incident from the therapeutic practice of a friend—one of the most distinguished therapists of schizophrenia in modern times. The incident is not especially unusual and may, therefore, suggest the flavor of the life within an institution devoted to the treatment of schizophrenia, as it might appear to an outsider.

My friend the therapist had been treating a schizophrenic young man for about a year and a half. The therapy had had its ordinary portion of difficulty, impasse, silence, violence, and the like, but, at the time of this incident, seemed to be moving along satisfactorily. My friend owned a fountain pen of which he was very fond. It was an excellent pen, valuable, distinctive in appearance, and reliable. Not only did it give him pleasure on all these counts, but it also had personal significance for him, having been a birthday gift from his father. My friend used this pen constantly, carrying it with him in his breast pocket wherever he went. Somehow, in the course of a therapeutic session, the pen came to the attention of the patient, who seemed to admire it. He watched attentively as my friend used it to make notes, then hesitantly reached his own hand toward it. Noticing this gesture, the therapist, instead of returning the pen to his pocket, put it into his patient's hand and said, "Pretty, isn't it? Do you want to try it out?" The patient slowly fondled the pen, then suddenly unscrewed the cap and fell to making marks on a sheet of paper the therapist had placed before him. Totally absorbed, he hunched over his work, manipulating the pen with care and deliberation. Although solemn and silent, as was customary, he seemed to be enjoying himself. Heartened by this responsiveness—if only to his fountain pen—and reluctant to ignore any opportunity for relation, the therapist said, "Look, how would you like to keep the pen until tomorrow? Maybe you could write a letter with it tonight. You can bring it back to me at our hour tomorrow." The patient stopped marking the paper and gazed down at the pen, then up at the ceiling, then out the window, and finally into the therapist's face. "Thank you," he said. The remainder of the hour went very well.

The following therapeutic session came and went without mention of the pen. And the following one. And the one after that. And then several more. At last, after some weeks had passed, my friend inquired politely about his pen and mentioned how convenient it would be to have it back again. The patient said nothing, but appeared to have heard the therapist's remarks. A few more therapeutic hours passed with no sign or mention of the pen, and finally one day my friend said, "I don't want to press you about this, but the matter of my fountain pen is increasingly on my mind. I'm sure I didn't mention it to you at the time you borrowed it, but that pen means a great deal to me. I realize this may be sheer childishness on my part, but, you see, it was a present from my father, a little while before he died, as a matter of fact, and I'm very attached to it. Of course, I could easily just buy myself another pen, or use a pencil, and forget the whole thing. But, as I've explained, I'm especially fond of that particular pen. This may all seem quite silly to you, but surely you know how people sometimes become devoted to certain objects . . . Well, maybe it *is* silly, but the fact remains that I *am* devoted to that pen, and I'd appreciate very much having it back. So, would you please bring it along with you next time?" There was no answer, but my friend assumed he had made his point and that it had registered. However, the fountain pen failed to appear at the next interview, or the next, or the next. A few sessions later my friend introduced the subject still another time. "About my pen. . . . You've had it six weeks now. Don't you think that's about long enough to keep a borrowed fountain pen? I've explained it all very carefully to you—why I'm anxious to have it back, and so forth. Now, please don't fail to bring the pen with you tomorrow."

And, two meetings later, "My patience is wearing thin. I mean to have that pen, and I don't want any more foolishness about it. Time after time I've asked you gently and politely to return it; I've explained how I feel about it, and why I insist on having it back, and all this has produced no result whatever. You don't return it, you won't discuss it. Now what the hell is all this about? Can you tell me that?"

After a long silence the patient murmured, "It's lost."
"It's *what*? What do you mean *lost*?" No answer.
"Are you trying to tell me that you no longer have
my fountain pen? You don't have it with you? It's
not in your room? In other words, it's *gone*?" Again
the patient made no answer; in fact, he remained absolutely silent throughout the rest of the hour, while
the therapist thundered at him and stomped about
the office.

The interview concluded on this uncordial note,
and the patient returned to his room. Immediately
the therapist summoned two hospital attendants, and
the three of them marched off toward the ward where
the patient lived. When they reached his room, the
therapist gave a curt order, and the attendants flung
wide the door, bounded inside, and in a matter of seconds had the startled young man on his back, pinned
to the floor. My friend then entered the room, and
without taking the least notice of his gasping and as-
tonished patient, made a rapid but efficient search for
his pen. He found it in the drawer of the desk. He
picked it up, regarded it a moment, glanced briefly
at his pinioned patient while he jabbed the pen into
his breast pocket, then wheeled about and stalked
from the room. As he was making his exit the patient
raised his head from the floor and shouted past the
attendants toward his retreating therapist, "My God,
what a madhouse! All this fuss about one little fountain pen!"

I am at pains to point out that my friend is a cour-
teous, civilized person, whose normal manner—at least
among friends—is gracious and reserved and ironic.
Ordinarily, he is simply not given to such carrying on
as I have described. It would be more characteristic,

in such a circumstance, for him to acknowledge that the problem of the borrowed-pen-gone-astray is the inevitable concern of anyone who has—and lends— cherished possessions, and, after polite efforts to retrieve some item had failed, he would, without undue commotion, replace it. This display over his patient's failure, or refusal, to return his pen is curiously uncharacteristic and might even be said to be enacted somewhat larger than life. But we must be careful with our interpretations at this point. My friend is no method actor, who will facetiously describe to his wife during dinner the experimental situation he engaged in with his patient, re-enacting his gestures and lines for her amusement. At no time, either while with his patient or when recounting the incident to his wife, does the therapist imagine himself to be *acting* at all. In talking with his wife, he will declare, quite sincerely, that his exasperating patient provoked him beyond all human endurance, driving him to take the measures he took. The one thing about the incident that would surely strike an observer will just as surely escape the attention of the therapist himself, namely, that this collision of wills has been shockingly naked, clothed by none of the artifices that usually conceal willfulness. If my friend has been theatrical, his theatricality has been effective enough to deceive himself. He may be ruthless in rooting out his motives for this violent action; he will call them "countertransference," which will enable him, by convicting himself of a vanity that led him to offer the pen in the first place, to seize full psychological responsibility for the whole encounter. Still, he will not be troubled by the quality and scope of his performance, nor is he likely to consider the possibility that the whole affair could be a fictitious alternative for some real moral dilemma confronting him and his patient. As a matter of fact, once he has thrashed out his motives—alone or, more commonly, with the assistance of his wife or a colleague—he may decide his handling of this incident has been direct, even courageous. Naturally, to come to this conclusion he will have to forget that the hospital situation stacks the deck in his favor; without a tremor, bravely, and in full view of the audience, he has shot the villain with a stage revolver loaded with blank cartridges.

Let me mention another incident, this one from the practice of the late Dr. Frieda Fromm-Reichmann, one of the most gifted people to work with schizophrenia.

Dr. Fromm-Reichmann was seeing an extremely disabled young man who had been schizophrenic for years. He was habitually dirty and disheveled; he rarely spoke and even more rarely achieved much coherence in what little speech he did produce. Without question, therapeutic work with this patient was a grim business, affording scant hope, little satisfaction, and few of even those fleeting rewards so precious to the therapist who specializes in the treatment of schizophrenia. One day, during a therapeutic hour, as this patient (mute, as usual) was sitting with Dr. Fromm-Reichmann in her office, she noticed that he was fingering his genitals with one hand that was crammed deep into the pocket of his trousers. It was also plain to her that he had an erection. She pondered this situation for a moment, then said to him, "If it will make you feel any better, please go ahead." Whereupon the young man unzipped his fly and proceeded to masturbate, while Dr. Fromm-Reichmann sat quietly across from him, her eyes down, her hands clasped in her lap.

Anyone who knew Dr. Fromm-Reichmann at all knew that she was a well-brought-up, refined, upper middle-class, German Jewish lady. During Georg Groddeck's last years, prior to his commitment to an institution, she performed the offices of his hostess with fastidious skill. Once or twice a year, she helped Groddeck to assemble at his estate a group of distinguished European psychiatrists. It was her duty to arrange for food and wine and cigars and in general to put these guests (many of whom did not know one another) at their ease, to ensure a comfortable social atmosphere out of which might come the sort of conversation Groddeck wished about matters psychoanalytic. Once the group had gathered, following all her work of arrangement and preparation, she was required, as the only woman present, to assist in the setting of the scene and in the maintenance of the appropriate tone to the occasion, but always without calling attention either to her assistance or to the novelty of her presence. But, of course, it might happen that in the consideration of some question of feminine psychology, Groddeck would suddenly turn to her and say, "Frieda, we men cannot really know about these things. As a woman, Frieda, you must instruct us." At such moments, I am sure, she was more than rewarded for the physical and emotional labor of these occasions, not to mention the irritations involved in dealing with a person as crotchety and difficult as Groddeck became in his later years.

Dr. Fromm-Reichmann was always a marvelous hostess, and something of her quality as hostess appears in the incident I have recounted about her and

the mute young man who was encouraged to masturbate if it would help him to feel more comfortable.
But I doubt that as this man sat masturbating in her
quiet office, full of tasteful mementoes of her European past, she found much resemblance to her life as
Groddeck's hostess. To some extent a hostess resembles an actress, in that she plays a role (in this
case, one of amiability toward a group she may not
know); she is not required to believe that her role is
anything more than a role. As with an actress, believ-
ability is central to the effectiveness of the performance, but in order that it be achieved, actual personal
sincerity—in regard to the scene itself—is unnecessary, if not irrelevant. In therapeutic encounters, on
the other hand, the therapist's actual personal sincerity is considered absolutely essential to the occasion.
I think that as Dr. Fromm-Reichmann described this
incident with the mute and masturbating young man
at a staff conference, she might well have blamed herself for some awkwardness in her invitation, and she
would have been quick to acknowledge any erotic
titillation she experienced. But she would have re-
sisted the suggestion that there was anything unusual
about her behavior, that while committed, in full sincerity, to her duties as psychotherapist she had suddenly found herself enacting the role of hostess. Her
private conviction, I suspect, would have been, as in
our previous example, that there was something real,
something "down-to-earth" about this incident.

It does not actually matter if the part an actor
plays is not really relevant to his life, because he
knows (I am speaking ideally, of course) that he is
playing a part. The therapist, however, is not granted
such distance; he may be theatrical, but he is not

playing a part. (Unlike the actor, he may believe what he will or will what he believes.) As he comes to believe in the reality of these overblown therapeutic encounters, so rich in the materials of strife and sexuality, it is his ordinary life outside the hospital that may come to appear artificial and pallid. It is not unusual for the therapist, as he settles into his work with schizophrenia, to begin to prefer the company of schizophrenics, even those who are mute. Given the extraordinary difficulty of treating schizophrenia, it might be expected that with experience, status, and income, the older therapist would try to restrict the hours he spends with schizophrenic patients. More often than not, the opposite is the case: he tends to fill more and more of his waking hours with such therapeutic work, and to feel quite bereft and impotent and lonely, when, for reasons of illness or vacation or grants, he is deprived of the schizophrenic's company. I shall return to this unusual preference later.

In telling the story about the therapist and the borrowed pen, I suggested that the whole incident had a quality of being somehow larger than life. But it is not merely the therapeutic encounter which is habitually writ large in this way; something of this quality passes over from the event to the man, and not infrequently the gifted therapists themselves come to be writ large. They begin to resemble certain spectacular personalities—often, but by no means exclusively, actors and show people—in that they no sooner enter a room than they fill it. Room after room after room, differences of setting and occasion mattering not at all, confronted with a room they fill it, in what becomes a characteristic style of their own, yet not predictable—as mere idiosyncrasy of manner is—and flexible enough to adapt itself to any particular situation. Just *how* they accomplish this, time after time, must to some extent remain a mystery; but what we have noted about their therapeutic life may give some clue to this quality of compelling social, or personal, presence, shared by a surprising number of therapists who have spent years in the company of schizophrenics, a quality that seems gradually to unfold to full-flower—quite a *large* flower, usually—in them over the years. Let me be quite clear here: filling a room is not merely—and sometimes not at all—a matter of talking long and loud; even silence may, on occasion, produce a unique resonance, affecting an entire scene. Nor can this capacity be attributed merely to physical manner. Manner is not unimportant, but it is more likely to be the vehicle (or perhaps only the packaging) of the effect than the key to its cause. It is true that *what* is said is usually less important than *how* it is said, but even here both the what and the how tend to vary with the therapist's dramatic feel of the occasion. There is, however, one general statement that we can make about such a man and his manner: what he cannot or will not countenance is distance and—as a result—any real absorption in subject matter. His province is relation: not the relation that may slowly emerge out of content, nor even the relation that may come from a leisurely exchange of personal forthrightness, which always risks alienation as its culmination, when two people strive (with success or without) to reveal themselves to each other. In one way or another, this room-filling therapist manipulates and forces the spell of relation, willfully exploiting whatever personal expedients come to mind.

In order to understand better this connection between will and relation—which I believe to be crucial to our subject—let us remind ourselves of the nature of the therapeutic life with schizophrenia. In Chapter 8 of *The Ways of The Will* I attempted to portray something of the agony of the therapeutic life with schizophrenia that may end in what I have called "the therapeutic despair." But, as some of my older friends have reminded me, despair is not inevitable; in fact, they would prefer to believe such despair is a morbid consequence of this work—as unhealthy, perhaps, as my own preoccupation with the subject.

I would like to suggest that avoiding despair by reducing it to a merely "morbid" or "unhealthy" state of mind—and thus refusing to conceive it as belonging inescapably in some measure to our lives as human beings—may be more malignant than despair itself. (It was Kierkegaard's belief that the worst of all despairs is that in which one does not know he is in despair.) It sometimes happens that despair itself provides the very condition of urgency that brings a man to ask those serious—we might call them tragic—questions about his life and the meaning and measure of his particular humanness. When despair is repudiated, these questions go unasked, and it may be exactly here, in the failure to confront these questions, that there occurs a turning in one's development that is false.

Let us consider again the situation in which the therapist, knowing that even the wrong approach is better than none, may muse or soliloquize aloud to his silent partner. For most therapists who persist in this field, such soliloquizing becomes their principal refuge or solace—or, from their standpoint, the form in which their therapeutic powers find their most vigorous expression. While the schizophrenic may be largely unresponsive to the social event, every therapist holds the premise that the patient hungers for relation at the same time that he lacks the ordinary personal grace that might bring such relation about. Moreover, he fears that should he venture an overture he might, owing to his gross deficiency, increase his estrangement by revealing himself as even more unacceptable than he already appears. Given the schizophrenic's incapacities, not to mention his experience in hypocrisy and betrayal, the overtures of others will seem to him even more dubious than his own. Obviously, such a situation imposes a formidable constraint on what may be said.

How may we characterize this constraint? There is, of course, the fact of inequality between these two people: one is patient, the other, doctor; one is confined, the other, free; one is mad, the other, sane. And this essential inequality must be contended with—validly or invalidly. Equally important is the choice and treatment of subject matter. Of what shall the therapist speak? And in what manner, from what view, to what point? If he were to talk about the daily events of his life, however scrupulously he stripped them of color and meaning and relevance, he would still imply a world in which he lived and worked, a world from which he himself was not estranged. And, aside from the effect on the patient, such a drab recital might very likely be dispiriting to the therapist, so eager himself to make some relational thrust into this seeming vacuum. (I am, of course, taking for granted that he will carefully avoid all those topics that might impinge on the patient's delusional propensities.) Since we may assume with some safety that the therapist himself is not schizophrenic, we will expect that in addition to having a world he lives with*in* rather than with*out*, he is also blessed by affectionate connections with friends and, very possibly, a family as well—all of which, for our present purposes, can be called relation. Unless he is sadistic, frantic, or simply stupid, he is hardly likely to expatiate to his schizophrenic patient over moments of intimacy with friends and family. If he chooses to speak of these people at all, it will probably be in order to emphasize whatever estrangement exists or has existed, seeking to appeal to his patient on the level of a fellow sufferer. The danger here, postponing momentarily the insidious effect this device may have on the therapist himself, is that often, to the patient, such talk about estrangement will serve to invoke intimations of those times when estrangement is (or was) either overcome or absent altogether. To forestall this danger, the therapist, almost without realizing it, may overstate and overgeneralize his case. Not deliberately, of course, since he is not being dishonest, but, in his need to join his patient, he may inventively overextend and exaggerate the oppressiveness of the situation he describes. And, since he is not an actor playing a part, and, more important still, since his own sincerity is essential to his convictions, as well as to the assurance with which he believes he must address his patient, he may succeed in persuading himself that through his work with his pa-

tient he has discovered patterns of pathology in himself and in his private life whose significance he had
not heretofore appreciated, or perhaps even suspected. This is not the only way certainly, but it is
an important way in which the therapist seeks, and
often finds, kinship with his patient: discovering (or
so he believes) his own schizophrenic possibilities.
As he pursues such objectifications of himself and his
life and his past, he comes to speak with a clarity
about himself as a psychological dynamism that is
not only excessive, but that may be quite false. But
again, being no actor, he may, as the years in this
work roll by, begin to confuse this deterministic construction with himself. And the assembling of this
construction is, of course, aided and abetted by the
fact that it will seldom, if ever, be challenged or
affirmed by the patient. Since determinism itself is
not necessarily an evil affair—it may be appropriate or
inappropriate, simple or complex—is there anything
we can say about the nature of the construction that
the therapist contrives to represent himself? By and
large, so far as I have been able to tell, regardless of
the particular school of psychoanalysis to which he
belongs, the therapist comes to view himself as victim, acted upon by forces of nature, society, or family
in such a manner or at such an early age as to render
him powerless. Whether he finds his victimization
during the first six months of his life, when he failed
to surpass the "paranoid position" postulated by
Melanie Klein, or locates his trauma in the anxious
mothering he received, according to Sullivanian theory, or—in modern fashion—discovers the "double
bind" in which his parents trapped him; his story will
be the familiar one of hero-as-victim irreversibly op-

pressed by the will of others. "I am this way because
. . . ," he announces to his patient as casually as possible, implying that it *is* possible to live this life in
spite of devastating victimization. Or, "The mood I
inflicted on you yesterday has its explanation in a
conflict I have been having with your ward adminis-
trator." Or, "My failure to hear you has always been
provoked by withdrawal, whether yours or my mother's." Or, "Last Thursday night I had a dream in
which I raped you. I tell you this so that you may
understand my coolness these last few days." And so
on. Such remarks will be regarded, not as acknowledgments of moral limitation, but as manifestations
of "countertransference," usually referring to personal attitudes acquired in the past and now inappropriate. We should notice here the easy and translu-
cent clarity of these statements: in vain will we seek
here for a hint of mystery, ambiguity, paradox, surprise, or uncertainty. Our visitor to the sanitarium,
hearing several such therapists in conference (naturally they speak to one another about themselves in
much the same way as to their patients), might, if
he were impressionable, briefly believe that he had
stumbled on a small band of mendicant monks, so
brutally honest did their confessions seem. But, as he
listened further, the utilitarian nature of this seeming
candor might soon strike him; he would note that such
"countertransference" explanations by and large af-
forded whatever meaning it seemed possible to provide in a painfully chaotic situation. Of course, he
could not help but observe that these confessions
were delivered, whether to patients or colleagues,
rather cheerfully, unlike his own halting and an-
guished acknowledgments of weakness and evil. Fi-

nally, he might wonder whether *confession* was quite the proper word to describe such remarks as, "I am this way because. . . ."

The realm of causation is treacherous ground for a man interested in the truth about himself. Although it is certainly probable that most phenomena of this world, human and otherwise, do have causes of one sort or another, an absorption with the role of causation in human affairs may lead to an habitual reduction of any human event to its (postulated) cause. It is apparent how such reduction promises refuge to a man beset by the necessity to "confess": once he turns his attention to cause, his personal responsibility (whether he acknowledges this or not) is diminished, along with any undue stress or discomfort he may have felt in facing what he believes to be his absolute worst. No matter what scandalous detail about himself he may reveal, he follows such revelation with "I am this way because . . . ," and everyone relaxes. Given the customary forms of psychology and a close-knit society of colleagues all trained to abide by these forms, and given in addition the harrowing, threatening, and chaotic environment of a sanitarium for schizophrenia, it is hardly a wonder that the solace of causation persistently tempts these therapists and appears most seductive when they are speaking with one another about themselves and their lives with their patients. Even should a therapist's account of himself on such occasions include no direct reference to cause, his remarks are apt to lack that hesitant, hard-come-by quality that tends to characterize the statements of a man truly involved in making a moral confession.

Our visitor, as his stay in the sanitarium lengthened, might—depending on the degree of his disenchantment—soon find the atmosphere oppressive, sickly, somewhat like living in a hothouse where, in the midst of lush vegetation, the temperature was always too hot, the sunlight filtered and indirect, the humidity and fertility always controlled, with none of the accident of sudden cold or wind. Particularly as he listened to the therapists in conference, admonishing and even reassuring one another with countertransference interpretations, he might choose another image to describe the stifling effect on himself: a chamber of distorting mirrors, such as one finds in amusement parks, in which all that may be seen are reflections of reflections of reflections—of the psyches of the therapists. Failure, principally, but also the occasional therapeutic success finds its cause and its meaning, by default of other sources of meaning, in the materials of countertransference, which constitutes a fashionable form of psychological determinism among those who treat schizophrenia.

Much of the responsibility for this absorption with countertransference lies in the nature of schizophrenia itself, which is a disorder consisting of a double failure in areas that might loosely be called meaning and relation. The intellectual defect, so strikingly displayed in the awkwardness with language, has been variously described in studies of schizophrenic thinking. Such civilized qualities as discretion, reticence, humor, judgment, and logic are poorly developed, if they are present at all. In the imaginative realm, what we usually call the capacity for metaphorical thinking is morbidly deficient, causing the schizophrenic's understanding and perceptions, as well as his efforts to communicate, to be uncomfortably literal. This disability of imagination may be mistaken by the therapist for the workings of the bared unconscious—as though the unconscious were not subject to refinement. Here, he is apt to regard as symbol either what properly is not symbol at all, or what could fairly be called only the rudiments of symbol. It is as though the therapist imagined the schizophrenic to contain inside him a nonschizophrenic poet, who manipulated and molded his symbolic utterances and gestures, concealing in some inside pocket that texture of meaning that symbols may achieve. However, it is more likely that this nonschizophrenic poet, if he exists at all, resides not inside the patient, but in the head of the therapist, who attributes to his patient's utterances a richness of meaning that is simply not deserved. I should mention that there are certain desirable aspects to the therapist's attribution of meaning to the verbal or gestural productions of his schizophrenic patient; not only does the patient need such imaginative assistance, if he is to recover, but such an exalted view of his capacities also incites an enthusiasm for his work on both sides that urges its continuance in the teeth of the discouragements that are intrinsic to the therapeutic situation.

Nevertheless, there is a hazard to this investitude. Should the therapist forget the degree to which he has supplied meaning to a patient unable to provide any for himself, he may come to regard the schizophrenic as a sort of oracle with whom he sits each day—a truly ragged oracle, untutored, unverbal, and naturally unappreciated, who has the rare power to cut through the usual hypocrisies and pretensions of ordinary life, thereby arriving at some purely human meaning. His illness now appears as an appropriate response to the impurities in the therapist's heart, even to the deceits and contradictions of the world in which he lives.

Take the example of a schizophrenic young man whose disagreeable habit—in his family's home as well as in the ward—was a thunderous clearing of the throat, often followed by spitting on the floor. We may guess how disruptive this habit was to ordinary conversation and how furious his father became when the young man chose the hour of his father's favorite television program for his most explosive performances. Some of us might even have commiserated with the father when, on one occasion, he angrily switched off the set and said, "One or the other, not both. Either I sit here and listen to you, or else you quiet down so that we can watch this program." It is not entirely unreasonable, I think, to regard this young man's carrying-on as a contemptuous and willful bit of self-assertion. On the other hand, if we had been closeted with him for many months and had come to regard him as an oracle, we might see his behavior as an appropriate social protest against the bourgeois dishonesties of his family life, of which television represented only one. Hocking and spitting might appear to be the only valid or truthful event that ever occurred in this family. When approached as an oracle, the schizophrenic seems not only more perceptive, but more "real," which helps to explain the therapist's growing attraction, even addiction, to the companionship of schizophrenic patients.

Whatever may be the real "real" life that our oracular patient provides, language is not one of its virtues. Nor, for that matter, does it include those areas of knowledge or imagination that live through language: literature, history, philosophy, and so on. What tends to be celebrated is what is vaguely termed "the nonverbal," as though this were a department of gesticulation that need have no lively connection with language. Often accompanying the therapist's exaltation of the nonverbal may be an active intolerance toward, or even disparagement of, language. "Just words" will be a recurring phrase among those who share this view of language; it will suggest that words in general, any words, are crude and deceptive tools when compared to that superior, and at the same time more elemental, mode that dispenses with words altogether. Once the therapist embraces this view, not only does his own language, spoken or written, fail to develop, but he also finds it increasingly difficult to deal in a discriminating fashion with the spoken or written language of others. I have known several therapists who, after years with schizophrenic patients, gave up reading altogether—and not with shame, but proudly, as though they were glad to leave this brand of conformity behind them. What language they retained took on a pedantic, self-assertive quality that did little service to the development of their ideas, but seemed increasingly to resemble physical gesture.

Let me mention one further consequence of endowing the schizophrenic with oracular powers—a consequence (for the therapist) that has been implicit in what I have already said. Partly because he has helped anoint this oracle by supplying meanings that the oracle did not possess, partly because the work itself has required him to assert meanings with an assurance he himself did not at first possess, and partly because his audience was both captive and unresponsive, the therapist, by virtue of the prolonged apprenticeship he has served in the most self-indulgent kind of self-expression, may gradually be led toward both the posture and, ultimately, the belief that he, too, is an oracle—well-dressed rather than ragged, affluent rather than impoverished, legally sane rather than clinically schizophrenic, and yet possessed of the same charismatic power to grasp the real truth in any situation, regardless of what his intellectual or educational limitations may be. With the assumption of this toga, that dramatic room-filling quality to which I have referred will have unfolded to full bloom. Though mad in that private sense in which he seems to have fallen away from his own particular direction in life and to have lost all relation to the shy, studious, thoughtful young man he may once have been, he will appear eminently wise, although possibly rather florid and eccentric, to those younger therapists whom he will train in the intricacies of the therapeutic life with schizophrenia.

We can now return to that most important aspect of our subject: the issue of the connection between relation and will. I believe that this unholy conspiracy characterizes, in an important sense, the behavior of both therapist and schizophrenic, not only in their relationship with each other, where it achieves its most dramatic form, but also, and equally importantly, in the relationship of each to his world, to all others, and to himself. In spite of the fact that the intellectual life of the schizophrenic is as fearfully impoverished as his capacities for relation with others, we must assume that he is still human enough to hunger for relation and, should it be even fleetingly achieved, to dread and to be enraged by its loss. In such an extreme state, much of his delusional and hallucinatory life will either reach for consummation, even glory, or else proclaim his repudiation of such a possibility with a web of corroborating, though fantastic, details. By his impoverishment, he is reduced in his attempts at relation, or in his repudiation of relation (and often the two are intermingled), to what I choose to call his isolated will—or willfulness, if we define it as *Webster's* does, namely, that state in which one is governed by will without yielding to reason; obstinate; perverse; stubborn. It is a most important part of schizophrenia, and one that has been relatively neglected in the literature, though aspects of it have been considered under other categories. I would say that willfulness not only accounts for much of the schizophrenic's behavior, but authors a great deal of his delusional material. Without the assistance of the imagination, the will invents in its own image; this means that the will contrives plots in which will is pitted against will, its subject matter being, roughly, power. In delusion, the willful one may be an outside agent and the schizophrenic his victim, but, regardless of who is villain and who victim, the plot represents a crude example of what Yeats called "the will trying to do the work of the imagination." To some extent power *is* a real and ubiquitous motive in the world. Thus, if the therapist is adept at supplying texture and meaning to the plot, it is easy to see how he may come to endow his schizophrenic patient with an oracular vision of how power controls and corrupts the affairs of all men.

Willfully, then, the schizophrenic grasps at, and withdraws from, relation—sometimes simultaneously.

Sullivan once remarked that he thought that, with the exception of periods of panic, the schizophrenic's life with others was largely hysterical in character. Although my understanding of hysteria is quite different from Sullivan's, I think I know what led him to this observation. It was, I suspect, the violent, flamboyant, impulsive, often explosive and destructive quality of the schizophrenic's social movements that reminded him of hysteria. In this regard we should remind ourselves that one or two of the first hysterics Freud and Breur studied would today be diagnosed as schizophrenic. To take but one example: the muteness of a particular schizophrenic may have originated in panic, when talk led him into such terrifying confusion about reality that his distress, instead of being relieved, was not only perpetuated but intensified. But as his panic subsides, his muteness may become, and remain, a willful refusal to talk, in response to what he regards as the demand to talk being made on him by those about him. Reduced to his own will, the schizophrenic perceives himself continually assailed by the willful demands of others. Examples of schizophrenic willfulness, whether or not they had their antecedents in panic, and despite the often confusing nature of their delusional elaboration or justification, are numerous: the refusal to eat, waxy inflexibility or the refusal to move, untidiness and nakedness, even smearing. All these may be willful responses to what seems to the schizophrenic to be willfulness on the part of those responsible for his care. Most of these examples are expressions of rejection of relation, but it should be said that the schizophrenic's sexual attempts to force intimacy can be equally willful, as with Dr. Fromm-Reichmann's mas-

turbating patient, seeming almost assaultive in their
grotesque lack of the nuances that usually assist the
life of affection.

Not until the willfulness of the schizophrenic is
recognized can it be understood why the therapeutic
life with schizophrenia is such a bloodcurdling affair,
its melodrama underscored by screaming invective,
physical grappling of a brutal order, and all manner
of obscenity. Even the mildest, most unassuming
therapist, if he continues in this work, will soon find
himself hurled into an arena where will is pitted
boldily against will. He may even come to count himself fortunate to have this semblance of relation, no
matter how degraded, instead of none at all, which is
his more frequent lot.

It is hardly surprising that the more violent forms
of the therapy of schizophrenia should seem to be life
in the raw, making all ordinary civilized existence
trivial by comparison. But the problem for the therapist is more serious than this. Whether he is locked
in frantic physical encounter with his patient, or else
trying, through monologue, to breach his patient's
muteness, he is thrown back on his own isolated will
in his efforts to provoke relationship. Even in defeat,
he may resort to a silence that is as willful as the silence of his patient. It can be said that both therapist
and patient have a will to relation and a relationship
of wills. But this is a rather reckless use of the word
"relation." Relation, understood in any decent sense,
cannot be willed: it happens or it doesn't happen,
depending on what human qualities are brought to
the event: honesty, imagination, tact, humor, and so
on. By contrast, the willful encounter—a far cry from
the chancy and fleeting mutuality that occurs from

time to time between people, and that we designate by the honorable term "relation"—will have a special binge-like excitement, even though its center is hollow. Its intensity is of the moment; unlike friendship, when the moment vanishes, little remains. This is the reason that the addictive possibilities of this therapeutic life are considerable. (In this regard it is no accident that two of the best-known therapists in the field have attempted to give ontological status to the experience of loneliness.) As the therapist returns again and again to the excitements of this drama of wills that passes for relation, he becomes increasingly impatient of relation, although it is unlikely he will cease believing, and asserting, that the capacity for relation is his special power. Gradually, but not casually, he develops into an apostle of relation who can no longer abide relation. It is an unhappy fact that when, through drugs or life-situation, one finds more and more scope for willfulness, those other human qualities I have mentioned are not merely held in abeyance, but fall into the atrophy of disuse. And, with such atrophy, the ordinary amenities of the world become not only no longer sustaining, but actually disturbing, making recourse to the drug ever more compelling. As the therapist continues to will what cannot be willed, those attributes of character to expand and harden will be precisely those public, self-assertive gestures that are unfaithful to the person he might have become.

Schizophrenia, of course, is not contagious. In no way do I mean to suggest that the therapist, by virtue of prolonged exposure to schizophrenia and of the possibility of his eventual addiction to intimate association with its victims, actually succumbs to this par-

ticular infection and turns schizophrenic himself. He
does not become schizophrenic; but as I have said, he
tends to become something other than the person he
is, or was, or was meant to be. It has been my intention in this discussion to propose that the curious
nature of the person he *does* become may best be understood as a particular and personal, and characteristic, response to that particular disorder of human
potentiality that is schizophrenia.

Laing's Models of Madness*

BY MIRIAM SIEGLER, HUMPHREY OSMOND,
AND HARRIET MANN

BRIGHT YOUNG SCHIZOPHRENICS, like bright young people generally, are interested in reading about their
condition. From the vast and varied selection of literature available to them, they appear to show a
marked preference for a book called *The Politics of
Experience*, by R. D. Laing (1967). The authors, like
other members of the "square," older generation, are
of the opinion that they know what is best, and that
this book is not good for these patients. It is an appealing book, and emotionally there is not a false note
in it. This alone makes it important. But it contains
treacherous confusions, and while we do not presume
to make choices for our young friends, we do feel
that it is our duty to clarify the alternatives as presented in this book.

We have evolved a method for picking our way
through the jungle of theories about schizophrenia:

* This work was made possible by funds from NIMH General Research Support Grant 1-SO1-FR-05558-01 and initiated by support from the American Schizophrenia Foundation, Inc.

the construction of models (Siegler and Osmond, 1966; Siegler and Osmond, in press). Briefly, our models are constructed by taking a single theory or point of view and asking its author or authors as to what schizophrenia is, how it might have come about, what is to be done about it, in what direction it is likely to alter over time, how the people involved with it ought to behave, and other such questions. We have labeled these questions "definition," "etiology," "treatment," "prognosis," "the rights and duties of patients," and so forth, and they constitute the dimensions of the model. The answers to these questions make up the content of the model itself. The dimensions must be consistent with each other within any one model. When two or more such models have been constructed, they can be compared, dimension by dimension. In the physical sciences, workers are in the habit of comparing theories and showing in what way one is better than another, but in psychiatry, stemming as it does from empirical medicine, eclecticism prevails. Our models are an attempt to borrow from the physical sciences a certain orderliness which we find enviable. Thus far, we have constructed seven models of schizophrenia: medical, moral, psychoanalytic, family interaction, social, conspiratorial, and impaired. We have also constructed a model (Siegler and Osmond, in press) from Goffman's paper, "On the Characteristics of Total Institutions" (1961) and identified it as a conspiratorial model. We now propose to apply our method to *The Politics of Experience*.

Most books and articles on schizophrenia are written either to express some point of view or theory about schizophrenia, or else to report some research on a problem that arises within a particular theory. In either case, it is usually evident from the start what model the author holds. In Laing's book, however, it is not immediately evident what kind of model will emerge from this process. In fact, it soon becomes apparent that the dimensions can be filled more than once, i.e., there is more than one model. The task, then, is to locate all of his statements which fit any of our dimensions, to put together all the dimensions which are compatible with each other, to see how many models result from this process, and to see what dimensions, if any, are missing from the identifiable models. Using this method, we find that Laing's book contains two more-or-less complete models, and a fragment of a third model. Of the three models, two have been described before (psychoanalytic, conspiratorial) and one is entirely new (psychedelic).

In the two models which are more-or-less complete, we have filled in the missing dimensions so that they are consistent with the existing ones. The dimensions which we have supplied in this way are bracketed, so that the reader may easily distinguish them from Laing's own statements.

We have filled some of the dimensions with Laing's own words, and in all these cases, the quotation marks and page numbers are given. We have done this in order to convey the flavor of his argument, which might otherwise be lost. The method of model construction inevitably distorts the author's intentions, which are conveyed in part by the "mood" of the book, the order in which things are presented, the style of writing, and other means which lie outside of the argument itself. Arranging a theory as a model often destroys the uniqueness of the author's point of view, and yet it is precisely this uniqueness which prevents the comparison of one author's theory with another. We have used the author's exact words whenever feasible, then, in order to minimize this distortion without sacrificing the comparability which our method makes possible.

All statements in the dimensions which are not bracketed or in quotation marks are paraphrases of Laing's statements.

I. Laing's Conspiratorial Model of Madness

A. The Model Described

1. Definition

Schizophrenia is a *label* which some people pin on other people, under certain social circumstances. It is not an illness, like pneumonia. It is a form of alienation which is out of step with the prevailing state of alienation. It is a social fact and a political event.

2. Etiology

Alienation, of which schizophrenia is one form, ". . . is achieved only by outrageous violence perpetrated by human beings on human beings" (p. xv). We are driving our children mad. We are intolerant of different fundamental structures of experience.

The social system, and not individuals, must be the object of study if we are to understand the etiology of schizophrenia. The blame cannot be laid at anyone's door; "very seldom is it a question of contrived, deliberate cynical lies or a ruthless intention to drive someone crazy . . ." (p. 79).

3. Behavior

". . . Behavior that gets labeled schizophrenic is a special strategy that a person invents in order to live in an unlivable situation." (p. 79).

Transactional analyses are insufficient explanations of behavior. Electronic systems can play games which can be analyzed in this way, but human relations are transexperiential.

Psychiatrists have tended to pay more attention to the patient's behavior than to his experience.

4. Treatment

What is called "treatment" is really getting the patient to abandon his subjective experiential perspective for the therapist's objective ones. The patient's experiences are interpreted away by the therapist, and said to mean something other than what the patient says they mean.

5. Prognosis

Once the label of "schizophrenic" is applied, it sticks, and treating someone in terms of this label reinforces the very behavior which caused the label to be applied in the first place. It is a vicious circle.

6. Suicide

(Suicide is a way out of the vicious circle.)[1]

---

[1] Suicide is discussed in another of Laing's books, *The Divided Self* (London: Tavistock Publications, 1959). The model in use in this book is the psychoanalytic model.

7. Function of the hospital

The hospital is a total institution which degrades and invalidates human beings. Once in the hospital, the patient hardly ever leaves, because he manifests more and more of the behavior for which he was hospitalized.

8. Personnel

The personnel for this model are all the people who come into contact with the person labeled as schizophrenic except the schizophrenic himself. "The person labeled is inaugurated not only into a role, but into a career of patient, by the concerted action of a coalition (a 'conspiracy') of family, G.P., mental health officer, psychiatrists nurses, psychiatric social workers, and often fellow patients." (p. 84).

9. Rights and duties of patients

"The 'committed' person labeled as patient, and specifically as 'schizophrenic,' is degraded from full existential and legal status as human agent and responsible person to someone no longer in possession of his own definition of himself, unable to retain his own possessions, precluded from the exercise of his discretion as to whom he meets, what he does. His time is no longer his own, and the space he occupies is no longer of his own choosing. After being subjected to a degradation ceremonial known as psychiatric examination, he is bereft of his civil liberties in being imprisoned in a total institution known as a 'mental' hospital. More completely, more radically than anywhere else in our society, he is invalidated as a human being. In the mental hospital he must remain, until the label is rescinded or qualified by such terms as 'remitted' or 'readjusted.'" (p. 84).

The schizophrenic has no rights and no duties.

10. Rights and duties of families of patients

(The family has driven the schizophrenic crazy, although they probably did not intend to do so, labeled him schizophrenic, and hospitalized him in a total institution. In doing so, they have forfeited the usual rights and duties of families toward one of their members.)

11. Rights and duties of society

(Society [i.e., all members of a culture] seems to have the right to maintain the status quo, and in order to do so, the status quo is represented as part of the natural order, or as a natural law. Society appears to have the right to lock people up in mental hospitals as a means of maintaining the status quo. It is not clear whether society has any duties toward its members in this model.)

12. Goal of the model

The goal of this model is to maintain the status quo by "treating" as medical patients certain individuals who, due to the strength of their inner perceptions and experiences, are exceptionally eloquent critics of the society.

B. The Model Discussed

We have identified this model as conspiratorial because it fits the description of that model given in our original paper (Siegler and Osmond, 1966). It has as its main concern the violation of the rights of the person labeled as schizophrenic. Since it is denied that the person so labeled has an illness, his incarceration in a building called a "hospital" is inexplicable. And so it is said that there is a conspiracy among those surrounding the "patient" to exile him to a total institution which is called a hospital but is really a kind of concentration camp.[2]

A conspiratorial model is a view of the fate of schizophrenics minus the medical context. We must now ask what it is about the medical context that disturbs Laing so much. First, Laing finds the practice of assigning diagnostic labels to patients unacceptable. He says: ". . . It is wrong to impute a hypothetical disease of unknown etiology and undiscovered pathology to someone unless *he* can prove otherwise." (p. 71). Laing is certainly entitled to believe that this is wrong, but it is only fair to note that the practice of medicine consists to a great extent of imputing hypothetical diseases of unknown etiology and undiscovered pathology to patients who are in no position to prove otherwise. All diseases are hypothetical, all are labels. There is no such thing as diabetes, there are only individuals who have certain experiences and physical symptoms which are said to have some relation to the hypothetical disease. Yet such a disease entity is an extremely powerful category, for all its philosophical inelegance. Without it, medical research would be unthinkable, and practice chaotic. When doctors see "a case of pneumonia" or "a case of tuberculosis," they bring to bear on each

[2] Laing actually uses the word "conspiracy" on p. 84, but in parenthesis and with full quotation marks around it, which seems to suggest that he wished to qualify the word somewhat.

case such knowledge as they and other doctors have accumulated about this hypothetical entity. Diagnosis is one of the principal functions of the physician. In the conspiratorial model, to label someone is to discriminate against him, but in the medical model, to label someone is to bring the knowledge of medicine to bear upon him. It is an essential step which precedes and determines treatment. It may save his life.[3]

Another aspect of medicine which seems to bother Laing is that when one removes the medical context from a medical interaction, one is often left with an extraordinary situation. He describes a clinical examination, taken from Kraepelin's lectures, in which Kraepelin demonstrates a young girl's psychotic illness but noting her reactions when he attempts to stop her movements, forces a piece of bread out of her hands, sticks a needle into her forehead, and so forth (p. 73). Laing correctly notes that this is very peculiar behavior, taken out of the context as experienced and defined by Kraepelin, i.e., a clinical examination. The medical context permits people called doctors to perform all kinds of unusual actions on people called patients, and this enables them to treat illnesses. On the whole, people feel that the advantages of the medical model are such that it is worth preserving the social fiction which is required to sustain it. But not everyone is of this opinion; some people, for example, Christian Scientists, feel

---

[3] Diagnosis has another important function: it is a necessary step in conferring the sick role. Patients are anxious to have a diagnosis because without it, their status as patient is dubious. They might otherwise be frauds, malingerers, or hypochondriacs.

that other values take precedence. As an individual, Laing is quite free to put forth any view on these matters that he chooses, but as a physician, he is not free to put forth the view that the social fiction called medicine is more harmful than helpful.

In the dimension of "behavior," Laing correctly notes that psychiatrists tend to pay attention to behavior to the exclusion of experience. To the extent that they do so, they fail to behave like medical men, for a doctor does not simply observe his patient's behavior, but makes inquiries and, if possible, tests of what is going on "inside" the patient. The thermometer measures the inner experience of the patient, and is more accurate and useful than watching the patient mop his brow. Doctors ask their patients to tell them where it hurts, and they listen carefully to this information, in order to map out the nature and extent of the illness. Psychiatrists who no longer listen to the reports of their patients' experiences, or who interpret these experiences symbolically instead of using them as information, are not using the medical model.

One of the dimensions which is missing from Laing's model is suicide. Within the medical model, suicide is a medical risk in certain illnesses, especially in schizophrenia (Osmond and Hoffer, 1967). The doctor must be alert for signs of possible suicide, and he must use his clinical experience to avert it if possible. But in Laing's model, as in Goffman's, suicide is conspicuous by its absence. Since the staff in this model seem to have rights in relation to the patient, but no duties toward him, it is not possible to say that it is the duty of the staff to prevent the patient from committing suicide. Laing and Goffman might have taken the stand that suicide is the patient's (or rather, "patient's") business, and that no one else has the right to interfere with it, but they do not do this; they prefer not to discuss it at all. Yet suicide is just the sort of moral dilemma which makes medicine the model of choice in the case of schizophrenia. The medical model is the only one which can simultaneously try to prevent death, and account for it if it occurs. In all other models of which we are aware, death must be seen as someone's fault. In medicine, as long as the doctor behaves like a doctor, he is not blamed for deaths which occur in his practice.

In addition to suicide, there are two other dimensions missing from Laing's model, the rights and duties of the patients' families, and the rights and duties of society. Since this model has as its central focus the rights of the person labeled as schizophrenic, it is not surprising that those of the other participants are ignored. Laing clearly wished to redress the balance in favor of the person labeled as schizophrenic. He appears to believe that the reason why the "patient" has lost so many rights is that we are "intolerant of different fundamental structures of experience" (p. 50). That is, he sees the family and community as repressive forces, unwilling to permit the schizophrenic to experience his unusual perceptions without interference. Because they fail to accept his experiences as authentic, Laing argues, they elicit frustrated and peculiar behavior from him, label it as schizophrenic, and extrude him from the family and community until he learns to see things their way. Given this picture of the "patient" as a victim of repressive forces, it is little wonder that Laing is not moved to consider the rights of the family and community.

We are in agreement with Laing's contention that most people cannot accept the fact that others experience the world in a radically different way from themselves (Mann, H., Siegler, M. and Osmond, H., 1968). On the whole people know very little about other experiential worlds. Many experiences are difficult to put into words, and some people are not as articulate as others, so most people do not guess how very different the experiences of others may be. However, we disagree with Laing's contention that it is in the area of experience that the schizophrenic comes to grief; his difficulties lie in the area of behavior. As long as a schizophrenic manages to behave normally, no one will show the slightest interest, kindly or otherwise, in his unusual experiences. A person may, with impunity, experience himself as walking down the street without any clothes on; it is only when he actually does this that the community will take action against him. The community is generally indifferent to and ignorant of the inner experiences of its members, but it does punish misbehavior by curtailing the rights that are contingent on acceptable behavior. Although the behavior required varies enormously from culture to culture, and from family to family, all cultures and all families exchange certain rights for certain behavioral conformity. When this breakdown of reciprocity occurs, the person in question loses his usual rights and moves into some new role, which has other rights. The possible roles for such a person of which we are aware are: bad, eccentric, prophetic, mad, analysand, impaired, sick. Today, since there are schizophrenics in each of these roles, one might ask which are best off.[4]

Schizophrenics who occupy the "bad" role may be found in prisons or in home-made, family-run jail cells. In the former case, they are offered the rights and duties of prisoners, including a determinate sentence for some specific infraction of the law. Some people believe that this is a kinder fate than the mental hospital, but unfortunately the advantages to the schizophrenic are often outweighed by the fact that the non-schizophrenic prisoners recognize that there is something wrong with them, and will not accept them into the highly normative sub-culture of the criminal. Foucault (1965) describes the situation which arose when, in eighteenth century France, criminals, schizophrenics and the indigent were all locked up together: the schizophrenics quickly became highly visible, because they could not conform to the daily life of the prison. This situation is still reported today.

The role of eccentric is open to some schizophrenics. It has the great advantage of being an acceptable social role, but most communities cannot tolerate more than a few eccentrics, and there is no room for the enormous number of schizophrenics.

The role of prophet, like the eccentric role, is one which is open to very few people, whether they are schizophrenic or not. A schizophrenic who wished to occupy this role would find himself in competition with normal people whose temperament allowed them to excel in this way.

Schizophrenics labeled as mad, a category which

[4] To our knowledge, no one has offered schizophrenics a choice of these roles, although some schizophrenics have moved or been moved from one role to another.

seems to be about half-way between bad and sick, are very likely to be mistreated. Whether they are driven out of towns, put on a ship of fools, or locked up in madhouses, the role seems to have hardly any protection for them. It appears to be a social role designed primarily to keep the rest of society from being disrupted by them, and perhaps comes closest to being a social role without rights.

The role of analysand is open to a small number of well-to-do schizophrenics who live in a few Western countries, and whose temperament permits them to engage in the psychoanalytic form of communication. In general, working class people are barred from this role both financially and culturally. Its main advantage is that a great deal of personal care and attention is lavished on the schizophrenic occupying this role. Among its disadvantages are that it creates financial and emotional strain in the analysand's family; the analysand feels guilty if his condition does not improve; and the analysand role is constantly being confused with the sick role.

The impaired role (Siegler and Osmond, in press) is a kind of second-class citizenship, designed to offer support and protection to people who have disabilities. The blind, the deaf, the crippled, and the retarded are all examples of impaired people. These people are expected to behave as normally as possible in exchange for reduced demands upon them by others. Unlike that of sick people, their situation is not expected to change. Many schizophrenics, especially those in hospitals, occupy the impaired role, but unfortunately, it does not quite fit them, because most of them have fluctuating illnesses: they may be quite normal at some times, and very ill at others. Those mental hospitals which are really homes for the impaired are neither equipped to give real medical care to the very ill, nor are they set up to allow normal living to those who are not ill at any given moment. While the impaired role is an improvement over the mad role, in that the schizophrenics do receive at least a minimum of protection and care, it causes a great deal of unnecessary suffering for many schizophrenics.

Some schizophrenics occupy the sick role. That is, they perceive themselves as having a major illness which, like many major illnesses, does not have an agreed-upon etiology or a wholly successful treatment. They understand that they are not able to carry their full adult load of social responsibility because they are unfortunate enough to be very ill. They consult their physicians, take medication as directed (ideally), report changes in their condition when they occur, go into the hospital when their illness gets worse, follow the progress of medical research, talk with other patients with the same illness about their mutual difficulties, and ask their doctor if he thinks they will ever be really well again. Their lot is not an easy one, but they do occupy an ancient and respectable social role, that of the sick person. If they occupy the sick role fully, they do not blame themselves or their families for their condition. This relieves them of the additional burden of family strife, not a small matter for a young adult who may have to live with his family long past the time he would normally leave if he were well. The schizophrenic in the sick role may gain such comfort as he can from the knowledge that other major psychiatric diseases, such as general paresis and pallagra psychosis, have yielded to medical research.

II. Laing's Psychoanalytic Model of Madness

A. The Model Described

Only two dimensions of this model are present in Laing's book, etiology and treatment.

1. Etiology

"... To the best of my knowledge, *no* schizophrenic has been studied whose disturbed pattern of communication has not been shown to be a reflection of, and reaction to, the disturbed and disturbing pattern characterizing his or her family of origin." (p. 78).[5]

[5] Although it may appear that Laing uses here a family interaction model, rather than a psychoanalytic one, this is not so. In the family interaction model as we have described it (Siegler and Osmond, 1966), the essential feature is that the disturbance is seen as lying *among* the members of the family, all of whom are, together, "the patient." Laing nowhere in this book shows the slightest concern for the experiences of the other members of the family. He simply uses the information provided by the family interaction model to reinforce his argument that the schizophrenic patient has been driven mad by his family, a statement which is meaningless in the other model. The purists among the family interactionists believe that only the analysis of the whole family together can alter the family pathology, whereas Laing maintains that psychoanalytic view that treatment occurs between two people, therapist and patient. In another book on schizophrenia (Laing, R. D. and Esterson, A., *Sanity, Madness and the Family*, Volume 1, Families of Schizophrenics. New York: Basic Books, 1964), Laing also sees the function of the therapist to be the exploration of the patient's experience, rather than that of other family members.

2. Treatment

"Psychotherapy must remain an obstinate attempt of two people to recover the wholeness of being human through the relationship between them." (p. 32). "Psychotherapy consists in the paring away of all that stands between us, the props, masks, roles, lies, defenses, anxieties, projections and interjections, in short, all the carryovers from the past, transference and countertransference, that we use by habit and collusion, wittingly and unwittingly, as our currency for relationships." (p. 27).

B. The Model Discussed

We have identified this model as a psychoanalytic model, even though Laing is not an orthodox psychoanalyst, because it has the essential features of such a model: the source of the person's difficulties lie in the past, specifically in his disturbed family relationships, and the treatment consists of a special kind of corrective relationship between two people, patient and therapist. These features are not true of any other model.

It is interesting that only these two dimensions of the model are present, for these are the dimensions on which the strength of the psychoanalytic model rests. Diagnosis, for example, is of little concern in this model. Whereas the process of diagnosis is seen as prejudicial labeling in the conspiratorial model, and as an essential step toward determining treatment in the medical model, it is seen in the psychoanalytic model as a useless diversion. Why bother to determine what category a patient falls into, when the treatment is the same in any case, and every relationship between patient and therapist is unique?

The psychoanalytic model is opposed to the medical model at almost every point. Yet psychoanalysts are often medical doctors; in some countries, they must be. This has created the utmost confusion for schizophrenic patients, since they usually go to a doctor because they perceive themselves to be ill, and wish to be treated; they then discover that the treatment offered them carries with it a set of rights and duties, i.e., the role of analysand, which is incompatible with the sick role. The analyst uses the authority which derives from the fact that he is a physician to put forth an anti-medical view. It is almost as if a priest used the authority vested in him by the church to put forth a doctrine which was completely irreconcilable with that of the church. The difference between the two institutions is that the church strives to be overtly consistent, while medicine has a covert, unverbalized consistency, which is undisturbed by the peculiar and often outrageous opinions which doctors voice from time to time. The fact that doctors are not thrown out of medical societies for putting forth anti-medical views shows that the true consensus in medicine lies elsewhere than in verbalized doctrines. It is a tribute to the enduring qualities of the institution of medicine that doctors can advocate and even proselytize anti-medical views among patients without destroying the basic doctor-patient relationship between them.

But schizophrenic patients do not emerge unscathed from these encounters. The underlying assumption of psychoanalysis is that progress toward a "healthy" personality is possible, given hard work, good faith, enough time, and enough money. In medicine, there is no such contract; an illness may become suddenly worse, for no known reason, in spite of everyone's hard work and good faith. In the psychoanalytic model, these sudden reversals must be explained "dynamically," i.e., they are somebody's fault. Either the family does not really wish the patient to get well, or the patient has been damaged too severely to get well, or the patient is "afraid" to get well, or the analyst has not solved the countertransference problem. The fact that failure must be explained, either implicitly or explicitly, as someone's fault places a great additional burden on the schizophrenic and his family.

Laing's conspiratorial model is an account of how he thinks schizophrenics are presently treated; his psychedelic model, to follow, is an account of how he thinks schizophrenics ought to be treated. His psychoanalytic model, which seems to have crept into the book by mistake, is an account of what he actually does. He is a psychotherapist, with a very deep regard for his patients, and he tells us, in these fragments of a model, that he forms meaningful and authentic relationships with them. Since it appears that the psychoanalytic model is the one which he actually uses, we feel it is incumbent upon him to inform his patients fully about it, so that they may compare it with the alternative models.

III. Laing's Psychedelic Model of Madness

  A. The Model Described

    1. Definition

        Schizophrenia is " . . . itself a natural way of healing our own appalling state of alienation called

normality . . ." (p. 116). "Madness need not be all
breakdown . . . It may also be breakthrough. It is
potentially liberation and renewal as well as enslave-
ment and existential death." (p. 93). It is not an illness to be treated, but a "voyage." Socially, madness
may be a form in which ". . . often through quite ordinary people, the light begins to break through the
cracks in our all-too-closed minds." (p. 90).

2. Etiology

"We have been processed on Procrustean
beds. At least some of us have managed to hate what
they have made of us." (p. 47).

3. Behavior

"The madness that we encounter in 'pa-
tients' is a gross travesty, a mockery, a grotesque caricature of what that natural healing process of that
estranged integration we call sanity might be." (p.
101). It is distorted by our misguided attempts to
"treat" them. If we really understood our patients,
we would see behavior which was a reflection of the
natural healing process, a desire to explore the inner
world.

4. Treatment

Instead of the degradation ceremonial of
psychiatric examination, diagnosis and prognostication, we need, for those who are ready for it, ". . . an
initiation ceremonial, through which the person will
be guided with full social encouragement and sanction
into inner space and time, by people who have been
there and back." (p. 89).

5. Prognosis

(If a schizophrenic person were intelligently guided through his voyage into inner time and space, he would emerge a better person than he had been before; perhaps one might say that he would be "enlightened.")

6. Suicide

(If a schizophrenic person commits suicide while being guided on a voyage, that is just one of the risks—voyages are dangerous. There are no guarantees.)

7. Function of the hospital

We need a place which has the right atmosphere for guided voyages into inner time and space. The schizophrenic person would leave this place when the voyage was over.

8. Personnel

The appropriate personnel for guiding these voyages are people who have been there and back, including ex-patients. "Among physicians and priests, there should be some who are guides . . ." (p. 97).

9. Rights and duties of schizophrenic persons

(The schizophrenic has the right to a well-guided voyage, in a setting that is conducive to inner exploration. He has the right to be spared psychiatric diagnosis and treatment which is designed to make him give up his own existential view. He has the duty to accept being put in a padded cell if he is too much for the others.)

10. Rights and duties of families

(The family has the duty to let the schizophrenic person make his own choice about where and how to undergo an inner voyage. The family does not have the right to label a family member as "schizophrenic" and then hospitalize him for "treatment.")

11. Rights and duties of society

(Society has no rights in relation to schizophrenic persons, certainly not the right to label people and then lock them up in "hospitals." Society has the duty to organize itself in such a way that alienation is not "normal." Society has the duty to allow more "breakthrough.")

12. Goal of the model

The goal of this model is to enable certain people, now called "schizophrenic," to develop their potentialities for inner exploration. If such people can be allowed and encouraged to move in this direction, all of us will benefit.

B. The Model Discussed

We have called this model "psychedelic," although Laing does not use the term in this book, because it is obvious that he thinks that schizophrenics may have, sometimes have, and ought to have the same kinds of experiences that normal individuals seek when they take mind-expanding drugs. From our point of view, Laing has failed to distinguish two very different kinds of experience, psychedelic and psychotic. We share his opinion that schizophrenics sometimes have psychedelic experiences, particularly at the beginning of their illnesses (Bowers and Freedman, 1966), and it is certainly true that some schizophrenics have been able to make creative use of their unusual experiences. It must be noted, however, that some creative individuals have always been able to make use of the experience of having a major illness to further their own self-development. During the era when well-to-do tubercular patients lived in Magic Mountains," some were able to use this experience, with its enforced leisure and unusual physical sensations, to arrive at a different view of themselves than they might have otherwise achieved. Simply staying in bed for a long period may be a great boon to a contemplative individual. Even terminal cancer has brought out the best in some people, and in some family relationships.[6] But it is heartless to suggest, without the most exact explanation and qualification, to those suffering from tuberculosis, cancer, or schizophrenia that they should look on this as a rare opportunity for self-understanding. For most people and their families, a major disease means the end of hopes and plans, however modest. It almost always means a severe financial drain on the family, and families are sometimes destroyed by the disruption which a disease brings in its wake.

There is one dimension of this model which deserves mention, that of "personnel." Laing has suggested ex-patients, some physicians, and some priests as guides for the voyages of inner exploration. It is clear why he thinks that ex-patients and priests might be suitable, but we are at a loss to understand why

[6] See, for example, John Gunther's *Death Be Not Proud* (New York: Harper and Brothers, 1949) and Lael Tucker Wertenbaker's *Death of a Man* (New York: Random House, 1957).

physicians are considered for this role. Medicine is a
dirty, rough business. It favors the thick-skinned person over the sensitive one, the practical person over
the imaginative. Men of unsuitable temperament who
chose medicine by mistake are often weeded out during medical training. Doctors who like their work
enjoy coping with emergencies; they are cut from the
same cloth as sailors and farmers, masons and car-
penters. They see machinery and the human body in
much the same way, and they are respectful and
knowledgeable about the workings of both. They are
accustomed to being obeyed, not because of their individual personalities, but because they are doctors,
and they believe that they have been commissioned to
deal with urgent matters of life and death. Making
gurus out of doctors seems to us like making a silk
purse out of a sow's ear, hardly worth the trouble
when there are so many unemployed ex-patients
about. Laing ought to make it clear what qualities of
doctors he feels make them likely candidates for
psychedelic guides.

Perhaps the most important point to be made about
Laing's psychedelic model is its implication that schizophrenics will benefit from being seen as persons em-
barked on a voyage of self-discovery. It would be
closer to the truth to see most of them as voyagers
who have been shanghaied, for unknown reasons, on
to a ship which never reaches port. Psychedelic voyages
are usually voluntary, and the person usually knows
what the agent of his changed perceptions is. Schizophrenia is involuntary, the person rarely knows the
cause of his strange new perceptions, and he is unlikely to receive much helpful information about it.
In a psychedelic experience, a "bad trip" can usually

be avoided by surrounding oneself with known and trusted people, by choosing a setting that is secure and aesthetically pleasing, and by showing prudence and caution. In a psychotic experience, on the other hand, good people can be perceived as bad, so that it may be even worse to have beloved people around than those who are indifferent, for nothing is worse than to hate those one normally loves. Another critical difference between the two experiences is the absolute length of time that elapses. A psychedelic experience is necessarily short; it is usually counted in hours, not years.[7] But a psychosis may last ten or twenty years. A "bad trip" is an experience, whether drug-induced or naturally occurring, which is moving in the direction of being a psychosis but is still perceived as something that will end. Whether a "bad trip" will end, or will turn into a psychosis depends in part on the benevolence of the surroundings, but much more on the continued presence in the body of the chemical substance which initiated the experience. People who "turn on" without drugs do not have "bad trips." They achieve altered states of consciousness with the aid of music, colored lights, meditation, deep breathing, and so forth, but are at liberty to interrupt or end the experience at any time, since the stimulus can be removed.

In addition to these differences in circumstances between the two states, there are many experimental differences. Some of these are listed below. We do not wish to imply by this that the two states are entirely comparable; even less, that they are at opposite

---

[7] Those embarking on psychedelic voyages may make use of substances such as niacin to terminate the experience. They do not want interminable journeys.

ends of the same continuum. They can be seen as overlapping if one fails to take into account the length of time that the experience lasts, and its place in the total life of the person involved. It is understandable that these states are often confused, since the "bad trip" lies between the psychedelic and the psychotic experiences. Confusion between these states can lead to someone on a "bad trip" being mistakenly hospitalized, when all that is required is the guidence of a psychedelic adept. More tragic, even, is the fate of the psychotic individual whose anomalous experiences are seen as temporary, and who therefore is not promptly treated. We feel it is important to emphasize the differences between these states, in whatever dimensions they are observable.

PSYCHEDELIC EXPERIENCE	PSYCHOTIC EXPERIENCE
1. Time dimension	
Liberation from time.	Frozen in time: nothing will ever change.
Expansion of time dimensions.	Shrinkage and collapse of time dimensions.
Internal or external time may speed up, increasing possibility of quick and decisive action.	Internal and external time may slow down, inhibiting action and creating despair.
Ability to modify past, present, future.	Inability to influence any of the temporal categories.
The future is the realm of ambition and motivation.	The future is the realm of anxiety and danger.
2. Space dimension	
Expanded depth.	Reduced depth.
Enhanced distance.	Reduced distance.
Distance perception stable.	Distance perception highly variable.
Distances so vast that one feels liberated.	Distances so vast that one feels isolated and alienated.
3. Affect	
Feeling that everything is meaningful and exhilarating.	Feeling that everything contains hidden, threatening meanings.
Feelings of love, empathy, consideration, affection.	Feelings of isolation, fear, hatred, suspicion.

PSYCHEDELIC EXPERIENCE (Continued)	PSYCHOTIC EXPERIENCE (Continued)
Euphoria.	Depression.
Feeling of delight with oneself.	Feeling of disgust with oneself.

4. *Thought processes*

Thought changes are sought for, expected, valued.	Thought changes come unawares, are not welcome, are seen as accidental.
Seeing more possibilities that can be acted upon, which makes life exciting.	Seeing so many possibilities that action is impossible.
Seeing beyond the usual categories.	Seeing only fragments or parts of the usual categories.
Seeing new connections which have always been possible.	Seeing connections which are not possible.
Ability to see things objectively.	No objectivity, inability to disengage from total involvement.
Ability to see things subjectively.	No subjectivity, estrangement from self.
Ability to explain thought changes.	Desperate attempts (delusions) to explain thought changes.

5. *Perceptions*

Clear and distinct vision.	Blurred and distorted vision.
Augmentation of perception.	Diminution of perception.
Unusual perceptions seem to emanate from greater-than-human spirit or force.	Unusual perceptions seem to emanate from mechanical or sub-human forces.
Perceptual changes may be experienced as exhilarating, exciting, novel.	Perceptual changes may be experienced as frightening, threatening, dangerous.

6. *Identity*

Feeling of unity with people and material objects.	Feeling of invasion by people and material objects.
Experience of the Self.	Experience of the No-Self, ego fragmentation.
Feeling of being at one with the world.	Feeling of being opposed to and in conflict with oneself and the world.
Feelings of humility and awe as one sees oneself as part of the universe.	Feelings of smallness and insignificance as one feels at the mercy of the universe.
Feelings of integrity and identity.	Loss of integrity and identity.
Pleasant, creative fantasies that one can control.	Nightmarish fantasies that one cannot control.
Feeling that one can join the company of other enlightened people.	Feeling that one is less and less human, more and more isolated.

Perhaps the best analogy from everyday life for these experiential states is the difference between good dreams, bad dreams, and nightmares. Dreams, whether good or bad, have always been of great interest, and much has been written about their interpretation. Far less interest has been shown in the interpretation of nightmares. When a person relates a nightmare, it is usually immediately after he has had it, when he wishes to be reassured that the nightmare is not real. People learn from both good dreams and bad dreams, but they seldom learn from nightmares. A good dream is one in which the symbols clearly manifest some aspect of the person's life or inner potentialities. A good dream is like a "good trip," a good psychedelic experience, or a naturally-occurring experience of enlightenment. A bad dream is one which draws its symbols from the darker side of life; there may be feelings of sorrow, anger, fear or regret. But as with the good dream, the bad dream tells a meaningful story. It is like a chapter in a fairy story in which evil temporarily triumphs, but will eventually be overcome. A bad dream is like a "bad trip." Nightmares may or may not tell stories, but when they do, the story only mounts in horror and never resolves itself. Most people have no desire to remember their nightmares, although they may wish to re-tell dreams years after they have had them. Nightmares are like psychotic states. People who have had psychotic illnesses do not usually want to talk about them or remember them; what they want most is just what the person wants who is coming out of a nightmare: to be told that the events in it did not really happen, that the "real" world is still there, and that it is over.

Another way to emphasize the difference between

the psychedelic world and the psychotic world is to look at the accomplishments of both. The psychedelic world has provided new music, new fashions in clothing and the decorative arts, new vocabulary, new life-styles, and a new inter-generational dialogue. But not a single new art form has come out of the mental hospital. While individual schizophrenic patients may return to a creative life which they had before they became ill, or may, if they are very lucky, take up a new creative life when they leave the hospital, groups of schizophrenics cannot create any new style together, even in the small private psychiatric hospitals which house some of our most privileged young people. Even Dr. Laing's patients are not known to us for their contributions to music, poetry, or mysticism; we only know of them because Laing writes about them.

DISCUSSION

It is not surprising that *The Politics of Experience* is appealing to bright young schizophrenics. Most of the possible roles open to them are of lower status than that enjoyed by normal people, and some roles, like the sick role, are of special status. But Laing has made a very bold move: he has offered them a status above that of normal people. They can hardly be expected to ignore this fine offer, especially when their daily lives are so miserable. Furthermore, Laing has cast his offer in a style that is very much in tune with the times. He is genuinely sympathetic with today's young people. His psychedelic model of schizophrenia is a timely one, and timeliness is a potent asset in a model. That is why we believe that his point of view must be scrutinized, in spite of its flaws and omissions.

Young schizophrenics are serious about Laing, and so we must be serious in examining his ideas. But how serious is Laing himself? This is a question which must be raised because he is a physician who uses the authority which derives from medicine to advocate a nonmedical model. As Hoffer puts it (1966): "If schizophrenia is madness, then Laing is incompetent to deal with it, for he is not qualified by experience and training to deal with madness. Neither, as a psychiatrist, am I. If schizophrenia is madness, society will deal with it as it did during the days of the Inquisition when devils were driven from the mad in order to save their souls by methods which were generally approved of for many years. If schizophrenia is madness, Laing must give up his medical degrees since they are no longer of any value to him, and society has given him no special right (or responsibility) for dealing with madness, and it had better be left with counsellors of the mad, ministers, rabbis and such like, who are much more conversant with saints or devils than are psychoanalysts."

We wonder if Laing appreciates how much more serious he would seem if he gave up his medical identity. It is no great problem to do so. In the United Kingdom, one simply applies to the General Medical Council to revoke one's license to practice. There is a good precedent for this. Sir William Arbuthnot Lane, one of the greatest of English surgeons, became convinced that dietary reform was more important than surgery. He relinquished his practice in order to run a special health magazine. He apparently recognized that the clinical medical model was different from one dealing with problems of prevention. According to Alex Comfort (1967), "To silence invidious comment, he withdrew from the medical register the better to propagate his ideas."

Surely the young people who turn to Laing for help deserve to know what hat he is wearing, what role he offers them, what model he uses, what authority he speaks from. In this book, he offers three models which can be disentangled only with the greatest difficulty. None of them is the medical model, from which we believe he derives his authority. If Laing wishes to be a guru or a philosopher, there is no doubt a place for him, but young people who are suffering from schizophrenia may prefer to entrust themselves to a doctor who will treat their illness as best he can.

SUMMARY

In this paper, we have analyzed Laing's book, *The Politics of Experience*, using our method of constructing models. There appear to be three models of schizophrenia in this book, two which we have described before (psychoanalytic, conspiratorial) and one new one (psychedelic). We have discussed the shortcomings of each of these models, especially in relation to the medical model, which Laing does not describe, but which provides the source of his authority. We have also pointed out some of the differences between psychedelic and psychotic experiences, which we believe Laing has confused.

REFERENCES

BOWERS, MALCOLM B. and FREEDMAN, DANIEL X. (1966). "Psychedelic experiences in acute psychosis." *Archives of General Psychiatry*, 15 (No. 3), pp. 240–248.

COMFORT, ALEX (1967). *The Anxiety Makers* (London: Nelson).

FOUCAULT, MICHEL (1965). *Madness and Civilization* (Trans. by Richard Howard) (New York: Random House, Inc.).

GOFFMAN, ERVING (1961). "On the characteristics of total institutions," in Asylums (ed. Goffman) (Garden City: Doubleday and Co.), pp. 1–124.

HOFFER, ABRAM (1966). Correspondence in *Psychedelic Review*, No. 7, pp. 127–128.

MANN, HARRIET, SIEGLER, MIRIAM and OSMOND, HUMPHRY (1968). "The many worlds of time." *Journal of Analytical Psychology*, 13 (No. 1), pp. 33–56.

OSMOND, HUMPHRY and HOFFER, ABRAM (1967). "Schizophrenia and suicide." *Journal of Schizophrenia*, 1 (No. 1), pp. 54–64.

SIEGLER, MIRIAM and OSMOND, HUMPHRY (1966). "Models of madness." *British Journal of Psychiatry*, 112 (No. 493), pp. 1193–1203.

SIEGLER, MIRIAM and OSMOND, HUMPHRY (In press). "The impaired model of schizophrenia." *British Journal of Psychiatry*.

SIEGLER, MIRIAM and OSMOND, HUMPHRY (In press). "Goffman's model of mental illness." *British Journal of Psychiatry*.

Schizophrenia, R. D. Laing, and The Contemporary Treatment of Psychosis: An Interview with Dr. Theodore Lidz

INTERVIEWERS: ROBERT ORRILL, ROBERT BOYERS

Q.: *What is your reaction to recent criticism of the traditional categories of psychoses? Some psychotherapists argue that categories such as schizophrenia, if understood in the same terms as physical disease, are misleading. Others seem to believe that these categories are simply instruments of social control, pejorative terms used to brand people who behave in ways different from most of us.*

LIDZ: I think that those of us who were trained in the Meyerian tradition have always taken the categorizations, that is that they are not things in themselves, not discreet entities but more or less arbitrary ways of differentiating, just as the division of the color spectrum into separate colors is a cultural matter and somewhat arbitrary. We divide it into certain primary colors but other cultures divide it differently. I personally, as you may know, do not consider schizophrenia a disease or an illness, but rather a type of reaction to a sick organization, a personality disorder. However, I think that it would be very difficult to get along without the concepts of psychosis and neurosis. At one time, you know, syphilis of the central nervous system was a major category of psychosis, and one of the points in coming around to having a declassification was to differentiate between what we now call schizophrenia dementia praecox and the deteriorating diseases due to syphilis of the brain. We always have to try to differentiate between the so-called functional psychoses and the organic psychoses. That's the first step. Beyond that, I'm not sure I know what the criticism you refer to really amounts to, though there are differences in the way we describe our patients. While I use the word schizophrenia, for example, I think I would never say a patient *has* schizophrenia. We say a patient *is* schizophrenic. It isn't something that has control over him, it is a disturbance of his functioning.

Q.: *Do you think such things as shock treatment, chemotherapy, and surgery have any place in the treatment of schizophrenia? Laing objects strongly to them, and implies that they are widely misused.*
LIDZ: While I think surgery has no place except maybe in some extraordinary condition, I don't think we know enough about lobotomy to speak with perfect certainty. In the department as a whole, I don't think there have been any in the 20 years I have been here. Shock treatment may have some value in acute disturbances where the patient is apt to injure himself and nobody can make contact, but this is a rare occurrence. We use relatively little shock treatment,

just enough to calm down the acute excitement. As to tranquillizers, many of us feel that treating really disturbed schizophrenic patients without tranquillizers is almost malpractice. If one wishes to treat them psychotherapeutically, they should not get so much drugs that they can't think or act but simply enough to tone down the anxiety and cut down the over-stimulation by excessive sensory input. So it has become possible to establish a psychotherapeutic relationship much more easily than it used to be, and the small amount of drugs does not interfere with the patient working. Anxiety is useful in pushing therapy in neurotic patients and to some extent with psychotic patients, but when anxiety gets to be overwhelming it is not therapeutically useful. The patient gets paralyzed and can't really work.

Q.: *Laing writes in* The Divided Self *"The therapist acts on the principle that, since relatedness is potentially present in everyone, then he may not be wasting his time in sitting for hours with a silent catatonic who gives every evidence that he does not recognize his existence." Does this statement capture the essence of the therapeutic endeavor, relative to schizophrenia?*

LIDZ: Well, I agree, except that I think this is now a rarity. We are not in this position very often any more, though we were 15–20 years ago when I would sit with the patient sometimes day after day making occasional comments, waiting to find areas of interest, sometimes even avoiding anything that might obstruct the patient from finding something we could talk about. I can think about one of the first schizophrenic patients I treated about 30 years ago. She was a very sick schizophrenic girl with acute excitement. After a while I found out from her family that she was studying to be an art historian, and I would say that for some months we talked about European art galleries. Of course, you could talk about them and gradually move into the problems that were very disturbing to her. I don't think this was very necessary, really, and now with a good milieu and the use of a moderate amount of drugs one can communicate at some level with most patients. Even with the catatonic patient today we know, or have pretty good guesses about what is going on inside him and may decide to make tentative remarks in that direction.

Q.: *You have learned this sort of thing from experience?*

LIDZ: From experience, yes. A patient may be catatonic, rigid catatonic, because he thinks that any move he makes will affect the balance of the universe, or that this will destroy the city, and he is caught between positive and negative emotions. I may make tentative remarks about that. I may say to a patient: do you think that everything depends on you, or are you caught between heaven and hell? The patient doesn't have to agree but sometimes the patient gets the notion that there's not this great crucial isolation he had felt, and he will respond. Another thing that we recently discovered, that is I recently discovered, is the surprising frequency with which catatonic episodes happen when the parents are about to break up, and we use this kind of knowledge in making tentative approaches.

Q.: *You mentioned the importance of a good milieu. Can you elaborate on this?*

LIDZ: About good milieus? Well, I should say that I am currently in the minority because many people feel that keeping a schizophrenic patient in the hospital causes regression and will prolong the illness. Our goal is to set up an institution in which regression is not fostered and yet which can be a retreat from whatever actual trouble may have precipitated the psychosis. A place where patients can learn to deal with peer groups, work out problems, learn various aspects of socialization, sometimes stay while going back to school at the start, and these depend very heavily on the patients helping one another and also in governing the activities of the hospital. You have patients-staff meetings every week, group therapy a couple of times a week, patients government meetings, patient officers; the patient has a broad say in deciding who is ready to start going out, going back to work, going to school. They can't have the absolute final say, but we find they have pretty good judgment after they have been here awhile.

Q.:   *How do they help one another?*
LIDZ: They help one another often by talking, supporting one another. I can give you some specific illustrations. One I can think of sticks in my mind. It was some years back. We took in a girl, a young woman really, who had been hospitalized in another hospital for 10 years, I think, before that institution closed. We saw that this was a girl who had been used to soiling, that her functioning was badly disturbed. We had a bad time with the girl because, as we might have expected, her parents were extremely difficult. We noted that after a while, the girl was still not talking to anybody, or going near anybody. We then

had a men's sleeping room area and a girl's living
room area, which were not actually separated, though
the men slept in one wing and the girls in another.
This girl wouldn't stay within the girls' part but
walked around, walked up and down the men's part so
that anybody who came along in the hall she would
carefully stay away from, keeping within five feet
away from them. Then she would just stand there.
After a while we noted that she would be watching a
checker or chess game, standing off at the side, and
the men very carefully thought whether they could get
her interested in a game. They said nothing for a
while and she moved gradually closer, and after a few
days they had a chair ready for her to sit on that nobody else was sitting in and they had her finally right
there with them, making a few comments and so on.
This is a very tangible illustration.

Q.: *Is this a general illustration?*
LIDZ: Well, I have another one that may support
it. A few years ago we had taken in five or six rather
severe upper middle class delinquents, kids who
would be in jail if they weren't in psychiatrics. After
they were with us a while, a young schizophrenic boy
eloped and the patients were all standing around
thinking: now where would he have gone? What has
he told us about where he has friends or relatives?
What would he be interested in doing? The delinquents were thinking: let me out of this place. They
are nothing but a bunch of stoolies around here. But
the patients knew perfectly well that this escaped kid
was not in any way ready to take care of himself. We
do, you know, have some of our patients running off,
but very few. While we do have a closed floor, it is

to some extent only symbolically closed. Anybody who wants to put his mind to it can run off almost any day he chooses. The floor has to be at least symbolically closed to give the patient a sense of a limited area to live in.

Q.: *Could you describe the psychotherapeutic treatment of schizophrenia in greater detail?*
LIDZ: Well, I can try. I suppose the first phase is setting up a degree of trust and communication—it's hard to develop a trust without communication. And we have to decide how disturbed is the patient. Sometimes we can tell more easily than with a neurotic patient who is somewhat delusional but is communicating pretty well. Usually it is a matter of really finding out what a patient is saying and letting him know that you hear, at least tentatively. This is not a matter of interpretation. Most of us develop a technique of responding to the patient in a way in which we are saying: is this what you mean? And we don't say: is this what you mean because of this tone in your voice? And sometimes one says: are you saying or do I hear you saying or are you trying to tell me, and sometimes it is a matter of rephrasing what the patient is saying in a way in which, if it is what he is saying, he will accept it and if not he will turn it down. But we may not, as one sometimes will, hear a therapist say, approach the patient with, well, that means you say this and that means so and so. The patient has to have his area of freedom in which he can hold the door open until he is ready to allow you to come closer. Another critical thing is one's attitude, and I think I would take issue with some things Dr. Laing has written more recently here. One has to be

tremendously interested in the patient, and it has to be real. You can't be interested in a patient before you know him and there is no use trying to pretend you are. But if one doesn't really become interested in the patient, he might as well quit therapy, as it will then be like just going to work. The therapist is going to have to take a great deal of trouble and tribulation in the process of the treatment. He must not *need* the patient of course, for this can create great dangers. One of the critical problems, we feel, is that the patient has been used and needed in one sense by one or the other parent, so that he has never been able to become a separate individual in his own right. And if he begins to feel that the therapist is using him for his purposes or perhaps for somebody else's, everything is lost. One mustn't be treating him because one must have a therapeutic triumph or for the sake of the patient's parent or for one's prestige. And one must not love the patient in the sense of there being a diminution of the boundaries between the therapist's self and the patient. He must get the patient to utilize his own perceptions of things, not depend on his therapist's, to validate his own perception which has been denied over and over again in the family, very much as Dr. Laing has written.

Q.: *You seem then to agree with Laing that very much of what the schizophrenic is saying is obvious and quite literally true.*
LIDZ: Well, if you can understand it. There are misunderstandings too. We talk about the patient's great sensitivity, and it's there because most schizophrenics or many schizophrenic patients have grown

up in such confused communications in the home that they become attuned to understanding the unspoken as being more reliable than the spoken. And they very much relate this way to the therapist as well who often gets this uncanny feeling that the patient knows what he's thinking and feeling. But, you know, they are not mystical. What they see is often correct, but it is often incorrect. I can give you a simple example I wrote of in an article. I had trouble with my back some years ago and had difficulty getting up out of my chair. Now I would say all my patients noted this. It was obvious that it was troublesome for me to sit down and get up. I had a schizophrenic woman I was treating at the time who had noted that I usually would get up and open the door for her when she was leaving the office. Well, now I couldn't and the patient took this to mean that I no longer had any respect or regard for her because I was no longer getting up and opening the door. It was an understandable interpretation, but it was a misinterpretation.

Q.: *What happens once you establish a trust?*
LIDZ: Well, we work for different things, though I suppose you might say we work to undercut the delusional material by finding out what it is the patient really feels persecuted about and maybe has been persecuted about rather than having it transposed to a delusional form—that is one aspect. In recent years my tendency has been to get the patient to recognize, especially younger patients, that his parents are not omnipotent or omniscient and that he can provide his own protection, that he has to stop seeing through their eyes and filling their needs and

begin to direct his energies towards his own life rather than to theirs. Now this goes into a whole theory about the etiology of the schizophrenic.

Q.: *Can you tell us about it?*
LIDZ: This isn't so easy. My wife, Dr. Ruth Lidz and I were recently in Norway for a conference and talked for four days without making much of a dent. I think some of these things we can't answer in half a day.

Q.: *Is there very much danger that therapists working with relatively intractable patients will begin to search for meanings that aren't there and read things into patients' words?*
LIDZ: Oh, I think that treating a schizophrenic patient is very demanding and very trying, but I don't think that a psychiatrist who is reasonably stable and has been decently analyzed should be drawn toward the delusional material. I really don't. I mean if this happens with one of our residents, as it does sometimes, we get him out of that situation and into therapy damn fast. One can become very anxious in our work, and I think people who can't tolerate anxiety have no place in treating the schizophrenic patient. The therapist also has to be able to admit to the patient that he becomes anxious or upset by what's going on, because it can't be hidden. There are many trials, such as when you have a patient who is going along well and suddenly swoops down into some kind of abyss of bitter gloom or suddenly becomes unapproachable. You feel, everything was going well, what did I do, what went wrong. This is a very preoccupying business, to say the least.

Q.: *This involves a strong sense of responsibility for the patient?*

LIDZ: In treating out-patients particularly. There was a time in Baltimore when Dr. Ruth Lidz and I were each treating three or four out-patient schizophrenic patients. I'd say it was a rare night that we slept. The phone would ring until 2 or 3 o'clock in the morning, 3 or 4 nights a week, where somebody was in terrible shape. There's a limit to how much one can take. We found one camping in the woods in a sleeping bag. We knew the patients were apt to be wandering around the house, had to be prepared for this kind of thing and the infringement on our privacy. It is different when you are treating patients in the hospital—we may be worried about them but we know the limits to which they can go.

Q.: *Is there a limit to the number of years one can spend treating a patient, and do former patients ever try to renew contact?*

LIDZ: Well, people are very, very different. I know one therapist in Washington who has been treating a schizophrenic patient for 15 years or more. I don't know what's happening in that case. Some of us at times feel that the kind of investment of ourselves we make when the patient is severely psychotic is such that after a time it's better that he go to another therapist—we feel we've submitted ourselves too much to achieve a proper and worthwhile treatment. The shift may be a beneficial one. As to whether patients come back after leaving therapy, the answer is sometimes. I can think of a man I treated some years ago and who was doing, for him, very well, but every once in a while I would get a call. I didn't do very much, but

I think just knowing that I was here and available was enough to keep him going.

Q.: *Do most hospitals have the luxury in terms of time and money and staff to treat schizophrenics psychotherapeutically?*
LIDZ: Well, state hospitals generally don't, though some with decent residents and a good staff will have doctors take 1 or 2 patients. But this isn't going to affect the general population of the hospital. Very few hospitals actually have their people doing intensive psychotherapy with schizophrenic patients. And we may say that it's a luxury that some of us feel is an essential luxury, that this is how we are going to learn enough about schizophrenic reactions to do something by way of prophylaxis.

Q.: *I get the impression that sometimes the hospitals are, in a sense, driven to drugs and electro-shock treatments because they don't have time to do anything else.*
LIDZ: Oh, I don't think there is any question about that. The state hospitals, for example, keep giving the drugs while the general hospitals use shock treatment and drugs, keeping patients in the hospital for brief periods, getting them out again on drugs, seeing them occasionally, maybe having them involved in group therapy, giving them something to hold on to. We try to do more than that. We try, for example, at the general hospital where we keep patients for a short time, to see to it that either the patient or the family has some change in attitude that will make things more feasible than before.

Q.: *I thought I'd ask you again about the danger to which the therapist exposes himself when he deals with the schizophrenic patient. Dr. Leslie Farber, as you probably know, has discussed this idea at some length, drawing upon his experience with people like Harry Stack Sullivan and Frieda Fromm Reichmann. The danger, as Dr. Farber describes it, is that the therapist may be drawn progressively into a schizophrenic orientation, corresponding at points rather closely to his patient's.*

LIDZ: I'm not sure there is a general answer I can make to that question, but I did know Sullivan and Fromm Reichmann somewhat, and so I can say something that may be helpful. Most people who knew Sullivan knew that he was at least potentially unstable—working as closely with schizophrenics as he did, and given the tremendous empathy he had for them, it would almost have been remarkable if he were not at least mildly affected in the way that Dr. Farber suggests. In fact, the first notable description of the schizophrenic mother is buried somewhere in an old article of Sullivan's, and so vivid is the account that the reader feels quite certain Sullivan is talking about his own mother. There must have been certain special difficulties for him in treating patients in the light of his own precarious equilibrium—perhaps some advantages as well. But I don't think that Sullivan was ever really so upset that one would want to call him schizophrenic, really.

Fromm-Reichmann could be depressed, especially in her later years, but there never seemed to be any question of her adopting the thought-patterns of her patients. Sometimes it is true that she threw herself

so entirely into her task that she may well have
blocked the therapy. She would, for instance, sit in a
patient's urine with him to show there was no difference between them. Or a patient would give his feces
as a gift, and she would take them. Perhaps she did
not always maintain, could not, all of the necessary
distinctions, but I'd be surprised to learn that she ever
got terribly mixed up with her patients. She seemed
pretty much on top of what she was doing.

Q.: *If we could leave the subject of therapy for a
moment, I would like to ask if we are getting any
closer to agreement about the nature of schizophrenia?*
LIDZ: There is so much we don't know as yet
about schizophrenic reactions that I don't want to
sound positive in what I say here. We are working
with presumptions rather than hard facts, for the most
part, but we have to get on with our work, to help
people, and to find out what we can based on working hypotheses. That is the point we are at. I have
attended meetings at which somewhat viable approaches to schizophrenia stressing the hereditary factor were presented in papers. But the data found in
these papers is not very much different from the sort
of thing we found in studies of tuberculosis years ago.
The hereditary tendency is assumed, and it is found
in particular experiments that tuberculosis runs in
families. What is difficult to work on is the primacy
of the environmental factor or genetic susceptibility.
Children could have been infected, after all, and become clinically tubercular only later in life. But we
don't know just how closely future developments in
our research with schizophrenia will resemble this sit-

uation. There may well be a tendency for some people to be schizophrenic, but what does this amount to, we ask. Two good studies have recently been completed, one in Finland, the other in Norway. In the Finnish experiment, it was found that in one of twelve sets of identical twins studied, both children were schizophrenic. In the Norwegian study it was learned there was a 20–35% chance that, if one identical twin was schizophrenic, the other would be as well. Now, of course, identical twins may be expected to grow up more or less alike under the best of circumstances, and so we are not sure about the validity of these experiments as explanations of our problem.

At the moment other studies are being made involving the adopted children of schizophrenic mothers. Attempts are being made to go back to see if there is more psychopathology in the adopted or the biological families. These are studies that can't be done in this country, but their importance may be very great. Years ago we were quite sure that the biological family would show more psychopathology than the adopted family. Now we don't really know. I should mention that a rather good paper recently held that the hereditary factor is not viable. Even if we accepted as sound the studies that find heredity a significant element, we would still find only 10% of the cases tested explainable in that way.

Q.: *How do you personally regard the etiology?*
LIDZ: It is something we are studying, like others in the field. I am among those, however, who make the assumption, or accept the hypothesis, that schizophrenic reactions are developmental, have to do with personality rather than with anything organic. I'm

not about to argue the point, but I do feel, as I've indicated, that we have to get on with our research. This is a hunch I prefer to follow, and we think it has paid off, that we can make sense of things that didn't make sense before.

We have seen results of research conducted in many parts of the world, and one thing is clear: there has never been a schizophrenic who came from a stable family—at least we can't find any. The hallmark of the thought disorder we identify as a schizophrenic reaction is that is does not lie simply in the patient. There's something wrong in the communication of one or both parents, a disturbing quality in the pattern of the family's interpersonal relations that one can begin to bet on. We can't say this is all there is to it, but patterns are surely apparent.

Q.: *How do you regard Laing's description of the family's interpersonal relationship?*
LIDZ: Laing describes the family very well from what is essentially a phenomenological perspective, but he doesn't really analyze the patterns sufficiently. Then too there is an ideological connotation in what he says, as in his discussion of mystification in families. The concept itself is nothing new, but Laing doesn't mention that my colleagues and I in the middle fifties published papers covering similar ground. We did not describe the double-bind, or mystification, but dealt with irrational patterns of communication in the family as a whole. What we saw, and what Laing puts very well, is that being paranoid is a normal mode of behavior in certain families. Some fathers have such a paranoid attitude that they vir-

tually teach children to be inordinately suspicious of outsiders, sometimes even of the mother.

Q.: *Are the patterns so regular that it is legitimate to generalize about these families?*

LIDZ: You have to categorize somewhat if you are to speak of general patterns. There are types of schizophrenic families. We knew very early in our studies that a large number of families of schizophrenic patients were severely disturbed. In describing the nature of this disturbance it is common to find that in many families parents do not get along, are in fact in open conflict with one another much of the time. But here, in the schizophrenic family, one parent undercuts the worth of the other to the child. The parent tries to win the child's support in the conflict with the other parent. Each tries to give the child the sense that he needs this support. It happens more commonly with a girl who gets caught in what we call a schism in her family. If she sides with one parent she must necessarily be rejected by the other, a variation of the double-bind. The child can never be right, and thus finds herself in an untenable situation. Commonly the girl sides with the father and becomes psychotic. This should not be at all surprising, for the child needs a positive role model from the parents, especially from the parent of the same sex with whom she can in some way identify. When the child grows up feeling different from her mother, a negative orientation is established. The father encouraged the view that her mother is no good, that she must be different from her mother to be cared for by him. And the girl knows, somehow, that no matter what she does she is not going to be cared for by the father. He will never really be satisfied.

This is an area in which we have done a good deal of work, but Laing has misrepresented the whole thing in a way that I don't understand. In our work to which Laing refers, we were talking about a family model, not actual family transactions. In certain kinds of schizophrenic families there is apt to be a breakdown of boundaries between the two generations. The child is being used by a parent to complete his life. Often in such a situation there is a good chance for the reversal of role-models—the father, for example, will not be a proper male model, and so on. Also in a schismatic family, although the mother may seem concerned for the girl, there will be something inimical in her manner of relating—she will not be able to show proper, convincing affection. And as the mother fails in not being affectionate or maternal she provides a great handicap to the girl's development as a mother, should she conceive herself in these terms.

Of course it is not always obvious what is wrong in the family milieu. In a family in which the mother really seeks completion from the son, she is frequently unable to set up boundaries between them, for she does not know what is going on either in herself or in the son. Often the very fact that she is a woman makes the mother feel that she cannot achieve anything like completion, that she must turn to the son. The child is given a laxative, and why? Because the mother is constipated. She cannot grasp that the child will begin to see the world differently than she does. And in such families the pattern is not countered by the father, who in these families is typically passive. The mother in fact married him because he was passive and would not interfere. We find that the mother is usually near psychotic, as manifested in peculiar ways of talking and of calling the family together. And there is a markedly excessive concern to keep the child from others outside the family, especially other children. In such relative isolation from outside norms, without a proper male role-model, a boy will be thrown back on the need to be special, different from his father. In this pattern, as in others, communication problems lead to the schizophrenic reaction in the child.

Q.: *Can you describe the precise nature of these communication problems? Are they linguistic problems?*

LIDZ: We have to learn more about language and language development before we can explain these things precisely. Sometimes it is almost linguistic imitation that is involved in the development of a schizophrenic pattern. A mother imposes herself upon a child, hounds him so persistently that he can't make sense of what he does or see clearly how he can break loose of her. She insists upon knowing exactly what happened to the child from the time he left for school to the time of his return, or during a date with a girl. Should the child become disturbed he may well tell us how he imitated the way his mother talked, talked, talked all the time and never said anything. But this is rather unusual. It's really a matter of a whole array of things that go wrong. To describe this is to get into the problems of boundaries between the self and others, the problem of egocentricity and the development of language. To talk of experience we must divide our perceptions into discreet categories, in contrast with the continuity of experience as we feel it. It has been pointed out that one of the first steps in this process is the division into I and others, self and object world, and this takes place at a number of levels. The anthropologists point out how vital in every society are the taboos placed upon things that force the self to conceive what is not-self. In the way we teach children to look at their own feces, for instance, we have the establishment of ego-boundaries.

We psychiatrists stress the process whereby the mother is differentiated from the child. Ordinarily the mother takes the lead in this by weaning the child from his dependence, fostering a sense of autonomy. Between the ages of two and four the child moves out, becoming a member of a family beyond the simple mother-child unit. We feel this is the essence of what doesn't happen in the schizophrenic family. The mother-child dyad doesn't become a dyad but remains a symbiosis far too long, all through the child's life to some extent. This interferes with the learning of categories in a vital way. Basically the mother doesn't foster in the child the self-assurance to move out. In some cases he feels it is his function to complete the parent's life. The parents are hampered by their failure to understand the child's needs, but the child is worse off because he doesn't even have the egocentric orientation of his parents. His is a parent-centered orientation that doesn't even have roots in a life-project of his own but works in support of the parental project. This affects the entire communication pattern of the child and keeps him rather confused.

Q.: *Are schizophrenic reactions more likely to occur in members of any one socio-economic class?*

LIDZ: According to current figures they are more common in lower socio-economic classes. There are two hypotheses that have been recommended here. One is that the incidence of schizophrenia is comparable to the incidence of broken homes, not on a 1 to 1 basis, but enough to make us ask more questions here. It is possible that where the surfaces of family life are disturbed we may have a greater possibility of schizophrenia, though the disturbance would have to assume particular forms, as I've suggested. The other hypothesis has to do with the quality of thinking, the capacity to conceptualize we find in families with minimal education. In such families children may be more prone to schizophrenic reactions, though we're not sure why.

Q.: *Has there been much success in treating the parents of schizophrenics?*

LIDZ: There are those who feel that family therapy is the only way to deal with the problem, to make inroads into the entire communication patterns of the family. I'd agree this is a major item in our approach to schizophrenia, but it isn't easy. Parents are much older than the patient, have reached some kind of equilibrium in their lives which they are very reluctant to give up.

Q.: *Must the patient separate himself from the family if he is to get better?*

LIDZ: Well, our tendency is in this direction. At the Yale Psychiatric Institute we try hard to find another way for the patient to live, to avoid going back to the family situation.

Q.: *And how do the families respond to this?*
LIDZ: This is one of the things we can actually accomplish. We can help stop families from using the child as a pawn in the struggle with one another. We help the parents come together and agree that given their continuing differences it would be better if their son went to boarding school. Often it takes a year or more to bring the parents around to this position.

Q.: *Is it your conclusion, then, that schizophrenia is never a disease in one person?*
LIDZ: I wouldn't argue with that conclusion—in our experience the family is disturbed, the entire family, and needs attention. But there is, we must remember, a patient.

Q.: *It is possible that the fact of there being a schizophrenic in the house is what creates disturbed patterns of family interaction?*
LIDZ: No doubt, this is something we can't overlook. But we don't know just how important an idea it is because we haven't been able to set up adequate longitudinal studies as yet, though everyone in the field agrees these are what we need. We have conducted extensive interviews with family members, individually and as groups. We have carefully observed their interactions with one another and even with staff members. We have tried to recreate family situations through such interviews, going back to the time

of the parents' marriage up to the time the patient, the child, comes to the hospital. We have even tried to go back to the parents' parents. But what we really need are longitudinal studies that start with families before a schizophrenic patient appears on the scene. And since approximately one in every hundred children will turn out to be schizophrenic, such studies are extremely difficult to make. You'd have to study thirty families in order to get one family with a schizophrenic child. And you might by chance study a hundred families and still fail to come up with a single patient. Of course one can try to pick out likely families, but that's hard too.

Q.: *Why should these family patterns that lead to schizophrenic disturbances occur so often in this culture?*

LIDZ: We don't know that it's cultural—these are rather natural patterns to occur. The question is, how deeply are they established in a given culture? We expect that in societies unlike ours, in tribal cultures, for instance, where the nuclear family has relatively little effect on the child, the patterns we have been describing will not so readily take hold. Children in these other cultures will likely be raised by older women and other tribal figures. But we don't know enough about this, nor even about the incidence of schizophrenic reaction in children raised in the Israeli Kibbutzim.

Q.: *Are the dynamics of schizophrenic families sufficiently different from what we see in most "normal" families that the distinctions are always apparent? Some of us look at our own families, or the families*

*of friends with whom we grew up, and so much in the
patterns you describe seems familiar.*
LIDZ: There are all sorts of gradations, of course,
more or less bad families, more or less good ones,
more or less schizophrenic ones—provided you don't
think schizophrenia is a disease. But we have had
medical students observe family therapy sessions, and
their response has been "my God, I couldn't live in
that family for a week, there is something so malignant." So the family unit as the critical item in the
schizophrenic situation does seem to many of us per-
suasive, and it is not a notion originally established
by Laing but by Nathan Ackerman, I think.

Q.: *How do you define the schizophrenic psychosis,
apart from the conditions to which it is a response?*
LIDZ: The schizophrenic psychosis in contrast with
others, involves a disturbance in thought and language without degradation of intellectual potential,
a confusion of thought without impairment of the
intelligence. This is clear enough. What we are less
clear about is the nature of susceptibility to this reaction. We are all to one degree or another hemmed
in by the way we are taught to believe in reality. Our
hypothesis is that the schizophrenic's early background leads him to deal in certain ways with this
reality, usually by escaping from the culture's needs,
evading its demands upon him. Some people, on the
other hand, have problems that seem overwhelming,
but they develop severe physical symptoms in response—perhaps often of a very painful kind—and
yet they keep in touch with reality. They can't break
even if it might seem better to do so. It may be a
hereditary matter that some people cannot retreat

into an infantile fantasy life to remind them of how the world was before things fell apart.

Q.: *Laing is highly critical of acculturation of the sort you seem to recommend. What do you think of his views on this point?*

LIDZ: There is a radical difference at this point between his orientation and mine. Laing is in a tradition that now includes Marcuse and Norman O. Brown and others who have misunderstood and overemphasized Freud's ideas, especially those found in *Civilization and Its Discontents.* Laing's tradition stresses the fact that civilization impedes the development of human potential, and concludes that if we can only get rid of the repression foisted upon us we will all be happy. All we need are conditions that will allow the primitive, innate child within us to develop without restraint. This is the thing that contemporary youth finds so appealing in the tradition. But the human being is not able to escape—he is worse without the adaptive techniques required to live in a society. He doesn't have to continue adhering to the mores of his culture, but he cannot fall back on something called an innate quality—this is a fallacious concept of human development. We can't begin to understand the current hypotheses regarding schizophrenia unless we see that it involves a malfunction in the family's nurturing of the child. This has to do with basic roles that are taught, the instrumentalities of the culture, its language and so forth.

Q.: *How then do you regard Laing's statements about the importance of authenticity?*

LIDZ: It depends how he uses the idea. Laing's current usage varies from his earlier usage. I have relatively little quarrel with *The Divided Self*. While it's a different type of approach than I would use, I think it's a brilliant work and held out the promise of a really great mind in our profession. *Politics of Experience*, on the other hand, is a wild and whirling commentary that demonstrates little grasp of the reality of human development. In a sense authenticity means recognizing the reality of what one really is, but this is not just a matter of finding what is innate. Genes have a good deal to do with this reality, but we must also consider other things. You cannot suddenly say that you want to be an eskimo and swiftly become one. You have to learn from the time you are growing up how to be an eskimo, to have the proper frame of mind to be one. We must accept the fact that we live in the 20th century, in what is termed a civilized society. We can change that society, but we can't escape it.

Q.: *In* The Divided Self *Laing described schizophrenia as a process of self-annihilation. In the* Politics of Experience, *in a much quoted passage, he speaks of madness as not being a breakdown, but potentially breakthrough and liberation. Do you agree with the latter formulation?*
LIDZ: Well, I think potentially this is not impossible. There are those who go through madness, I would say, and who come out on the other side with a different understanding than before. But this is unusual, as we see even if we look at some of the greatest products, if I may put it that way, of schizophrenia. The playwright August Strindberg, for example, who had four years of his life during which

he was incapacitated, never emerged a really sound person. I also have the feeling, though, that his creativity may have been greater because of his schizophrenic reaction, though he continued to suffer the rest of his life. And there aren't many Strindbergs.

Q.: *Laing says that in future years we will come to look upon the schizophrenic person as a prophet. Do you agree, given what you've said of Strindberg.*

LIDZ: I understand how Laing could make such a statement, but I don't think it's valid. Let's come back to Strindberg. He said many things which contain deep and vital insights, but much of what he said people couldn't understand until Freud explained the various concepts in more reasonable terms. But yes, Strindberg was one of the prophets of the future, we might say, and so perhaps was Blake. Blake was maybe psychotic, certainly had insights other people could not have, but . . .

Q.: *Laing seems not to be talking only of such people, though, of great artists and men of genius, but of his own patients.*

LIDZ: There are many gifted people—we need not be speaking only of geniuses or great artists. But I would say that how a man sees while he is schizophrenic is in the nature of illusion, and delusion, and has very little to do with anything real or practical. This much we should be clear about. Of course, the perceptions of a schizophrenic may be different from anything you or I have, so closely in touch is he with things we have to block off. These special perceptions may have more to do with the things that myth deals with—with a deep understanding of human motivation often.

Q.: *Would you illustrate this for us?*
LIDZ: Well, Freud put us in touch with certain unconscious drives which we were unable earlier to see, incestuous feelings that the mother may harbor towards the son, for example. A schizophrenic woman may perceive this very clearly in herself and in other women she knows.

Q.: *Are these kinds of perceptions at all useful in enhancing the life of patients?*
LIDZ: I think they can be useful. Insights into other people, what motivates others, can surely be of use. But I take a very dim view of the things Laing proposes for the schizophrenic experience. He is recommending that people who feel they need it be encouraged to go through psychotic experiences directed by Shaman-figures who are taking drugs and prophesying what is to come. Schizophrenic patients should not be proposed as models for those seeking deeper insights than they can manage on their own. From what I have heard from people who claim to know what Laing is doing, he is currently arguing that schizophrenic patients are helped by taking LSD and being allowed to go back and increase the intensity of their psychotic experience. Most therapists I know would have to feel this is absolutely dangerous as hell.

Q.: *You seem to be committed to a process whereby the therapist tries to bring a person back to reality, whereas Laing encourages his patients to move away.*

LIDZ: He feels there is a more or less spontaneous process in which a psychotic patient can have some vital experience in breakdown, get some enlightenment, and emerge. And I'm sure this is possible for some people. Laing tends also to believe it is hospitalization that often keeps the patient from his happiness. I don't think this is true. I've seen hundreds of schizophrenic patients who have never been near a hospital. I used to work in the medical clinic of a hospital as a psychiatric consultant. Every day I would see at least one schizophrenic patient, and no more than one of twenty would I send to the hospital. Many of these people were unhappy, tied up in knots in some way, but they had a certain equilibrium and didn't cause anyone else special trouble. But they didn't get better. Schizophrenia tends to be a self-perpetuating condition in which people give up validating their experience.

Q.: *Are you saying that schizophrenics don't get well on their own under any circumstances?*
LIDZ: No, it isn't that lots of them don't get well. There are after all many more schizophrenics than psychiatrists ever see. They go through a psychotic period, survive it somehow, and then get well, or better. They might have delusions still, but they make compromises, and that's the whole thing. But in the most typical form, the person goes down-hill slowly in middle adolescence and becomes more and more withdrawn and aloof. This is not a self-curative experience. But again I emphasize there are those who come to some resolution on their own.

Q.: *We were speaking earlier of Laing's aversion to*

mental hospitals. Have you heard much about Laing's Kingsley Hall, which eliminates the traditional forms we associate with mental hospitals and tries to provide a protected place where the schizophrenic patient won't be intruded upon?

LIDZ: I don't know very much about it, but from what I have heard I haven't been encouraged to learn more, I must say. We've tried to get away from most conventions of the traditional hospital too, but we feel the situation has to be structured. One of the problems the schizophrenic patient has is the lack of structuring influences in his life. And also the idea of breaking down distinctions between doctor and patient doesn't appeal to me at all—we have to recognize that the patient has suffered usually from a lack of proper differentiation between himself and the parent. A goal of many therapists is specifically the development of ego-boundaries for the patient, and some therapists begin at the most elementary level, naively I think, with "this is your hand. You are touching this book, not me, not someone else." Some therapists go to the other extreme, almost saying there is no reason why doctors and patients should stay apart and not get so involved in one another's lives. But the patient is too damned involved in his parents' lives most often, and must learn to look out for himself as a separate individual.

Q.: *Do Laing's phenomenological descriptions of the schizophrenic, especially in his earlier books, assist therapists in a practical way at all?*

LIDZ: They can if they give therapists a better orientation to what is happening inside the patient. I have no real quarrel with Laing's description—it is a great clarification of several things, I think. He says a number of things that others customarily describe in other ways, such as his division between a subjective self and a kind of body-self, though that isn't exactly his term. Others would say that the patient lives or tries to live as if he were not tied down to the consequences of his actual actions, what his body does. The patient, in other words, feels he can live in the realm of pure subjectivity. It's a typical problem of adolescents which dissappears as they grow up and learn to conceptualize. As we begin to think about thinking, the discrepancy between solving problems in reality and thinking about solving them in our imagination becomes apparent to us. You cease to believe you can change the world simply by telling people what's wrong with your government. You learn that you can't solve problems in the mind alone, but have to transform them into actual operations. Some people become artists and create worlds of their own, but most of them know that these worlds are not reality. The schizophrenic is apt to retreat into a world in which he can solve things purely on his own. And he will not refer this world back to the real one at any point.

Q.: *Laing argues that fantasy and imagination play an increasingly diminished role in human development, that these faculties are blunted by the culture we live in. Do you agree? Are we becoming excessively rational?*

LIDZ: I think there is something in that. I was saying only the other day to my class that I didn't think there had ever been another society so little in touch with the mythic—and this carries considerable penalties with it. We have set out to solve all our problems by an objective scientific approach in which we think that by reasoning things out we'll be able to bring even essential problems into manageable focus. Mythical thinking, on the other hand, deals with eternal, recurrent problems in our lives, and sees each phenomenon as a particular manifestation, just another instance of universal phenomena. All people are born, must leave their mothers, go through puberty, marry and so on—these are common patterns, and mythic thinking would study these.

Q.: *How much of an influence has Freud been in your own life? Many psychiatrists have attacked him in recent years, claiming that Freudian theories are no longer applicable to current problems.*
LIDZ: The influence has been very great. I would never have become a psychiatrist without having read Freud as a young man. Nonetheless it is a pity that Freud's original concepts have remained in a dominant position for so long a period of time. I think it strange that psychoanalytic training institutes start their training periods by teaching the writings of Freud. Nobody does this in any other area of science. You don't start teaching neurology by giving students the work of Jackson, the equivalent figure to Freud in Anglo-American neurology. After a time students will go back and read some pertinent papers of Jackson, but it is acknowledged that neurology has developed way beyond the original perceptions of Jackson.

Q.: *Most of Freud's work, and he was insistent upon this, dealt with a phenomenon he called transference neurosis. In the light of this, are Freud's theories and concepts translatable into the understanding and treatment of schizophrenics?*

LIDZ: It is true that he stayed away from the treatment of schizophrenic patients. He felt that the transference relationship couldn't develop in the schizophrenic patients. But in the late 30's and early 40's it became quite apparent that it was not difficult to establish the relationship. Of course it's a much more primitive, infantile relationship than Freud was accustomed to that we can have with our schizophrenic patients. But those of us with sufficient experience find these relationships can be genuinely therapeutic, though they become so all-important to the patient that they are difficult to handle or resolve.

Q.:   *Why does analysis with these patients frequently go on so long?*

LIDZ: The problems are frequently overwhelming. In addition, though, many therapists want to work only with chronic patients. There is a difference of opinion among psychiatrists on this point, but I don't think we should devote our major energies and time to the most chronic schizophrenic patients. We would never cure any cancer victims that way if we dealt only with cancers that have been metastasized. We ought to be dealing with schizophrenic patients whose condition really became severe in the last week or the last month, before years have gone by in which aspects of the person's basic growth have been arrested.

Q.:   *I wanted to ask you a question that relates something you wrote years ago to some of Laing's views. You said that without a social system and its directives there can be no individual freedom. What do you think Laing's response would be?*

LIDZ: Laing seems to be saying that reality itself has become so crazy that anyone who accepts reality is himself crazy—the only sane people are those who reject this reality, while conventionally adjusted people are crazy. I don't agree with this at all as a general statement. We're living in pretty desperate times, but I'm not convinced that the irrationality of the way things happen is more pronounced than at any earlier time. But our expectations are different, and we may worry more because we believe more than in earlier times that the way a person turns out depends on the circumstances in which he is brought up. We are moved when we see people in poverty, or people who lack certain educational advantages. A hundred years ago it was taken for granted that a working class man might very well produce a working class son. It was readily accepted that some people were stupid and some people smart. We rebel against such things, and to a great extent we are justified in doing so, for we know that people who crack, our schizophrenic patients, are largely those who have had something wrong or especially unfulfilling in their families. But to suggest, as Laing does, that this sort of situation justifies a schizophrenic reaction is a grave error.

Q.: *Are you surprised to find books on schizophrenia so popular among young people today?*
LIDZ: I don't know that I was surprised to see this happening, but I was upset at first when I found that Laing was writing for a general public rather than for a professional audience. In the first place it's none of the public's business about these families, even though Laing may have changed details enough to make his

case studies more or less anonymous. We found that we could not publish accounts of most families we were working with. They were not anonymous or poor, and some were known rather widely and might have been recognized in the accounts we prepared. Some of our case studies run from fifty to eighty typescript pages, really wonderful documents, but we can't publish them. I will say, though, in support of Laing, that it's helpful to have in *The Divided Self* and the book he did with Esterson the description he provides even for the general public. It teaches people that schizophrenic reactions are functional disorders, that they stem from something wrong in the family background, that they are understandable and treatable.

Not strangely, it is much easier for parents of a patient to accept an explanation that attributes the problem to some genetic abnormality, or to a vitamin deficiency, than to accept that they've done something wrong. We don't think they've done anything wrong. They weren't trying to harm the child. I know this is somewhat in contrast with a number of things Laing has written—he feels the parents of the patient are frequently malicious. I think this is very rare. By and large the parents do the best they can—they can't be different than what they are.

Q.: *Are you concerned that schizophrenic patients are reading Laing? Is there a potential danger in this?*
LIDZ: Yes, I think *Politics of Experience* is doing a real disservice to a number of people who take it very seriously. I am speaking of the notion that it is good to be schizophrenic, or that one should force himself into a psychotic experience. Our experience is based on

very tangible situations, and we find that most of our patients do better when they are specifically limited. In our hospital at Yale patients know that on their floor they don't have to be constantly worrying about giving into some impulse they can't control. We don't lock them up as such, but we do provide a protective, supervized environment. Our patients feel that if they should suddenly decide to commit suicide a man will be there to stop them. Some patients have the fear they may want to rape another patient, but they know we will not allow them to. Many have the impulse to wander away, or to run away, thinking suddenly they may be able to evade their problems in this way, but they know we won't let them wander away, and usually don't try as a result.

Q.: *Why do college students seem to find* Politics of Experience *so compelling?*
LIDZ: It suits very well the current trends of a romantic period, encouraging the idea of doing away with limitations, the notion that we should be able to change things by an expression of good will. You know the attitude—if you let yourself go and blow your mind you'll really learn to understand the world. It's a way of gaining experience without having actually to go through it, a very romantic idea. I wrote a book called *The Person* a couple of years ago, as you know, and in it I show that the developing purpose of human integration is brought about in the early stages by directive talk in the home. This does not amount to putting a strait-jacket on the person, but involves providing an opportunity without which the person can't become anything. And there are

aspects of this situation that Laing seems not to understand.

Q.: *Laing says the schizophrenic patient is frequently devious, and clearly implies this is because of the way the therapist mishandles his patients. Laing makes the point vividly by referring to the psychiatrist Kraepelin and his approach to the patient, as you probably recall.*

LIDZ: The patient is devious, of course, but the therapist usually senses that in a peculiar way he is letting the doctor know what he's thinking about. The communications are cryptic, in part purposefully so, but I don't know many psychiatrists who treat patients badly in the way Laing suggests is so common. Sometimes a patient may feel he has been hurt by a therapist, and he may be right about it in a particular instance, but in general I'd have to say that Laing sets up a Kraepelinian straw man. If you examine contemporary textbooks in psychiatry you'll see what I mean—not in thirty years has a typical text corresponded to the Kraepelinian volume Laing uses as his example. Besides, there weren't any decent textbooks in psychiatry until the last ten years.

Q.: *Could this attitude of Laing's be the result of inadequacies in his own training?*

LIDZ: It's possible—at a number of English medical schools they have almost no psychiatric training at all. The point is that what Laing says is not comprehensible as commentary on the better training centers in this country.

Q.: *Did he perhaps adopt this line of argument to shock the general public?*

LIDZ: Well, he should have kept in mind the relevant concepts, the history of our profession. As I mentioned before, Kraepelin was differentiating dementia paralytica from dimentia senilis—that's why he finally came up with the term dimentia praecox for what he observed in his psychotic patients. The term defines a deteriorating disease of the brain that would inevitably lead to a fatal ending, the way paralytica or syphilis would. Adopting such a perspective on the psychoses he treated, Kraepelin had to have a fatalistic concept of his work with these patients.

Q.: *What about Laing's relation to the psychiatrist Thomas Szasz who has argued in a number of volumes that psychiatry in this country has a punitive rather than a therapeutic function?*

LIDZ: The situation in this country at the moment certainly doesn't warrant that sort of attack. At least I've never heard of anyone here involved in what they do with psychiatry in Russia—using it to lock up political dissidents. Of course it is possible that a number of people who should go to jail are being sent to mental institutions, but that is a different thing. Laing of course agrees with Szasz that mental hospitals are noxious places, and that people who seem disturbed do not have an illness as such. I've talked to Szasz about his position and pointed out to him that the whole American Meyerian tradition has refused to accept mental disorders as illnesses. But Szasz argues, perhaps rightly in part, that this applies only to an element of American psychiatry and that most American psychiatrists do speak of disorders and illnesses in the way he says. He points to the use of insulin and other kinds of medication in mental hospitals as cures for mental disturbances. He also points to the use of tranquilizers, but I believe this should be viewed differently. Tranquilizers do cut down the patient's agitation, the sensory input, and make him more available to other treatment. But there are very few people who think tranquilizers can cure schizophrenic patients.

Q.: *Since we've been speaking of Laing's relationship to Szasz, perhaps you can tell us what is your idea of institutionalizing patients without their consent—this is another area in which Szasz especially has been most vocal.*

LIDZ: We have the right to institutionalize a patient only for the protection of others or of the patient himself. Otherwise we have no right. Szasz overlooks the fact that society has the right to protect itself. He may say there are no dangers, but that's not the case. Some people shoot others when they are insane. Most people in state hospitals aren't really dangerous to others in this way, but it's also true that most aren't certified as being dangerous in this sense.

Q.: *What of the argument that crime is strictly a legal matter and not a psychiatric one?*

LIDZ: I don't think you can state that unequivocally. For one thing, it has taken psychiatry a long time to get crime out of being too much a legal matter. We have put patients through a very bad time, having them stand up in front of a court to have their sanity argued at an open sanity hearing. And the decision must often be reached by a jury that is not capable of deciding any way. We are getting around to taking these hearings out of the courtroom and relying on a couple of professional people to reach a decision . . . you know, habeas corpus proceedings are open to anybody at a state hospital who demands attention from the government. And from what I've seen proceedings are made available in this way. Others argue that this isn't true at the larger hospitals, that there are people who don't get hearings when they demand them. I'm not in a position to know whether this is true in certain cases, but I don't see why Szasz is so adamant about his position. Most hospitals, surely the ones I know, are trying to get rid of as many patients as they can.

Q.: *Laing emphasizes the concept of experience in his writings, the patient's experience, and this is something you do in your writings as well. Do you find his discussion of experience adequately intelligible?*

LIDZ: I have had some trouble understanding him, but it is true that both of us study the patient's experience, though we do not use the same terms. He would say the important thing is to study this experience phenomenologically, not to look for something underneath. In a recent article of mine on Adolph Meyer I discuss how this way of thinking entered so strongly into American psychiatry. Prior to Meyer, it was commonly agreed that it was scientifically legitimate only to study brain cells and chemistry, but he advocated taking experience as a fact in itself and seeing what could be made of it. This is very close to what Laing has said—very little of what he's proposed is at all new. What we all want to do is to find out what the patient said or did or meant in his terms, not ours.

Q.: *Has what Laing wrote in* The Divided Self *changed your own thinking at all?*
LIDZ: Well, his most important contribution is his own particular insight, his sense of what's going on in a schizophrenic patient—his sense of the whole thing is extraordinary and has helped us to comprehend more clearly what we were dealing with. And it has been helpful that he has examined and emphasized the interfamilial problems that are so much a part of the schizophrenic situation. This is in keeping with the work of a number of other people working in the field whom Laing generally ignores. My impression is that he feels he originated many of these concepts on his own pretty much—he writes from his own personal experience, as you know. I don't think he would try to deny the work of others, but he has probably been unaware of the practitioners in his field who have come up with comparable insights. And when he belatedly found them out, he didn't bother referring to them.

Q.: *I wondered though whether Laing had influenced you?*
LIDZ: Insofar as our work was affected by anyone outside it was by the work of Don Jackson and his group, perhaps more pertinently by the work of Wynne and Singer on communication problems in the families of schizophrenics. These people opened up new areas in a way Laing did not for us.

Q.: *What would you say has been the most important contribution to the study of schizophrenia over the last twenty or twenty-five years?*

LIDZ: I suppose you mean in terms of a general approach. As I said, the field was opened up a great deal by the work of Wynne and Singer. But you know, beyond the family relations aspect, there was a time when we thought it was important to find out whether the most important part of the schizophrenic's development occurred in the oral or the anal stage. At first we thought the development was related to the patient's progress from the oral to the anal to the phallic stage, to the whole process. Then we thought for a while that the anal stage was more crucial. Now we know there isn't a period in the schizophrenic's life that hasn't been extremely disturbed, and we've learned to ask broader questions: What is the family for, what can it do, what role precisely does language play in the creation of a disturbance. This has affected our therapy quite profoundly. When we started out, even before World War II, it was assumed that the patient was usually immature for some unknown reason, that he would cling to his parents and never become independent. Then we found that the parent was the dependent person, and usually dependent on the patient in a way that kept the patient unfree. I know this sounds like a complete reversal, but it's held up time after time. The patient is dependent, but only secondarily . . . Also, in answer to your question, we've tried lately to find out why there is an ego-weakness in the patient, whether this is an innate problem. We've learned to use the work of people in other disciplines —Talcott Parsons for instance has been very important to us, introducing a number of sociological concepts we've needed . . . we've also come to try to keep patients away from the noxious milieu from which they've emerged, and we do the best we can not to let them relate to us as they once related to their parents—this involves a careful patterning in therapeutic relations. We realize many things now in establishing these relations that we didn't know only a short time ago—what was considered regression, you know, bad habits, uncleanliness, was never really regression for many of these people. They simply never learned how to handle these things in the first place, were always backwards with respect to socialization. They were always misfits, never prepared by the parents to emerge from the home . . . taking all of these things together, I would have to say that we're better oriented in every way. We are confident that we will find meaningful material to work with rather than having to look upon the whole thing as some perplexing condition. You can see that we can almost lay odds on what the family relations of patients have been.

Q.: *What will the future bring?*
LIDZ: The thing that disturbs us most is that, if our hypotheses are correct, and in a way I hope they are not, there won't be any simple approach to the problem. There are no prophylactic leads we can see. What we must do are the longitudinal studies I spoke of earlier, and we don't think they'll be impossible.

Beyond that, we are in a period in the treatment of mental disturbance which goes against providing proper hospital facilities. Everything is in the direction of short-term care, getting the patient out of the hospital as fast as possible. This is dictated in large part by economic necessity. A large part of the money that goes into mental health is being used to try to cut down on the number of patients treated and to prevent the building of new hospitals. We feel that we need experience in treating more patients in the proper type of hospital milieu, and there aren't many of these places around. The common trend is clearly not to build them.

If you want to know, finally, where I personally would concentrate my energies in the future, I'd want to learn the precise relation between interpersonal problems in the patient's family of origin and the patient's peculiar thought disorder.

Q.: *Is there any chance that preventive measures will be developed?*
LIDZ: We would hope there will be, but we don't know how they can be as long as the current trend is to keep people out of hospitals. It's a strange thing, because we should be able to get some people into hospitals much more quickly. We must make hospitals useful and congenial enough for people to want to go to them when they feel they need help, rather than staying away. One of the obstacles to decent therapeutic treatment of schizophrenics is that they don't come in until they are forced to. If we got to work with them before the condition had congealed, we could look at the situation that was precipitating the psychosis at the time, rather than going back over a period of years. We would be in a much better position, as we are with the college students we are able to treat at Yale.

The other big problem we have at the moment is with drugs, psychedelic drugs, and we find that schizophrenic reactions are becoming much less of a problem to us relatively. We are much more caught up and concerned with LSD reactions and questions like, what is the relationship between psychoses that may be due to LSD and schizophrenic reactions? Which comes first in a particular individual: Do we have a boy who became schizophrenic and then started taking LSD, or what? Or do we have a boy who gets into a peculiar confusional state that looks more or less like schizophrenia but is due to drugs? We're quite confused about this.

Q.: *You've said in one of your books that the problems of schizophrenics are related to the problems of all mankind. Would you explain that?*
LIDZ: I meant that it is a disorder that all men are prone to—it is a human disorder that depends on the use of symbolic processes and on disturbances in those processes. When we learn more about this we'll learn more about how human beings function generally. Schizophrenia for instance is closely related to paranoid states, even those that are not pathological, and to simpler distortions people use to defend themselves. Schizophrenia is really the essence, the essential mental disorder, and we'll know a hell of a lot about all the others when we understand it.

Q.: *Many argue that neurosis is a historical phenomenon, that the kind of neurosis described by Freud was created by the conditions of his time. Would you extend this to say that schizophrenia too might be an historical condition?*

LIDZ: We have the historical element very much in mind, and we've wanted to do experiments, phenomenological studies, to see what schizophrenics today have in common with the patients we saw thirty years ago. It's time we stopped thinking of it in the old way. I've seen residents who have never seen a catatonic patient, where years ago we'd have whole wards of catatonics. Now this is due partly to the changes in hospitalization and partly to drugs that cut the tension down. Today if you treat patients properly they just don't get dilapidated—we don't have any who go downhill, though there are those who don't get better.

Q.:   *How do you regard these lines from the* Politics of Experience: *"Who is not engaged in trying to impress, to leave a mark, to engrave his image on the others and the world—graven images held more dear than life itself? We wish to die leaving our imprints burned into the hearts of the others. What would life be if there were no one to remember us, to think of us when we are absent, to keep us alive when we are dead?"*

LIDZ: There is some truth in that, I think, though we must draw nourishment from ourselves while we are alive. It must be dismal to die without thinking we have left something in our children or students to carry on. But to need these things with the urgency we hear in Laing must be a terrible burden, almost disastrous in itself. Laing's philosophy in the *Politics of Experience* is really a philosophy of despair rather than one of hope. And I can't help but wonder why I should look at things so differently than he does. I think maybe I didn't have such expectations of human beings as he has, and therefore I've not become quite as disillusioned as he. Laing also says that it is impossible to love—that is a personal problem of his, I think. In fact, one of the terrible things about the *Politics of Experience* is that Laing generalizes so much from his personal experiences. I can't imagine how else he can see the family as actually antagonistic to human development. Laing's is the attitude of Strindberg and Samuel Butler, that it is almost necessary to do away with the family because of its devastating impact on children.

Q.: *Some people who see all this hurt and suffering engendered in families are more despairing about it than you.*

LIDZ: I may despair too, but I don't see any other way. The family is a universal phenomenon, or almost universal, and I have just about arrived at the conclusion that the family is a necessary adjurant of man's biological nature. This biological nature allows man almost limitless potentiality, but no given direction. Human beings are like other animals in that they are equipped to adapt to a rather limited environment in which they can maintain themselves. But as we developed language we found we could transmit various adaptive techniques that we discovered to our children. By gradually communicating techniques we found we could move into broader and broader environments, and could adapt to each in a multiplicity of different ways. These ways have to be learned—human beings can't survive without being taught how to fit into a social group and communicate with other people. The basics are transmitted in the family, which also protects us, and the two functions are closely related.

Q.: *What do you suspect would happen if we tried to eliminate the family?*
LIDZ: I think we'd have tragedy. I considered this recently particularly in regard to the Chinese communes, where parents are kept apart from their children except for visits once a month or every few weeks. My feeling is that for most people, without meaningful family relationships and the feeling for children whom we must care for and help make life meaningful for, life will not seem worthwhile. A society of such people would, I think, ultimately disintegrate.

Q.: *How do you feel, as a psychiatrist, when you finish a book that concludes: "If I could turn you on, if I could drive you out of your wretched mind, if I could tell you I would let you know."*
LIDZ: I think that Laing, the man who wrote those lines, is in such a despairing state that he shouldn't do therapy. I don't think I could treat patients if I were in such a depression that I felt there was so little joy and creativity in *this* world. There is another statement Laing makes in *The Politics Of Experience* that I have found very disturbing. I have it here. It reads:

"A man may indeed produce something new—a poem, a pattern, a sculpture, a system of ideas—think thoughts never before thought, produce sights never before seen. Little benefit is he likely to derive from his own creativity. The fantasy is not modified by such 'acting out,' even the sublimest. The fate that awaits the creator, after being ignored, neglected, despised, is, luckily or unluckily according to point of view, to be discovered by the non-creative." I thought that was a terrible statement. If Laing doesn't understand that the reward of creativity comes from being creative rather than from the recognition of it, I think he's way off base. Though of course it is a pleasure to be recognized. You have to feel the world can be changed for the better and that one can be nourished by his work in it. Doing psychiatric work is a creative process, and there is a real joy in creativity. To pick up the basic scenes in a patient's life, and try to see them in a harmonious way, somehow is to be involved in something meaningful.

R. D. Laing and Anti-Psychiatry:*
A Symposium

PANELISTS:
ROBERT COLES
LESLIE H. FARBER (MODERATOR)
EDGAR Z. FRIEDENBERG
KENNETH LUX

FRIEDENBERG: In preparing to discuss Laing I was particularly pleased to find that Laing himself made an acknowledgment to the influence of Harry Stack Sullivan who has always struck me as the most useful of the psycho-dynamic theorists as well as being an upstate New Yorker and probably more immediately attuned to our kind of reality. He and Edmund Wilson, I think, have derived from this a capacity to understand what is happening to people around here that I trust I'm rapidly losing as a voluntary self-exile from Buffalo and other points in this country. But Laing does seem to me to epitomize what in Sullivan he finds to be most true. Sullivan's very much quoted statement is that we are all more

* What follows is an edited transcript of a symposium held on October 5, 1970 at Skidmore College, sponsored by *Salmagundi*.

simply human than otherwise. Now, it isn't a sentimental value that I attach to that but it is from this
that Sullivan reaches, with a great deal less sense of
being besieged about it than Laing, the conclusion
that there really is no such thing as mental illness.
There are merely different stratagems for living which
have to be learned earlier or later as the case may be
and which are more or less costly as the case may be,
and generally the more strategy you have to learn
sooner as a result of the politics of your particular
family the more costly the game is going to be. This
is fundamental to an inter-personal theory of psychiatry, as Sullivan called his work. I do remember, of
course, that Sullivan shared with Jesus and Socrates
and Confucius, though possibly not with Meher Baba,
the peculiar character of not having written
down any of his own work that was later published.
Students had to reconstruct it from lecture notes and
things that they had taken down, tape recording being relatively less common in those days, though possible. But certainly what Sullivan had in mind in
speaking of an inter-personal theory of psychiatry was
indeed that who gets to be deemed mad is in fact the
loser in games people play. And I think we are a little
surprised how Sullivan now strikes us as comparatively so tranquil about all of this, though he himself
was certainly not a man who turned his back on any
kind of suffering. Like any human being he needed
other people and he needed them desperately, but it
never seemed to becloud his judgment. And yet he
wrote in a way Laing does not and that I certainly
would not myself and do not now. As if in a sense
conventional sanity were possible. Sullivan still had
access, not to a different psychodynamic theory, but

to a different set of social norms, perhaps even something more concrete in his total experience of life that led him to believe society made possible a life that would certainly not be happy but that would not be alienated or would at least make sense. When I think about what tragedy must have been for Sullivan I go back to something like Edith Wharton's old Ethan Frome. Even if it does end in the double suicide of the lovers it's for a reason they both understand. And this is a long way from the Kafka-like state that Laing quite properly writes about. To call one of your books, and so appropriately, *Politics of the Family*, is to recognize that even this most immediate of all social institutions has in effect degenerated into a game about power. And what I think is really changed in this is that in Laing's time, which is ours, the power plays have tended to become empty and purely manipulative because the family no longer has a relationship to any set of experiences, opportunities or resources in which it can in effect make good on its demands. So that you have the added frustration, which I know many people growing up today must have, of feeling that you have taken on all of this load of anxiety, of the false sense of self, and in return have gained not even any power in your own life, but are totally vulnerable. It's for this reason I think Laing uses the phrase ontological anxiety and why he repudiates the Freudian terminology, much less the Freudian reality. Laing does not associate anxiety with what amounts to a fear of impotence or malfunction in certain characteristic and important organ systems. Laing's insight is that the self may be obliterated when it is forced to acknowledge there may actually have been no game all the time you thought you were playing a game. That in fact your parents in addition to everything else were wasting your time and substance and that not only can you not always get what you want but that if you try some time you may just find that you ain't going to get what you need either. And in fact there was never any question really that it was just a game being played with the doorman as in a Kafkan example that Laing draws on. Furthermore, as an official expatriate I think things have maybe gotten a little worse since this was written. I can no longer take seriously the question of whether there are people in mad houses somewhere who are more seriously alienated than Richard Nixon. I mean that is ridiculous. But I do think that the question of ontological anxiety is a real question. You've got to at least assume that if the person had been somewhat more fortunate, if this hadn't supervened quite so soon, if the parents hadn't been quite so completely manipulative and hadn't been using the kid as a counter in a game and so on, that then not merely the fear of obliteration but indeed the probability of obliteration might have been substantially less. So to that extent you see the person far gone in a schizophrenic process is at least guilty of some serious misjudgment in that he would, if he were not so absorbed, if he could take in more, if he dared have more of a real self, would in fact be in less danger and could indeed control more of the reality that was impinging on him and that he perceived as wholly threatening. Laing uses a quotation from Kafka to the effect that you are free to choose to try to avoid the suffering of life but in so doing you may incur the only suffering that you might indeed have avoided. Well, I find that a very moving point of view and I would like to still believe it but I have my doubts. As one who has lived in the city of Buffalo for three years, for example, I can say that it has made at least one enormous clinical advance. The people of Buffalo have completely eliminated paranoia. It no longer exists. There is nobody in Buffalo, I don't believe, with a delusion of persecution. What they fear is in fact more likely than not to happen if they stay there. I know one can argue degrees here, but the range of experience is so great that it seems to me that one has to start now with the assumption in social life that what used to look like anxiety may simply be fear, in which case the distinction between the mad and the sane really collapses. And what I'm trying to say is that I've reached the point where I don't even care whether many of my speculations amount to paranoia or not. As far as I'm concerned it is just happening around here too often to suit me, and I don't know how one behaves rationally in such a world. I don't think rationality is a thing you abandon. I mean it may vanish and when it does it may or may not come back, but that isn't so much a matter of choice either.

Finally I guess I could sum it up by saying that I've come at this point to regard even Laing as a transitional figure, with a person like Freud seeing the norms as relatively fixed though being right on about the dynamics with respect to the norm, Sullivan that the norms are not fixed but generated in the society but still viable and capable once people more or less agree on the rules of the game. Laing, and I would say also Norman O. Brown though from a different point of view, stress that the general shiftiness of the world we live in is such as to make the distinction between sanity and insanity hardly worth making. I think it is about time for someone to point out that perhaps we are coming back toward an equally rigorous though very much more threatening view of reality in which fears are solidly based on the kinds of threats inherent in the very real personal characteristics of people who emerge to power and retain power in a mass democracy. Perhaps there is not going to be as much trouble finding out what and why and who we really fear, although madness will certainly then provide no alternative or refuge.

COLES: I think Laing evokes in his readers a response that has to do obviously with one's own life and one's own way of looking at things and in that sense of course he is a gifted man, because he evokes in such a wide range of people, so many responses. My own particular response to him is a function of my own life. My hero in college, when I majored in English, was a man like Joseph Conrad. We studied the end of the rational tradition in American and English literature, and I suppose I look upon myself even now as someone who tries to make sense of things. That's always my first impulse. Try to figure something out, put it down as coherently as one can. And if one looks to that tradition in the essay form, to the Orwell's of this world, perhaps to an inspired version of Agee, one is still part of the whole Western religious tradition and the social and political reality that tradition has assumed.

I first came across Laing several years ago. A book of his was sent to me by the *New Republic* and I read it. I was quite shaken up by it, shaken up perhaps the way I had been shaken up by some of

Thomas Szasz's writing, because what I saw in both of them was that they were challenging the social and political reality of which my profession was a part. This is something that I had never done during all the years of my training in that profession. The only time I did it was when I was working in the South with children going through school desegregation and particularly with youth in the sit-in movement when I saw one young student after another being carted off not to jail but mental hospitals, and by the best men in the South. I mean the liberals, the finest judges, not the segregationists, not the racists but the men who went to Harvard and Yale and Princeton and returned South and became judges. They said, "these young people who are waging sit-ins, who are fighting their way into cafeterias, are obviously disturbed, are obviously troubled and we are not going to send them to jail. They are college students after all. They are some of them from very fine families and they belong in a place where they will receive medical care and psychiatric evaluation." Now the case histories (I use that ironically) of many of the men we now know a great deal about in American history, you will find begin in the mental hospitals of the South in the early '60's. They were sent off and seen and sent out with diagnoses like adolescent adjustment reaction, psycho-neurotic disturbance, borderline personality, and if one talks with them one hears again and again the psychiatric anamnesis being given back to one. The doctor saying "and how long have you felt rebellious?" And "did this start at this stage in your life or at that stage?" And when they try to say something about what they were trying to do or what they believed, the doctors then ask them again, how long and whether there had been any difficulty with a brother or whether they had always gotten along well with their father and their mother, etc.

Now this mode of interrogation institutionalized in the name of progress struck me as something to think about, particularly because I had been part of it and had never questioned it. I was brought up in a middle-class Boston home, I went to college and medical school and took a rigorous psychiatric and psychoanalytic training where my concern was with finding out what was bothering people and then helping them to get over that. So that they would feel better and of course be better adjusted to what the world was around them and to what Professor Friedenberg has spoken of as fixed norms. There is the world and there is one's self in it. If one is troubled one hopes to end the trouble. One takes for granted words like sickness, anxiety, apprehensiveness. Now in the Air Force in Mississippi, which is the way I guess I got away from all this, I was working with SAC pilots. I'll never forget one of them who had been on a bomb mission. He had just dropped atom bombs on various American cities, in his mind, but also on a mission for this government—a familiar routine for these pilots during the late '50's. That is, they were going on simulated missions, dropping atom bombs without dropping them. And he did this and he got particularly anxious after one episode and came to the hospital. He was a pilot who had been piloting a plane up to 1000–1500 miles an hour, but he got anxious taking an elevator from the first floor to the second floor of our two-floor neuro-psychiatric center. I noted that irony as we talked and then I asked him why this time, and he came up with something after a few minutes, something that could almost be called funny if it weren't so sad. He said, well, I've been dropping bombs and doing this for a few months but I never did it on Los Angeles before. And I said, oh. And do you know that his mother lived in Los Angeles and this is what I was able to get out of him. Now I could understand, or thought I could. Nichols and May can take over from here. But then I remember driving home, and I thought to myself, what is going on here. My job of course is to get him back to duty so that he can keep on doing this. And do it to Los Angeles as well as to other cities. And then of course the combination of that and a few experiences with youth, in the sit-in movement and one begins to wonder about what one has lived with all these years. I am here, then, to emphasize not so much what Laing says (at times to be candid, I do not understand him. I read and reread and I can't make sense of what he is saying), but to try to make sense of various responses to him. I think I understand, for example, the response of the American Psychiatric profession and a number of its associates. I can make sense of this kind of remark by Norman Holland who teaches English at Buffalo, the city Mr. Friedenberg spoke about. Mr. Holland in a review of two of Laing's books in the *Nation* talks about Laing in this way. He is greatly concerned with psychoanalytic approaches to literary matters and he says here, why does Laing's Mary Baker Eddy Stance appeal. Why does at this troubled moment a writer on schizophrenia become a General Seer? Why for example have my graduate students, in English naturally, taken most seriously for 3 or 4 years now this psychiatric writer little heeded and very often, like Norman

O. Brown some years earlier, not even heard of by
professionals? Well, he goes on to give his answer.
And his answer is in terms of oral, anal and phallic.
Laing is saying that orality is good, and that is what
youth wants to hear, and the contrast with Laing is
the predominant American culture which is phallic.
He quotes from Laing a quote that many of you have
heard, the famous quote about a little girl of seventeen in a mental hospital who told Laing she was terrified because the atom bomb was inside her. That
is a delusion Laing concedes, but the statesmen of
the world who boast and threaten that they have
doomsday weapons are far more dangerous and far
more restrained from reality. Holland says that Laing,
speaking to his oral admirers, wants to blur the boundary between sanity and madness out of existence,
while Agnew speaking for his phallic constituency
wants to make a maginot line. Neither guides us any
more truly than a TV commercial. Dr. Laing helps
this particular patient, but preacher Laing offers only
total immersion in already troubled waters. That is
Holland's commentary on Laing's experience. Oral,
anal, phallic, Mary Baker Eddy Stance.

Now another distinguished American psychoanalyst, Abraham Kardiner, responds to a review in the
N. Y. Times by a political scientist of Laing's books.
Some of you may have read that front page review by
Marshall Berman, and here is Dr. Kardiner's response. He argues that assigning a political scientist
to review the works of a psychiatrist implies that psychiatry is not a science or even a methodical discipline which needs any special training to master. A
political scientist could not possibly know enough
about psychological mechanisms or methods to ade-

quately evaluate the theories of Dr. Laing. Therefore he could not see what is misleading and destructive in Laing's thesis. Kardiner then goes on to talk about tendencies in the culture generally, and he says we see the substitution now of sensation for feeling, the demand for immediate gratification, the inability to identify or empathize with others, the sense of inner emptiness, the resort to drugs. These and many others are the problems of our times. Presumably these are problems that we psychiatrists have never had in more rational times. But in any event, he says that unfortunately unless we deal realistically (listen to those adverbs), unless we deal realistically with these issues, we will face social disaster. No society can survive when too many people are narcissistic or unable to function adequately in the reality of the society, however unpleasant. In chaotic times like ours when reality is war, poverty, pollution, too rapid social change, we need people who can accurately diagnose these problems and solve them rationally and pragmatically enough.

Another psychiatrist thinks to rebuke Laing in saying it is true that sane men commit terrible crimes and that crazy men write exquisite poetry, but that it does not follow that all criminals are sane and that all poets are crazy. As if Laing has ever said that. Then he says there is no question but that Laing would drive him crazy if he could and would expect you to thank him for his time and trouble, for to Laing craziness is next to godliness. Now in this kind of argument we see the ideological quality in much psychiatric and psychoanalytical thought. It is a quality that has been pointed out by some but that even now is not quite appreciated. I am speaking of name

calling through the use of psychiatric terminology,
the relationship between a particular profession and
the status quo in a particular society, the service rendered every day to any number of people who do not
want to face certain issues bluntly and who find men
of my profession palliative, suitably hazy, mushy to
the right degree, cooperative, willing to go before
senate sub-committees and talk about disturbed youth
and their Oedipal complexes and their permissive
child-raising, but not quite ready to look at the child
rearing that has produced a Lyndon Johnson or a
Richard Nixon and what their Oedipus complexes
might be. I speak of the willingness, in other words, to
selectively apply certain conceptual frames of reference to particular populations. And there is a method
in this madness, the method of Feuer's *The Conflict
of Generations*, for example, in which concepts
fought for, struggled for in certain historical contexts
are used cleverly as bludgeons, as mean devices and in
that sense used unethically. If we are against someone we owe it to ourselves to know that we are against
him and to take that position clearly. In that sense
the psychiatric mode as it is abused is doing no more
justice to those who resort to it, the senate sub-committees, the other abusers, than it is to the people being attacked. So what I see in Laing is his courage to
question not only concepts like sanity and insanity,
but the relationship between his own professional life
and a particular kind of society. In that sense he is
history minded. He is political minded. He is society
minded. And for all of his inwardness and, if one will,
narcissism, he transcends that in a way I fear most of
us in psychiatry and psychoanalysis never dare do.
We are much wrapped up with ourselves, haven't the

courage or the will to look outside and can therefore
be accused of the very things we so often throw at a
man like this. What I don't feel myself confident to
talk about, what I can not understand in him and
which I think at some point we will need a great deal
of help in interpreting, is his way of looking at the
people we now happen to call schizophrenics. This is
something I don't understand because it is out of
my own experience. I have never been able to work
very well with schizophrenics and I can in that sense
admire Laing and yet be glad that I'm not doing what
he does.

DR. LUX: I would like to approach the issue of
Laing from two perspectives. One as a psychologist
working on an acute hospital admission service to
psychiatric patients, mostly psychotic; the other as a
follower of Meher Baba. Since the second is a little
less immediately familiar than the first approach I'll
explain that a little further. Meher Baba is an Indian
spiritual leader who has had a significant effect on me
over the last several years. As a matter of fact, he got
me off acid about 3 or 4 years ago and that was a very
meaningful time in my life. Laing draws many parallels between mystical experience or transcendental
experience and schizophrenia. For example, he says
that in the schizophrenic experience some light of
truth breaks through our all too closed minds. Against
that let me quote a statement Meher Baba made a
number of years ago to one of his disciples in India.
It's a four line statement which covers the whole
panorama of mysticism, madness and spirituality and
for me clarifies some of the issues that Laing seems
to lump or join together. Baba says: Mind working

is man. Mind working fast is mad. Mind working slow is saint. Mind stopped is God.

Now that statement sets up a continuum of states of mind based upon how fast mind is working. Mind working at a normal pace is the average man. Mind working slower approaches the saintly state of existence, one leading to a mystical life. The mind stopped completely realizes God. We know this from many mystical traditions, including Zen, for example, in which mind must be done away with in order for the truth to be seen. Now, when mind is working fast Baba says we have a state of madness. So on this continuum of rate of mind Baba actually places madness and mysticism at opposite poles. Let's take this same distinction at another level, the level of the ego. Mystics have said you must abandon or get rid of your ego in order to see truth, and often this thing called mind is equated with ego. It is sometimes referred to as the ego mind. Or mind is the ego mind. So the mystics say the ego must be abandoned in order for pure transcendental truth to be realized. Laing implies that the person in a schizophrenic state has abandoned his ego, has gotten rid of it and therefore has approached the truth of the mystic. Baba implies that the person in a schizophrenic state has not gotten rid of his ego but has had his ego center fractured. The schizophrenic in fact has first to get his ego back together again before he can start to lose it in a mystical way. But while one is in this state of fractured ego it is easy to think of oneself as having lost it. And thus on an intense acid trip one is very likely to say "I'm the Buddha" or something to that effect. But it is only to be lost a short time later. Meher Baba implies that the mad person, a person in a state of madness, has to become normal again before he can move on. How is this done?

Baba says you can't take heaven by storm. So how do you do it? I'm almost ashamed to say. He says that it is only love that can do it.

FARBER: You can see where the subject of R. D. Laing leads us; it leads us in several directions at once. It certainly leads us to a consideration of this society and its relation to whatever we may call madness. I was very gratified to hear Mr. Friedenberg mention the name of Harry Stack Sullivan because my own impression is that Laing's theories are very Sullivanian in quality. They are societal theories of whatever you want to call these disorders. I think that I am also struck by the fact that the more serious thinkers on the subject, certainly in this country, are people who began to treat schizophrenia. This is true both of Sullivan and Laing. For them, the treatment of schizophrenia was the nitty gritty of this work, work that becomes rather less intense when it's moved to Park Avenue offices. And one reason I believe that Sullivan was so taken not only with the value of the work he did with schizophrenia but with the broader necessity of this work was that he saw in the schizophrenic patient a stretching of the human condition almost beyond endurance. So that something, to use Laing's term, something ontological was brought up. That is, what is called into question is the possibility of addressing what it means to be essentially human for one occupied in office practice and dealing with people who are complaining because they are not successful enough in this world. Now, I think that as a psychiatrist here I should

point out that both Laing and Sullivan, too, give a
primacy to the word experience. And we must discuss
what is meant by this kind of primacy. To Sullivan it
meant something he called countertransference. This
was his addition really to Freudian psychology. Not
that Freudian psychology had neglected this term,
but it hadn't emphasized the experience of the psychoanalyst to a sufficient degree. Now I happen to believe,
provided it is qualified carefully, in the primacy of this
experience. And certainly this is one of the issues that
I think has made Laing so very popular through his
book, *The Politics of Experience*. I would like to ask
the panel members how they conceive of the experience that Laing talks about. Is it some feeling, is it
something like counter-transference, is it both feeling
and thought, is it necessarily immediate, is it ideological, or what?

FRIEDENBERG: If I grasp the issue you are rais-
ing, I think the importance of his emphasis on experience lies in the denial or rejection of normative inter-
vention. The problem in any case is what the patient
feels it to be and the existence of a patient and what
he senses himself to be going through is in fact the
gravamen of the charge, as the courts would say. That
is, if you talk about *The Politics of Experience* and
put your emphasis on experience, then what is upper-
most is what the patient thinks, feels, in short what
he experiences, and what is played down is the question of any lack of correspondence between that and
official wisdom or the photographic record. What is
played down is what is precisely not experience but
consensus, for consensus is something which becomes
very treacherous in this kind of situation.

COLES: One thing I feel it important to point out
is what Laing stands for within the psychiatric and
psychoanalytical professions which the young people
not yet in that profession or any profession respond
to. If they sense in him a willingness to share and be
equal with the patient, in that sense he responds to
their concern for equality and for the breakdown of
the authoritarian situation and the staple positions
of doctor-patient. I think this in turn takes us to the
figure of Freud himself in the two great volumes on
dreams and in the *Psychopathology of Everyday Life*
in which he draws copiously upon his own experience.
He is willing to look into himself unashamedly and
with the thinnest of disguises offer to the reader evidence about himself. In that sense, and others have
remarked on this, Freud is in the tradition of St. Au-
gustine, Kierkegaard, of the great confessionals of
western literature. But this is hardly the sort of thing
we find in psychoanalytical literature these days. We
are very anxious for the public to understand how
carefully trained we are. That we too have been patients, have been endlessly supervized, have gone
through prolonged analysis—all of this to assure
everyone, particularly ourselves, that we are most in-
trospective and most aware of ourselves. And yet in
the literature year after year one searches in vain for
the kind of honest autobiographical quality to an
analysis of the countertransference. There is a lot of
talk about the analysis of the tranference. Countertransference comes up, there are papers on it in some
of the journals. But how honestly do we dare talk as
doctors, therapists, psychiatrists, analysts, whatever,
about our personal experiences? One finds a section
here or there in Searles, or Wheelis, and then one

hears them put down as troubled romantics, their
work an embarrassment. This is a very complicated
thing, this tradition to which Laing belongs, stemming as it does out of a particular man's need in a
crisis in his forties to tell himself and the world about
his dreams. There are other factors, of course, all part
now of history. And of course we get out of history,
in a way, only what we want to see, can bear to take.
So I think what Laing does is to say "look, this is
what it is about. We went into this as patients, as well
as doctors. We wanted to be healed. And God knows
that is part of us. Let's talk about it. Let's open ourselves up to this." In turn we find this embarrassing,
difficult, unwise. And then of course we turn on the
person who threatens us and call him crazy. He has
his problems. As if we all don't. We are experts at
labeling people. We have a language that enables us
to do away with those who threaten us, meanwhile
overlooking in others vast areas. And I think the experience that Laing wants to get at is the hurt person
who becomes healer no longer so hurt though faced
with hurt, and once again trying to unhurt, this time
another's hurt. Some sequence like that. And we eminently respectable professional men are bothered by
this.

FARBER: I want to press Dr. Coles a bit on what
he has just said. I think I would agree utterly with
everything he has just described about the use of psychology as a kind of name-calling, status seeking, etc.
What I want to ask him is if he believes Laing belongs in the tradition of the kind of confessional literature that he has described briefly. That is, does he
find it in his writing?

COLES: I think in a way I implied the answer earlier. I confess I can't understand even some of Kierkegaard. So that Laing should not be isolated. Laing and a number of other men confront me with my limitations.

FARBER: What I am trying to ask you is, does he confront you and your limitations through his limitations?

COLES: No, more he confronts me with my particular position in society. It is more a social thing than a personal thing. And I think that is a very important point for us to work at. What he confronts me with are questions like, what has my life been like, what are the social and political assumptions I was brought up to make that were inculcated in me in school, in college, in medical college, in residency training and that I am still fighting with? And that is how he unsettles me. But he does not unsettle me personally, in that sense.

FARBER: What would you think?

FRIEDENBERG: I wanted to raise another question about what Bob had said. Because I think that in a way probably both Laing's sense of divine outrage and Bob's anger at the abuses of psychiatry seem to me a general middle class industrial thing, and seems to kind of conflict with the picture we have been presenting here of Laing as in a way an unusually political, politically wise and "hep" author. I don't think that an experienced black activist would respond in this way and I can't myself. I mean I felt

like saying on a number of occasions, what did you
think a magistrate was? It may be that the observation "pigs are pigs" is enough to explain a great deal.
There isn't any hope, I don't think, for a society in
which the people with a stake in legitimacy will behave decently at a time when the society itself is falling apart and losing its legitimacy. You get the kind
of perception and prophecy that we find in Laing,
and find of great value in Laing, at a time when legitimacy is no longer possible. But I don't think you will
ever find a time in which judges, proconsuls, psychiatrists, and other licensed officials are more trust-
worthy. You just find a time when you can put up
with them, because the society itself is functioning
well enough that it takes care of enough needs of
enough people, so that you are not outraged by its
functionaries. But neither should you be deceived by
them. I remember early arguments with my old
friend Tom Hayden, at a time when, looking at it in
retrospect, I guess I was reproaching him for being,
as it seemed to me, too patriotic. That is it seemed to
me that Tom had certain confidence in the ultimate
fundamental decency of the American system, something which seemed to me simply empirically wrong
and probably dangerous. And as I go back to Bob's
earlier illustration of the bomber-pilot, and guilty
though I feel about it, I can't help feeling that even
with a lot of mothers there, a person who wouldn't
enjoy even thinking about dropping an atomic bomb
on Los Angeles is sick. Now maybe the old religious
categories stand us better than that. The Catholic
church has a very old sin. It is a venial rather than
a cardinal one, but one which is definitely on the record for this sort of thing. They call it scrupulosity.

But even if you reverse the values or abandon them there is that flatness of affect that has to be explained.

COLES: In that sense I can always say, you know, my mea culpas, because I was brought up to subscribe to the more messianic aspects of psychoanalytic psychiatry. That is the point. And by no means out of any madness, I don't think. But Freud wrote one introductory essay after another and took on one thing after another, religion, Moses, socialism and we were taught or led to believe, groping as we were in the 50's and more desperate than we had any notion that we were, that some combination of ten years of psychoanalysis and a little liberal juggling of the economy and by golly heaven would be right around the corner. And as we started calling one another this or that depending on what kind of car we drove or what slip of the tongue we made, there was always the fantasy that at some point there would be no more slips of the tongue and that somehow we would have the perfect car. There wouldn't be oral, anal or phallic; we would be mature, genital and just right. So with that as a background we are getting ours, today.

FARBER: I should like to return to Laing's experience with schizophrenia. Without going into any great detail on the subject my reading of him troubles me here. And I may as well say why. I find him guilty of a kind of romanticism about this condition which simply doesn't jibe with my own experience. The hospitals are full of very disordered people who are by no means potential poets or potential artists of any sort but lead highly disagreeable lives and who would lead even more disagreeable lives if they were outside. And I would like to know what you people think of this aspect of Laing, in which he says, and I have to caricature here, he says madness in effect is sanity. Now I understand that as a cultural comment which can be justified and I also understand it as a decent political observation. I appreciate it as Professor Friedenberg's comparison between President Nixon and others who are actually deemed mad. But nevertheless there is an issue here. And the issue has to do with what I regard as an extremely romantic view of this situation. What would you think, Dr. Coles?

COLES: Well I think that there are unhappy people in the mental hospitals by the thousands who would describe themselves as unhappy and sad and lonely and isolated and wretched. Then one would have to say that outside these mental hospitals there would be people who would describe themselves this way. Then one would have to say we would think that even many of those who don't describe themselves in these terms might in all honesty do so if they could. I also have felt, I guess the word is the romanticization of something which I found terribly unpleasant when I worked with severely disturbed mental patients as a resident. I did not specialize in the treatment of such people and felt their disturbance was something that I could not respond to. What I saw in the people and patients I worked with was something that I didn't want for myself, something that seemed not only strange in the sense of alien and exotic or enticing or for that matter challenging, but something terribly sad and terribly hurt. A kind of hurt that I didn't feel that I had. And I suppose this is where I don't understand Laing or what he is saying about these people. I don't know that I fundamentally disagree with him, for I have had but limited experience in working with psychotic patients. I feel quite certain that I did not brainwash patients I treated nor tried to keep them as they were, nor served as official agent of a mad society. I always felt that my patients wanted something that would get them out of what they were and if I didn't have it they could only be disappointed. Now I do not say that to call them sick and call myself well. I say that this was the experience I had as a young psychiatric resident. They wanted, and the image kept on coming to me again and again, they wanted me to throw them a life line and I often felt inadequate because I didn't have it to throw. Now this may be a judgment on me and my limitations but it may also be a reflection on some of the terror which an artist like Strindberg would know, that some people on this earth feel, and I think there is a danger in the social response to Laing among us, a danger that we will overlook such terror. It's very similar I think to the kinds of dangers involved in relating to southern black people, or Mexican-Americans, or hippies for that matter. I speak of people other than ourselves toward whom we reach but only with limited reaching, and I think the danger is that we fail at times to see what they are after. We see what we want them to be after or we see our vision of what they are after and frequently miss some crucial items. We tend to romanticize their condition as we do with mental patients. The patient, the schizophrenic, is struggling for something out of the context of a life and then we go and say "look at them, they are us. They're mad but we're all mad. We want what they want and they should be impatient and probably are impatient even as we are. And we are all together in this." But there is a difference between those middle-class white students and those black children they want to help in New Orleans, and I suspect there is a difference between us and the mad patients and I suspect that we don't know it quite as well as the mad patients do.

FARBER: I think we might open up this discussion now to the audience. Any questions?

AUD: I would like to ask you about Laing's methods in treating a patient. Does he use Freudian methods?

FARBER: I'm sure he doesn't. But beyond that I can't say very much. I don't know about his actual work with the schizophrenic patients or with families. Do you, Dr. Coles?

COLES: Well, the only thing I know is that a student of mine who is now a young psychiatrist has just come back from an interview with Laing this summer and is preparing what must seem to many of us a remarkable document. At least he describes Laing in ways that I never would have expected. He had a very quiet, thoughtful time talking with him and the interview was conducted in eminently sensible and rational terms and they talked about such things as methods of treatment. Laing comes off as someone concerned with the difficulties and hazards of treatment, the length of time required, the obstacles, the ambiguities of knowing when one is better so to speak, and it all struck me as a contrast, not only with remarks made about Laing but even with the sense we get from Laing's own writings. The document seems like the kind of thing one would get out of a serious, even respectable doctor who has spent a lot of time working with severely troubled people.

FRIEDENBERG: Laing of course relies as much as he can on case materials in his own writings, certainly in *The Divided Self*. You probably can find a reasonably good answer to your question in reading what Laing presents as case material. Beyond this, I think your question has sort of a false assumption in it. Freud, as I recall, did very little work with schizophrenics and was quite reluctant to undertake it. There isn't anything like a classic Freudian method of dealing with schizophrenics. Harry Stack Sullivan on the contrary did some of his best work with persons whom we would call schizophrenics, but I think the reason the method has not emerged very clearly from Laing is precisely because he does think of his patients so much all the time as people, so that what he pieces together is like an account that a good anthropologist gives in popular writing for a sympathetic reader to whom, however, not having done any field work, what it is like to live out there in the bush under those conditions could hardly be communicated in any case. But I don't think it would be sentimental to say, that what emerges in Laing, as in Rollo May's somewhat comparable writings, is simply a feeling of rather complete respect for the person. I gather there must be many patients who would remain to such an extent an enigma, but there is no evidence that Laing would therefore cast them in a special class of hopeless mess or anything like that.

AUD: There seems to be another paradox here. Getting back to the original concept of experience, Laing says "I can not know your experience and you can not know my experience." And yet implicit in what has been said is an underlying assumption that somehow I have to get into your experience or at least be there listening, making sense of your experience. And then of course, if I can't know your experience I can't do what Buber would say, be over against you. And if that's the case then how can I in effect help you. There is again that confusion.

FARBER: I think there is real confusion on precisely this point. If Laing does say not only that one can not know another's experience but that one can not even imagine another's experience, Buber's contentions must be meaningless to him. If one can't imagine the real in another's experience I fail to see how anything therapeutic would occur. I would assume that Laing is superbly able to do precisely this in his work. And since Professor Friedenberg has mentioned some of the extraordinary perils and agonies of this kind of work let me just underline them, as I myself have abdicated such work because it is simply too much for me. A friend of mine described the work with schizophrenia as rather similar to pro-football. You have a few good years and then you really have to get out of the game. I say that somewhat facetiously, though not entirely. But there is a hazard here. And the hazard has to do with my earlier question of whether Laing does not romanticize schizophrenia. Given that the work is so damned horrible and grinding and defeating, frustrating, we must ask whether one isn't really driven to find the meaning and the pattern that isn't there. And this is what I suggest can happen and does happen, certainly with friends of mine who stay in this field too long.

LUX: Whether we can get inside another's experience remains to be experienced. But we do have the experience of making contacts more or less. We experience a range of contacts with another person, either more or less contact. Hopefully there is something to that.

AUD: We have been speaking this evening about the problems of adjustment in a culture like ours and we have been trying to relate difficulties of patients in institutions to the general cultural difficulty all of us experience. In the light of this I would like to read a one line quotation from Laing having to do with therapeutic procedure, and I would like to know how you all respond to this. Laing says at one point that "If a person already does not know where he is, to question adjustment, to attribute falsity to adjusted actions is extremely confusing. In other circumstances it could be clarifying. One could become very confused if the therapist both accused one of not being adjusted and at the same time cast doubts on the validity of being adjusted." Does the therapist then assume that every patient in a mental institution or in an office has the same capacity to tolerate high levels of conflict that Laing apparently assumes all of his patients have? The question is, does one assume that the characteristic mental patient one finds in institutions is anything like the patient Laing describes in his books? Dr. Farber himself suggests that in mental institutions one doesn't find many patients who are about to create glorious works of any sort. Would one then suggest to these patients who are having a difficult time becoming adjusted to the norms of their culture that to become adjusted is a false proposal, something one should not aspire to?

LUX: One sad thing about mental patients, as I see it, is that they are really trying hard for that mode of adjustment. They really are trying to find the norm. And very few of them show interest in really going beyond it or really being critical of any social phenomenon, other than things within their immediate parental family. I find them really looking for that adjustment. That is a distressing thing.

COLES: I'm not quite sure what your question is, though I agree that there are dangers of the kind you suggest. What I want to emphasize, what we ought to keep in mind is that Laing is a writer and a poet, an aphorist, a symbolist. And in that sense what he does to patients is what Flannery O'Conner or Faulkner does to the Southerner in the courthouse. As a writer Laing etches out things, draws out things, emphasizes, points up as artists always do, and makes larger than life so that we will be somehow responsive to qualities in people and situations that we might ordinarily miss. So in that sense what he may be doing to us, is saying, look, we know the drabness, the horror, the degradation, the banality of this, even as there is banalty in all of those "wierdos" Flannery O'Conner has given us. But I saw it and it is here. It may go away. It isn't everything. It's not their every day life—and you people, the psychiatrists, you see other things as well and have to struggle with the horrors and the banalities. But to the degree that he forces us to look at a picture considerably more varied than we suspected it may have been, Laing *is* a seer.

AUD: I want to put a question that you have heard before, I suspect. It is very possible that the psychotic patient is basically psychotic. That is, it is possible that there is some malfunction in the system. The same way that somebody who has the measles has a malfunction. And it is very possibly in this light that we ought to look at the psychotic. Dr. Coles, I would like to ask you why you see the people in the South. What do you hope to do when you are there? I think the question someone asked earlier is, is it a perversion to make people adjust? Is it perverse to help them cope? I don't want to infer something unfair, but aren't we trying to help these people adjust or cope?

COLES: I hope the people I've worked with wouldn't think of it in that way. I guess I didn't go there, I was there and I saw and I stayed. Yes. Gripped by something. And I have wanted to communicate what I saw so that others would see it and I don't think I have made any bones about what I would like to see happen. The words adjust and cope have never entered my mind in working with these children. In fact I haven't really been working with them. We have been together and we have had our conversations. I guess I profigressively lost all interest in finding out about their psychopathology, which probably hasn't been too much different from my own. One finds oneself slowly. The mind is like Macey's basement. You will soon find anything in everyone if you look long and hard enough. And they never came to me because they were in trouble anyway. I came to them to get to know them. But to cope, to adjust—all those words. One hears them at conference after conference, and when it isn't coping there are the inter-relationships and the actualizing and the rest. Well, it takes a long time to get away from that and one never does really, but one struggles to. If you are asking if I am helping children to cope, I would have to leave the answer to them. Because I don't quite know. Nor will I ever know what went on between us. I guess that is what we were talking about. But people I speak to always assume I have had some significant impact on the children, must have played some major role in their adjustment to the stresses they went through in the South. And all I can think of is that here I am with my one life and one body, and I can think of those thousands and thousands of children that I have never seen and will never see and that have never seen the likes of me, the millions who have lived in American history before "psychs" were around, and shrinks, and copers, and adjusters and practitioners, mental health professionals. And these people somehow lived, and out of their lives came the blues and the work songs and the jazz and styles of behaviour that many of our students envy dearly and have come to accept as their own. And it is surely a tragedy that for three hundred years we have not had an American history that could deal with this experience.

FRIEDENBERG: I want to go back a bit in our discussion to a point Dr. Farber raised. If you were in daily contact with people classed as schizophrenics, and the meaning of your life depended on your own evaluation of your work with them, would you not find that whatever was wrong, whether it was with you or them or society or shared among you, was so refractory that it was arrogant really to assume somehow if people were simply freed of this interference things would be much better or would straighten themselves out? But this has little to do with the fact that however irreversible the damage is to certain individuals we call schizophrenics and however difficult it might be for us to bridge the gap between us, it is still almost certainly true that they are in mental hospitals because of the problems they create for us and not because they are better off there. They may or may not be but I suspect that given the way the power-dynamics of society operate this has been a very minor consideration. I don't consider it especially instructive to speak of analyzing cells to find imbalances of some kind in the enzymes or a defective insulation of the synapses or something of that sort. I suspect that it is a great deal more of a social question than that. And recognizing this I am still able to say, as a man who was in analysis for some five years with very creditable Chicago analysts, that the worst I can blame them for is that at the end I was convinced that my life was worth living, something they may have been mistaken about though I don't think so at this point. I don't really feel that they were brainwashing me or anything but the one thing that I am quite sure of is that if there was anyone trying to do any adjusting there it was I. And I am really quite convinced that if they had an impulse, if they were pushing me in any direction it was indeed towards something that has since been called, and by the existential therapists, authenticity. In fact it wasn't at all hard in the 1940's and 1950's to find analysts who would become quite restive if you tried to cop out and find better peace terms with the society that was giving you trouble. But then if you want to go back further it helps to read a biography of Charles and Mary Lamb. Mary Lamb if you remember became so discontented with their relationship to their mother that she slew her, a thing that you were not supposed to do in England at the time. Now we know the general level of mental illness treatment in England if you were lucky enough not to get hanged for what you'd done would have relegated Mary to something no better than bedlam under ordinary circumstances. But it just so happened that her brother was the servant of a member of Parliament, and though she never was allowed to be in a position where she could define and go out and try to lead what she thought was a normal life, what she got was not punitive. She seems to have spent the rest of her life in the hands of people who were an inconvenience to her because they had defined themselves as empirical scientists in this field before there was any theory to work with. And that certainly must have been a terrible drag. But there was already the modern conception of the task as the delivery of the patient into his own hands, especially if the patient happened to come from a sufficiently privileged segment of society. And perhaps this is always the case. The really important advice may simply be never to go mad in a society in which you don't have lots of "nachus" to begin with.

AUD: Dr. Farber points to Laing's view of schizophrenia as a very romantic one, and this is what we must not overlook. If therapists view the schizophrenic's experience as a beautiful, poetic sort of an experience, then they are going to have difficulty helping many people who are ill and who are not asking for an expansion of their awareness but are asking for some assistance out of a very difficult situation, a very painful situation that exists at that time. And I have the feeling that the panel is substituting words like 'coping' and 'adjusting' for the words that used to be oral, anal and phallic. As a therapist I assert that the therapist should help someone adjust if he wants to adjust. The therapist should help one grow if he wants to grow.

FARBER: Sullivan always used to remind the younger therapists he would supervise that it was their responsibility not to make the patient worse. That was the most he could say. Perhaps as good a point as any on which to conclude.

Madness and Morals

BY MORTON SCHATZMAN

Thou lovest Truth and Beauty and Righteousness: and I for thy sake say it is well and seemly to love these things. But in my heart I laugh at thy love. Yet I would not have thee see my laughter. I would laugh alone.

My friend, thou art good and cautious and wise: nay, thou art perfect—and I, too, speak with thee wisely and cautiously. And yet I am mad. But I mask my madness. I would be mad alone.

My friend, thou art not my friend, but how shall I make thee understand? My path is not thy path, yet together we walk, hand in hand.

Kahlil Gibran, *The Madman*[1]

THERE IS REASON TO BELIEVE that a society which sees people as 'mentally ill,' calls them 'mentally ill' and treats them as 'mentally ill' aggravates *by* those acts the condition which it calls 'mental illness.'

People in a group label behaviour which breaks rules of the group as bad, criminal, malicious, sinful, selfish, immature, foolish, idiotic, ignorant, and so on.

[1] K. Gibran, *The Madman, His Parables and Poems* (London: Heinemann, Ltd., 1963), p. 13.

They develop criteria to judge which behaviour breaks rules and how to label it. They cannot apply any of these labels to the behaviour of some individuals who persistently break rules. Men in other times and places ascribed this behaviour to witchcraft, spirit-possession, or demons. Today, men in the industrialized nations of the world see the same behaviour as 'symptoms' of 'mental illness.' [2]

Men in western society have created norms to define which items in the cosmos must be seen as real or unreal and as inner or outer. If a man sees as real what they say he should see as unreal, or vice versa, or as inner what they say he should see as outer, or vice versa, and if he argues the validity of his view by a style of argument which they consider abnormal or does not argue it at all, they are likely to see him as 'mentally ill.' Western society appoints psychiatrists as experts to examine some of its members who break rules to discern if they break those rules for which they can be called 'mentally ill.'

The tradition of scientific medicine teaches a doctor to keep distinct his moral attitude towards diseased persons from his non-moral objective attitude towards their diseases. But the *moral* views of western society define for a psychiatrist what persons he may diagnose as 'mentally ill' and whom he may treat. A psychiatrist, especially if he works in a mental hospital, is concerned with surveying morals and mediating rules. He must deny this if he wishes to believe that he adheres to the principles of scientific medicine. Although he sees 'pathology' in behaviour

[2] See Thomas J. Scheff, *Being Mentally Ill, A Sociological Theory* (London: Weidenfeld and Nicolson, 1966).

which breaks rules, *because* it breaks rules, he does not say so, and usually does not even say that he considers it to break rules. If he works in a mental hospital he imposes rules on 'patients,' rewards obedience and punishes disobedience, and calls these activities 'treatment.' In the more advanced mental hospitals he tutors 'patients' to think, feel and act 'appropriately,' and calls this 'therapy.' These manoeuvers confuse many patients and induce them to respond in 'abnormal' ways which the psychiatrist may see as more evidence of their 'mental illness.'

Many 'mental patients' have always understood this situation; now some social scientists, psychologists and psychiatrists do.[3] Drs. Ronald D. Laing, Aaron Esterson, and David Cooper are psychiatrists in England who saw the need to create alternatives to the traditional mental hospital ward. David Cooper led people on a ward in a mental hospital near London to question their premises and to change many customary practices.[4] The Philadelphia Association, Ltd.,[5] of which Laing, Esterson and Cooper were founder-members, has affiliated itself with several self-governing households in London in which people, most of whom have previously been diagnosed as 'mentally ill,' live outside the mental hospital system.

[3] Artaud's *Letter to the Medical Director of Lunatic Asylums* is an especially lucid and concise statement by a 'patient.' Antonin Artaud, *Collected Works*, V. I, trans. by Victor Corti (London: Calder and Boyars, 1968).

[4] D. Cooper, *Psychiatry and Anti-Psychiatry* (London: Tavistock Publications, 1967), pp. 83–104.

[5] The Philadelphia Association Ltd. is registered as a charity in the U.K. and U.S.A. Its major foci of interest are research into 'mental health,' especially 'schizophrenia,' and the training and education of others about 'mental illness.'

They are more like hippie communes than like the most liberal mental-hospital wards. I shall describe 'Kingsley-Hall,' the largest of them, after explaining the rationale for their existence.

Mental Hospitals

Present-day western men presume that their cultural forebears became enlightened around the end of the eighteenth century to a truth to which men had been blind for too long: that madmen are sick men. The modern experience of madness has been governed by the conviction of 'sane' people that madness is really an illness and by their belief that this truth has been firmly proven by advances in scientific knowledge. They have converted the asylums into medical spaces where doctors have assumed the dominant roles. The doctors have based their powers on the presumption that they have scientific understanding of the inmates. This has been a disguise and a pretension, says Michel Foucault, a French philosopher and psychologist.[6] Psychiatric practice in the mental hospitals has been a *moral* tactic, cloaked with the dignity of scientific truth. The asylum, as set up by the doctors, has been from the beginning, Foucault says:

. . . a structure that formed a kind of microcosm in which were symbolized the massive structures of bourgeois society and its values: Family-Child relations, centered on the theme of paternal authority; Transgression-

[6] Michel Foucault, *Madness and Civilization, A History of Insanity in the Age of Reason* (trans. by Richard Howard) (New York: Random House, 1965, and London: Tavistock Publications, 1967).

Punishment relations, centered on the theme of immediate justice; Madness-Disorder relations, centered on the theme of social and moral order. It is from these that the doctor derives his power to cure . . .[7]

Philippe Pinel was a doctor whom historians of psychiatry regard as the 'father' of the modern mental hospital, and whom apologists for the *status quo* call the 'liberator of the insane.' In *A Treatise on Insanity* he suggested how to 'treat' the 'maniac, who under the influence of the most extravagant fury shall be guilty of every extravagance, both of language and action.'[8]

. . . no more coercion is employed than what is dictated by attention to personal safety. For this purpose the strait-waistcoat will be generally found amply sufficient. Every case of irritation, real or imaginary, is to be carefully avoided. *Improper application for personal liberty, or any other favour* must be received with acquiescence, taken graciously into consideration, and withheld under some plausible pretext, or postponed to a more convenient opportunity. The utmost vigilance of the *domestic police* will be necessary to engage the exertions of every maniac, especially during his lucid intervals, in some employment, laborious or otherwise, calculated to employ his thoughts and attention.[9]

Although he recommended the use of baths and 'pharmaceutical formulae' like 'antispasmodics' to

[7] Ibid., p. 274.
[8] Philippe Pinel, A Treatise on Insanity, first published as *Traite medicophilosophique sur l'alienation mentale, ou la manie*, 1801 (trans. by D. D. Davis) and published in England, 1806 (New York: Hafner, 1962).
[9] Ibid., p. 87 (my italics).

calm the 'tumult' of mental patients, he said that the fundamental 'treatment' is *exclusively moral.*[10]

The extreme importance which I attach to the maintenance of *order* and *moderation* in lunatic institutions, and consequently to the physical and moral qualities requisite to be possessed by their governors, is by no means to be wondered at, since it is fundamental principle in the treatment of mania to watch over the impetuosities of passion, and to order such arrangements of police and moral treatment as are favourable to that degree of excitement which experience approves as conducive to recovery.[11]

He said:

The doctrine in ethics of balancing the passions of men by others of equal or superior force, is not less applicable to the practice of medicine, than to the science of *politics.* and is probably not the only point of resemblance between the art of *governing* mankind and that of healing their diseases.[12]

'The Importance of an Enlightened System of Police for the Internal Management of Lunatic Asylums' is the title of one of the six sections of this book.

The principles of 'treatment' have not changed since Pinel, but the techniques have become more sophisticated. Tranquilizing drugs, electro-convulsive shock and insulin coma maintain 'order' and 'moderation' more effectively than the strait-jackets and antispasmodics did, and psychotherapy and therapeutic community meetings are more likely to per-

[10] Ibid., p. 38.
[11] Ibid., p. 99 (my italics).
[12] Ibid., p. 228 (my italics).

suade 'patients' to conform than was the moral instruction of the governors of lunatic asylums. The 'treatment' which hospital psychiatrists give is still exclusively moral. Unlike Pinel, they do not say that it is.

Mental hospitals like prisons confine deviant persons, but they confuse their inmates more, since they do not tell them what rules they have broken, nor even that they have broken rules. The psychiatrist in the mental hospital tries to persuade *himself*, his colleagues in the medical profession, the staff, the 'patients,' the 'patients'' families and friends, and society that he practices medicine, and denies to himself and all others that any persuasion occurs or is even necessary. To frame his activities within a medical model he calls a trial, 'examination'; a judgment, 'diagnosis'; a sentence, 'disposition'; and correction, 'treatment.' If his 'patients' claim they are not ill they challenge his pretensions.

One must admire the ingenuity with which he copes with this contingency. He presumes that a basic 'symptom' of the 'mentally ill patient' is his failure to know that he is 'ill.' When the 'patient' disagrees with the doctor who says he is 'ill,' the doctor does not tell him that he should not disagree, but that he does not *know* what he is saying, and that he does not, *because* he is 'ill.' He hears the 'patient's' statement that he is not ill as evidence that he is 'too ill' to realize that he is 'ill,' and he tells him so. If a 'patient' feels healthy despite being told by his doctor that he is not, and says so, the doctor may tell him that he is not motivated to regain his health.

The psychiatrist outwits by another twist a person

who pretends that he is mentally ill to manoeuvre a
social situation for personal gain. The psychiatrist who
suspects a person of this 'diagnoses' him to suffer from
the 'syndrome' of feigning illness which he considers
to be a sickness with a poor prognosis (Ganser's Syndrome). If a man knows what is going on, but pretends that he does not, and knows that he is pretending, the psychiatrist may see him as a man who
thinks he knows he is pretending, but as really not
pretending, and as pretending to pretend.

Kaplan, an American psychologist, says in his introduction to *The Inner World of Mental Illness*, 'a
series of first-person accounts of what it was like' to
be 'mentally ill,'

> One of the salient features of the psychopathologies
> that are described in this book is that they are opposed
> to a normality which is intimately related to the major
> value orientations of western society. It may be asserted
> therefore that abnormality psychosis involves a negative
> relationship to prevailing social normative prescriptions
> —perhaps the most extreme and complete form of nega-
> tion that is possible. This is more than an abstract and
> logical conclusion. In the jargon of the moment we may
> call this 'alienation.' In this association of abnormality
> with a refusal to be bound by things as they are and
> with the striving to be different, we have what is at bot-
> tom a concern with the category of change and tran-
> scendence.[13]

The same is so for many of the 'mentally ill' who
have not published their ideas. The dis-ease spins off
a runaway feedback loop: those who negate the prevailing social norms are negated by those who uphold

[13] B. Kaplan (ed.), *The Inner World of Mental Illness*
(New York and London: Harper and Row, 1964), p. xi.

them, and the upholders are negated in their nega-
tions of the negators by the negators . . . not *ad
infinitum* but *ad* the ascription of 'mental illness' by
the upholders upon the opposers.

When Jeremiah broke an earthen vessel in the
Temple courtyard to pronounce and predict the de-
struction of Jerusalem, the Temple police seized him,
beat him and punished him publicly by putting him
in the stocks. They did not, as far as we know, suspect
him of 'mental illness.' Recently, a young man in the
NATO military forces, with a position in a chain of
command to push a nuclear-missile 'button,' decided
to refuse to obey orders related to his job. He told his
superiors they should not command any man to do
such a job. He was diagnosed as 'schizophrenic' and
was hospitalized.

All that is certain about 'mental illness' is that
some people assert that other people have it. Epis-
temologically, 'mental illness' has the status of an
explanatory concept or a working hypothesis. No one
has proven it to exist as a thing nor has anyone described its attributes with scientific precision and re-
liability.[14]

Since mental hospitals regulate the behaviour and
the biochemistry of their inmates to a degree un-
equalled elsewhere in the 'free world,' 'patients' rebel
and resist.[15] Official psychiatry trains the young psy-

[14] W. A. Scott, 'Research Definitions of Mental Health and
Mental Illness,' Psychological Bulletin, 55 (January, 1958),
pp. 29–45; noted in T. Scheff, op. cit., p. 46.
[15] Although many inmates of mental hospitals are there
because they deviate from social norms in the way they think,
feel, and act, mental hospitals insist they conform to a set of
rules that permit a narrower spectrum of thoughts, feelings,
and acts than society outside does.

chiatrist not to see what is in front of his face when it teaches him to class 'patients'' attempts to protest against their situation as 'signs' and 'symptoms' of 'illness.' He learns to label 'patients' as 'ill' with 'personality disorders' if they make problems for *others* by defying the authority of the hospital or of society. He is taught to see those who openly challenge the rules of others as 'sick' with an 'illness' called 'psychotherapy' or 'sociopathy,' and those who inhibit their challenge due to a fear of the consequences as 'sick' with 'passive-aggressive personality disorders.' He treats the 'victims' of these 'diseases' with drugs and may insist on bedrest too. He learns to see 'acting-out,' 'agitation,' 'excitement,' and 'withdrawal' as symptoms which disturb his 'patients' and not to see that they may be saying by this behaviour that *he* is disturbing them.

Some doctors in their first year of psychiatric training argue at staff meetings that their 'patients'' responses to their situation in the hospital are valid. I have heard their teachers tell them that they have not yet 'worked through' their own 'adolescent personality crisis.'

What I describe here is a special case of what Wittgenstein called the 'bewitchment of our intelligence by means of language.' [16] 'A picture held us captive and we could not get outside it, for it lay in our language and language seemed to repeat it to us inexorably.' [17]

Laing says,

[16] Ludwig Wittgenstein, *Philosophical Investigations*, Translated by G. E. M. Anscombe (Oxford: Basil Blackwell & Mott, 1958), p. 47.
[17] Ibid., p. 48.

The concept of schizophrenia is a kind of conceptual straitjacket that severely restricts the possibilities both of psychiatrists and patients. By taking off this straitjacket we can see what happens. It has been abundantly shown in the field of ethology, that observations on the behaviour of animals in captivity tells us *nothing reliable* about their behaviour in their own natural setting. The whole of our present civilization may be a captivity that man has somehow imposed on himself. But, the observations upon which psychiatrists and psychologists have drawn in order to build up the prevailing picture of schizophrenia, have, almost entirely, been made on human beings in a double or even treble captivity.[18]

The power to confine people in mental hospitals, involuntarily if necessary, deprive them of civil liberties, define their limits of legal redress and award to their medical governors license to formulate and execute rules to regulate their management and treatment derives from the State and is guaranteed by the Law. The confinement of the 'mentally ill' must serve a basic homeostatic function to sustain the social and political order in western society since so many people are confined and so many work to confine them.[19]

*   *   *

Here is a schematic version of an actual story. Matthew, aged twenty-three, is from a devout Christian

[18] R. D. Laing, 'Study of Family and Social Contexts in Relation to the Origin of Schizophrenia,' *Excerpta Medica International Congress Series No. 151: The Origins of Schizophrenia. Proceedings of the First Rochester International Congress, 29–31 March, 1967.*

[19] Lemert says that when people ex-communicate others they develop and perpetuate false beliefs about them. He feels this process plays an important part in the social life of human groups. Lemert, E. W. 'Paranoia and the Dynamics of Exclusion, *Sociometry*, 1962, 25, pp. 2–20.

family. When he was twelve his father died; since thirteen he has slept in the same bed as his mother, at her request, because she has feared to sleep alone. He meets a woman of his own age whom he likes and whom he kisses one evening. That night 'vampires' attack him in his sleep. When the nightmares continue, his mother takes him to a G.P. who tells her he shows early signs of 'mental illness' and suggests he go into a hospital before his 'disease' progresses further.

He enters a mental hospital as an in-patient. He says to his psychiatrist the next day, 'Please help me. You are a messenger from God. You will decide my fate: whether I will go to heaven or hell. Do I have any power to influence you? If I confess that I have masturbated, will I help my chances with God or hurt them?' The psychiatrist thinks Matthew is being 'grandiose' and 'overideational,' and *therefore* diagnoses him as a 'paranoid schizophrenic'—'grandiosity' and 'overideation' are 'symptoms' of 'paranoid schizophrenia.' The staff think the 'disease' is due mainly to an inherited constitutional biochemical defect. They believe the 'illness' appears now because the sexual excitement stressed his delicate state. They do not implicate his mother's feelings and behaviour towards him, or his towards her, as pertinent to the understanding of his 'illness.' They see his mother as 'nervous' about his health but they dismiss this observation as irrelevant. Besides, how can they blame her for her concern, especially since her husband has died from an illness? The hospital is a good place for Matthew: he will have a chance to rest because the rules forbid all sexual contact.

The psychiatrist treats him with a common tranquilizing drug which is thought to have an 'anti-schiz-ophrenic' action. As the dose is raised progressively he develops a new 'symptom': he says he is 'being poi-soned.' The common side effects of this drug occur at the same time: dry mouth, nasal congestion, blurred vi-sion, constipation, drowsiness, stiffness of the muscles of the mouth and occasional dizziness. The staff real-ize that the drug is responsible for these effects. Since the doctor has diagnosed him as a 'paranoid schizo-phrenic' they see his belief that he is being poisoned as a 'progression' of his 'disease' which is occurring *despite* the efficacy of the drug.

The doctor raises the dosage of the drug. Matthew now shows the effects of high dosage: a pill-rolling tremor of both hands, mask-like regidity of his facial muscles, a stooped posture, and short quick steps when he walks. He reveals to an attendant on the ward that he has phoned the municipal health depart-ment to complain that the hospital poisons its in-mates, and that he has done this to protect others. He frequently says that he is frightened. The staff now believe his 'disease-process' is worsening.

The doctor adds a second tranquilizing drug, ad-ministered by injection. Matthew develops a rash over a large part of his body. He says that the doc-tors are 'in league with the Devil' to arrange that he burns in Hell for his sins, and that he would 'rather die than suffer eternal damnation.'

The staff see him as 'deteriorating' rapidly despite the best modern 'treatment.' They see his 'illness' as '*unresponsive*' to drug therapy. The doctor orders electro-convulsive shock therapy. 'Patients' often ex-perience this therapy as an assault and they always suffer some memory loss after it. The doctor knows this but he wishes to help Matthew before it is too late.

The staff do not see his behaviour as a consequence of his experience of *their* behaviour towards him. Here is an outline of some transactions between him and them in which I infer his experience of his situation, and interpret his behaviour as an attempt to cope with *their* behaviour.

1) He sees from the posture which his psychiatrist adopts toward him and from what other 'patients' tell him that the psychiatrist can assume much control over him if he wishes to. He hopes that the psychiatrist will not, but fears that he may.
2) He sees that the psychiatrist does not see himself as a powerful master who controls his charges, but as a doctor who treats 'sick patients.' He fears that if he tells the doctor he fears his power he may offend him.
3) A nurse tells him that 'patients' help themselves when they reveal their innermost thoughts to their doctor and the staff.
4) A nurse tells him he is 'ill' and belongs in the hospital. A nurse's aide tells him that although he entered the hospital voluntarily, the psychiatrist can sign a form to confine him against his will.
5) He cannot obey the claims of both 1) and 3) unless he disobeys his consideration in 2). He cannot obey 2) unless he disobeys the demands of either 1) or 3), and if he makes a move to leave the situation he will disobey the advice of the staff and risk being confined involuntarily. He decides upon 6).[20]
6) He tells the doctor, 'Please help me. You are a messenger from God. You will decide what my ultimate fate

[20] See the 'double bind' in G. Bateson, D. D. Jackson, J. Haley, J. and J. Weakland, 'Towards a theory of schizophrenia,' *Behavioral Science*, Vol. I, no. 251.

will be, etc. . . .' His religious upbringing colours the content of what he says. His dilemma imposes the *necessity* to speak in metaphor.
7) He does not realize that these statements lead his doctor to diagnose him as a 'paranoid schizophrenic.'

Although staff 'treat' a 'patient' by frequently telling him that he is 'sick,' they usually do not tell him his 'diagnosis.' Nor do the staff tell a 'patient' which data his doctor thinks are pertinent to the 'diagnosis,' or how, or why he thinks the data are pertinent. If a 'patient' asks to know his information, to which all the staff have access, they generally reply evasively.

8) He is not sure why his doctor has ordered a drug for him. When he asks a nurse why, she tells him he is 'ill' and that the drug will make him 'feel better.'
9) He tells the staff that this cannot be the right drug for him since he had felt well before he took it and now feels ill.
10) His doctor says that the fact that he had felt well before he was given the drug does not prove that he had not been ill then since 'mentally ill patients' often do not realize they are 'ill.' The nurses tell him at a ward meeting that he should trust his doctor since the doctor is trained in this field and he is not, and that 'mistrust' is a 'symptom' of 'mental illness.'
11) He feels confused. He mistrusts those who tell him he was ill when he felt well and that the drug they give him can help him to 'feel better' when it makes him feel ill. He mistrusts them more when they tell him he is ill if he mistrusts them. How can he influence the doctor to change his 'treatment' and conceal that he mistrusts the 'treatment'?
12) He says he is being 'poisoned.'
In this way he both conceals and reveals his mistrust. Since he does not know the doctor has diagnosed him as

a 'paranoid schizophrenic' and has ordered the drug to 'treat' this 'disease,' he does not realize that by saying he is 'being poisoned' he brings about what he most fears: an increase in drug dosage.

I leave it to the reader to complete the analysis of the story from here to the doctor's decision to administer electro-shock therapy.

I have heard many ex-mental patients tell me of experiences in mental hospitals similar in *structure* to my inferences about this man's experience. I read this story to seven of them and they all confirmed that they had found themselves in predicaments like this one, with which they had found it difficult to cope in a sane way. Mental hospitals entangle all their 'patients' in knots which are so constructed that the 'patients'' struggles to untie them tighten the knots.

The staff's practice of translating interpersonal events within the hospital into terms of a medical model bewilders the inmates, many of whom are befuddled already before coming to the hospital. Goffman, a sociologist who studied the social world inside a large American mental hospital, says:

. . . whatever else these institutions do, one of their central effects is to sustain the self-conception of the professional staff employed there. Inmates and lower staff levels are involved in a vast supportive action—an elaborate dramatized tribute—that has the effect, if not the purpose, of affirming that a medical-like service is in progress here and that the psychiatric staff is providing it. Something about the weakness of this claim is suggested by the industry required to support it . . .

Mental patients can find themselves in a special bind. To get out of the hospital, or to ease their life within it. They must show acceptance of the place accorded them, and the place accorded them is to support the occupational role of those who appear to force this bargain. This *self-alienating moral servitude*, which perhaps helps to account for some inmates becoming *mentally confused*, is achieved by invoking the great tradition of the expert servicing relation, especially its medical variety.[21]

The mental hospital confronts hapless wayfarers, gives them conundrums to solve, and punishes them dreadfully if they fail. Shall we not find an alternative to this modern Sphinx before it destroys the unwary among *us* too?

The Anti-Psychiatry Ward

Dr. David Cooper in 1962 began to dehierarchize one ward within a large mental hospital near London. He wished to 'allow a greater degree of freedom of movement out of the highly artificial staff and patient roles imposed on people by conventional psychiatry.' He called his project an 'experiment in anti-psychiatry.'

The staff abolished role-bound behaviour such as organizing 'patients' into activity, supervising their domestic work on the ward and 'treating' them. An 'anti-rule' was set up that 'patients' decide their own leave period, attendance at meetings and getting out of bed. In response to external administrative pressure the ward staff partially restored their own role-bound behaviour.

David Cooper sees the result of his 'experiment' to be that 'the limits of institutional change are found to be very closely drawn indeed—even in a progres-

---

[21] E. Goffman, *Asylums, Essays on the Social Situation of Mental Patients and other Inmates* (New York: Doubleday-Anchor Books, 1961), pp. 385–6. (My italics)

sive mental hospital.' He suggests that 'a step forward means ultimately a step out of the mental hospital into the community.' [22]

Kingsley Hall [23]

'Kingsley Hall' is the name of a building in the East End of London.[24] It was built about sixty years ago. It is three floors in height. About thirteen people can live there comfortably, each with his own room. A large ground-floor hall, a 'games room,' a dining room, a meeting room, two kitchens, and three other rooms—used by the occupants now as a meditation room, a chapel, and a dark-room for photography—comprise the 'common rooms.' The roof is open and has a garden.

The building has been used in the past as a community center for meetings of various kinds, and as a settlement house. It has also served as a place of worship. Mahatma Gandhi stayed at Kingsley Hall when he visited London in 1931.

The Philadelphia Association, Ltd. leased the building from the Kingsley Hall Board of Trustees in June, 1965. The 'community' which I describe here

[22] D. Cooper, op. cit., pp. 83–104.
[23] I lived at Kingsley Hall for a year. This description of 'Kingsley-Hall' is derived mostly from that experience. I am grateful to the people who lived there when I did and to the members of the Philadelphia Association, Ltd. for making that experience possible. I also draw on the experiences of people who lived in the community before me, especially Drs. Joseph Berke, R. D. Laing, Jerome Liss, and Leon Redler. The views which I express here are my own, and no one else can be considered responsible for them.
[24] I sometimes call the group of people living there 'Kingsley-Hall' or the 'community.' (The place is no longer operational. Editor's note.)

began then and has included over one-hundred individuals.[25] The 'P.A.' also has affiliated itself with several other smaller communities similar in aim to 'Kingsley-Hall.' The people in each household make the rules which govern their life together. These households comprise a major social experiment.

Several members of the P.A. lived at Kingsley Hall in the year 1965–66. The residents are free to ask them for advice or help whenever they wish. The P.A. has sponsored lectures in psychiatry, 'anti-psychiatry' and phenomenology at Kingsley Hall, and has arranged seminars and meetings there with professional people in many fields.

The 'community' has been a link in a chain of 'counter culture' centres. Experimental-drama groups, social scientists of the 'New Left,' classes from the Antiuniversity of London, leaders of the 'commune' movement and *avant-garde* poets, artists, musicians, dancers and photographers, have met at Kingsley Hall with the residents in the last three and a half years. The 'Free School of London' met there for the first time.

The founder-members of 'Kingsley-Hall' hoped to fulfill in the 'community' their seed-idea that lost souls may be cured by going mad among people who see madness as a chance to die and be reborn. Laing says in *The Politics of Experience*:

No age in the history of humanity has perhaps so lost touch with this natural *healing* process, that implicates *some* of the people whom we label schizophrenic. No age has so devalued it, no age has imposed such prohibi-

[25] From 1 June, 1965, to November, 1968, one-hundred and nine people lived in Kingsley Hall for periods of three days or more.

tions and deterrences against it, as our own. Instead of the mental hospital, a sort of re-servicing factory for human breakdowns, we need a place where people who have travelled further, and consequently, may be more lost than psychiatrists and other sane people, can find their way *further* into inner space and time, and back again. Instead of the *degradation* ceremonial of psychiatric examination, diagnosis and prognostication, we need, for those who are ready for it (in psychiatric terminology often those who are about to go into a schizophrenic breakdown), an initiation ceremonial, through which the person will be guided with full social encouragement and sanction into inner space and time. Psychiatrically, this would appear as ex-patients helping future patients to go mad.[26]

When Freud returned to his patients' earliest memories (and his own) he found traumas which he saw had led them (and him) to repress regions of their (and his) being. He revealed feelings and energy which had been buried and 'bound' together with the forgotten memories of events which had occurred in childhood and infancy. Freud urged his patients to re-member their pasts, and to recover their lost feelings, in order to make themselves whole again. He also said he knew of acts of men who had lived before recorded history which survived as 'unconscious' memories in the minds of all living human beings and influenced their behaviour. He did not urge his patients to go back to that time, long before their births, to cure themselves.

Human societies in diverse times and places have relied upon a method of 'psychotherapy' which west-

---

[26] R. D. Laing, *The Politics of Experience* (England: Penguin Books, 1967), p. 105, and (New York: Pantheon, 1967).

ern man has forgotten and suppressed: the return to Chaos. To cure himself 'archaic' and 'primitive' man goes back beyond the experience of his personal past, beyond the experiences of his ancestors, beyond history, beyond prehistory, beyond the time of this world to enter a mythical, eternal time that precedes all origins. He disintegrates, or is disintegrated, as a person who exists in historical, egoic time and he undergoes psychic chaos which 'he' experiences as contemporaneous with the amorphous Being whose interior was ruptured by the cosmogony. His rebirth into existence repeats the creation of Cosmos out of Chaos.[27]

Several 'returns' of this sort have occurred at 'Kingsley-Hall.' It is too early to know whether cures by this method are feasible in western culture, even among an enclave of people who will permit them to occur. The 'rebirth' of Mary Barnes may encourage those who wish to explore this further.

Mary Barnes is forty-five years old. She came to live at Kingsley Hall three and a half years ago. Recently she wrote an account for me of her experiences. Here are some excerpts.

From the age of seventeen years until the time of forty-two years when I came here my time was spent mainly in hospitals. One year was in a mental hospital as a patient. All the rest of the time was on the 'staff side' of several hospitals. I was a Sister, later a Tutor. Kingsley Hall is where I have experienced real healing. . . .

---

[27] See Mircea Eliade, *Shamanism, Archaic Techniques of Ecstasy*, translated by W. R. Trask (New York: Bollingen Foundation, 1964); and M. Eliade, *Myths, Dreams and Mysteries* (trans. by Philip Mairet) (Great Britain: Marvill Press, 1960).

Through the experience of a schizophrenic breakdown
twelve years before I came here, I knew what I wanted:
to go down, *back to before I was born* and to come up
again.

She felt she needed to return to the point where she
had taken a wrong turn, and to come back again by
another path.

In the mental hospital I had got stuck in my madness.
Mostly I was in the pads (padded cell) . . . No one
knew why—least of all me.

She got out of the hospital and 'somehow I kept
out of hospitals as a patient.' 'Eventually,' she came
to R. D. Laing. He told her he was looking for a
place where it would be possible for her to live
through the experiences she sought, but he did not
know when he would find one. She chose to 'hold on'
until he did. Nineteen months passed before Kingsley Hall became available. She 'held on' during that
time.

After moving into Kingsley Hall she began to go a
long way back.

At first so great was my fear I forgot what I had come
for . . . Quite suddenly I remembered, 'I've come here
to have a breakdown, to go back to before I was born
and come up again.'

For several weeks she continued to work at her job
at a hospital which was an hour away. She worked
during the day and 'regressed' at Kingsley Hall in the
evening. Then she wrote a letter of resignation to the
hospital.

Life soon became quite fantastic. Every night at Kingsley Hall I tore off my clothes, feeling I had to be naked.

Lay on the floor with my shits and water, smeared the walls with faeces. Was wild and noisy about the house or sitting in a heap on the kitchen floor. Half-aware that I was going mad, there was the terror that I might not know what I was doing away, outside of Kingsley Hall. Her resignation at the hospital was accepted.

The tempo was increasing. Down, down, oh God, would I never break.

The others found it difficult to live with her when she smeared faeces on her body and on the walls of her room. Her room was next to the kitchen and the odour diffused through the wall. Should they permit her to do this? Does a person have a right to a 'smell space' that extends beyond the four walls of his or her room?

She stopped eating solid foods and had to be fed milk from a bottle. People took turns feeding her. She stopped talking and lay still in bed for long periods.

In bed I kept my eyes shut so I didn't see people but I heard them . . . Touch was all important . . . Sometimes my body had seemed apart, a leg or an arm across the room. The wall became hollow and I seemed to go into it as into a big hole. Vividly aware of people, I was physically isolated in my room, my womb. . . .

That was three years ago.

Eventually, I 'came up'—was 'reborn.' I wanted new clothes, nothing black, the colour I used to wear . . . I was coming out of the web, working free. Coming to know I was a separate, distinct person.

She has 'come up' again in the views of those who know her. When she was 'down' she began to paint, which she had never done before 1965. To make her

first paintings she smeared faeces with her fingers on
the walls of her room. For the past three years she
has painted with oils on canvasses although she still
uses her fingers. She has sold many paintings and has
scheduled a public exhibition. She also has written
some poems and short stories. Here is a story which
she wrote last year, called *The Hollow Tree*.

There was once a tree in the forest who felt very sad
and lonely for her trunk was hollow and her head was
lost in mist.

Sometimes the mist seemed so thick that her head felt
divided from her trunk.

To the other trees, she appeared quite strong, but
rather aloof, for no wind ever sent her branches to them.

She felt if she bent she would break, yet she grew so
tired of standing straight.

So it was with relief that in a mighty storm she was
thrown to the ground. The tree was split, her branches
scattered, her roots torn up and her bark was charred and
blackened. She felt stunned, and though her head was
clear of the mist, she felt her sap dry as she felt her
deadness revealed when the hollow of her trunk was open
to the sky.

The other trees looked down and gasped, and didn't
quite know whether to turn their branches politely away
or whether to try to cover her emptiness and blackness
with their green and brown.

The tree moaned for her own life and feared to be suf-
focated by theirs. She felt she wanted to lay bare and
open to the wind and the rain, and the sun, and that in
time she would grow up again, full and brown, from the
ground.

So it was that with the wetness of the rain she put
down new roots, and by the warmth of the sun she
stretched forth new wood.

In the wind her branches bent to other trees, and as

their leaves rustled and whispered in the dark, and in the light, the tree felt loved, and laughed with life.

Not everyone who lives at Kingsley Hall desires or *needs* to undergo an experiential drama of this magnitude. Many wish to be free from the well-intentioned, misguided harassment of their families or mental hospitals or both. They want to live in a haven where they can simply be, or be *tzu-jan*, translated as 'or itself so,' 'spontaneously,' 'expanding from within.'[28]

To discover the intelligibility of a social situation one must undergo an experience which is constitutive and regulative of it and which is constituted and regulated by the experiences of each of the others in the situation.[29] Information about the *experience* of living at Kingsley Hall is revealed only to observers living within the building. I asked my fellow-residents at Kingsley Hall to discuss with me their experiences there. Here is what four people said to me.[30]

1. My first experience at Kingsley Hall was that I was taking a role very different from any other role I'd ever taken: instead of being one always looking at other people . . . um . . . like father figures . . . I think I was mainly in the position where I was told what to do and

[28] Alan, Watts, *Nature, Man and Woman* (New York: Pantheon Books, Inc., 1958).

[29] See R. D. Laing and D. C. Cooper, *Reason and Violence: A Decade of Sartre's Philosophy 1950–60* (New York: Humanities Press, 1964), especially pp. 11–14.

[30] I told each person living in the building in December 1968 that I planned to write about 'Kingsley-Hall,' and that I wished to include his view of his experience there. Everyone talked about his experience to me, alone. I wrote down what each person said verbatim. I chose to present these excerpts because they represent views that are generally shared.

somehow expected this . . . looking for some sort of guidance, I suppose. And then initially when I came here I seemed to be the one who was arranging things and making decisions—arranging things and taking quite an active part. . . .

I think one of the best things here is that one *doesn't have to be right* . . . Being here, anything goes—sort of. I think of a word—an 'acceptance' of people as they are which I've never found anywhere else. . . . Here one can make a kind of contact—a kind of understanding—it's easy to make some sort of contact without words, whereas outside one is limited to making certain sorts of sentences. There is something very unique about it . . . You're not bogged down by conventionalities of having to be polite or make statements which are regarded as conventional forms of politeness, things like: 'Come and sit by the fire' and 'Have you had a good day?' and the other person is expected to go through what sort of a day he's had . . . Here people don't do that. One feels under no obligation to do that. I think it's more honest. People aren't afraid if they don't particularly like the person—they're not afraid not to be friendly.

2. You have to decide here what you want to do because no one is around to tell you what you should be doing. Like most places I've been in there was always a reason I had to go out—or go to lectures at the university. If I didn't, someone would drag me out or say, 'Are you ill?' Now, no one is telling me I ought to come out and be mixing with people. I can decide if I want to leave my room. There is no external structure, or authority, or formality to fall back on to decide if you ought to do something—it's really up to you . . .

There are little things for me like playing the piano. I'm very unmusical. I can't play an instrument. I've never played an instrument I didn't know in front of anyone. I find here I can do this: bash around and make noise. I don't feel absurd. I can dance too. I never could dance in front of people before. Here, it's just O. K. And also, for the first time since childhood, maybe in my life, I can really play with another person . . .

3. The main thing about my family and mental hospitals as opposed to Kingsley·Hall is that here a number of divergent people come together to meet and to try to live out a life with one another where they can live out their differences—have rows, disagree intently, decide to do things in ways that will offend others—and still for them to be tolerated, and for people doing this gradually to become aware of other people and their intereffects upon one another. I'm convinced this *doesn't happen in a mental hospital*: I know it doesn't.

There, in mental hospitals, it's very difficult to relate to people at all in any sense other than the part they want you to play—so you've got to learn what rules they want you to carry out in their scheme of things: whereas here you find various people and you can open up to them and talk, and relate, and build 'up understanding. Not where one person tells another what he should want, how he should dress and eat . . . One of the things between Kingsley Hall—between a free situation —and a bound situation is that here a person can do something and isn't made to conform his behaviour in relation to a model of what others think is right and wrong.

4. One becomes here increasingly sensitive to the importance to people who maintain those very deluded mystiques of where it's at—who keep cheating themselves. When I'd be at home it would seem quite important that the table would be set in a certain way and that one ate one's sweet with a fork—and how in all those little things the justification is claimed to be just solely: that this form of behaviour is right because it exists . . .

I was always taught that work was a 'good thing' be-

cause it was, just because it was work—and 'everybody
worked, didn't they?' I feel that it is of course necessary
to do work of some kind in order to keep myself alive.
However, I don't believe any more in the very complicated mystique surrounding the necessity for work—I
mean pointless and unfulfilling work—which has nothing to do with this fundamental physical necessity.

I've discovered this here because here I find that many
people question things with a greater honesty. People
with obvious honesty question many things that one has
been taking to be unconditionally true and valid . . . I
feel that this very situation which makes *retreat from social reality*—well, external reality—possible; in fact
eventually, paradoxically, makes facing *reality in general
almost unavoidable*.

The people who live near Kingsley Hall never let
those who live inside the building forget, that the
inside is inside an outside, that has a different view of
what is True and what is Real, where the source of
Light is, and who is in Exile and who is in the Kingdom. At half-past eleven one Friday night, four men
who had been drinking in a nearby pub broke into
the building and shouted that we were 'looneys,'
'drug addicts,' 'lay-abouts,' and perverts' who 'stank'
and were 'desecrating' a community shrine by our
'foul' behaviour. A lady in a nearby shop called us
'a bunch of nutters and homosexuals.' The neighbourhood children continued the eighteenth-century
French custom of weekend visits to the lunatic asylum to view the inmates: they frequently entered the
building by self-invitation, just to look around and
giggle. Boys broke with stones the windows facing the
street so many times that we decided to freeze one
winter rather than spend money to repair them again.

Children unscrewed the front-door bell, smashed the front door with an axe, and several times put dogs' faeces on the floor of the ground-floor hall.

The disagreement between the people who live in the building and those who do not is about morals. All people decide which thoughts, feelings, acts, persons and groups of persons to call right or wrong, good or bad, clean or dirty, true or false, real or unreal, sane or insane, and so on. Western society interrogates people or groups of people to learn if they assign to particular thoughts, feelings, acts, persons and groups of persons the labels which it believes they ought to. Those who live at Kingsley Hall often do not apply the labels 'correctly,' and know it. If people in western society do not, do they have a right to live outside a mental hospital? Those who live at Kingsley Hall affirm that they do. Not all who live outside the building agree.

When residents behave in ways which are considered strange, they alarm some people outside the building. A man, aged twenty-eight, who lived at Kingsley Hall would walk into neighbourhood pubs and coffee shops and, without saying a word to anyone, would pick up glasses from tables or counters, drink the contents and walk out. If a door to a house was left open he would enter and sit on a chair in the drawing-room until someone of the house would see him. Then he would get up and walk out quietly. He never said anything to threaten anyone and he never touched anyone, but he unnerved people. People would approach him in the street to offer the unsolicited advice that he would 'feel better' if he were in a mental hospital. One resident kept people in the house next door awake at night by playing his record player as loudly as he could. He was experiencing his body as 'numb' and found he could give it 'life' if he played music loudly. He did not wish to disturb anyone; when those whom he disturbed complained, he stopped, and apologized.

The residents of Kingsley Hall have tried several times to begin a dialogue with people in the neighbourhood. We have felt that the children, when they harassed the 'community,' were refracting upon us their parents' fears and resentments of us. Once, the people at Kingsley Hall invited several hundred people in the neighbourhood to a tea to discuss with them why they lived together and to answer any questions. Only about twelve people showed up and by the time they left they still did not seem to have grasped the purpose of the 'community.'

Some neighborhood groups, for instance an 'Old People's' group and a boys' club which had met regularly in the large ground-floor hall before the P.A. leased the building, continued to meet there. One of the residents sometimes played his guitar and sang to the 'Old People.' When I lived there we let the hall one afternoon a week for a few shillings to a ballet class of about twenty girls and their teacher. These services by the 'community' created more rapport with people who lived outside than any teach-ins would have, but the children never ceased their hostilities.

People who live, work, or play together make rules to govern which parts of one's body one may bring into contiguity with which parts of the bodies of others. To know which rule applies in a specific case one must know the sex of the persons, their age, their marital status, their feelings towards each other, whether each has consented, whether those who are nearest and dearest to them have consented, how visible to others is the relation, and so on. People forbid each other to talk about some of these rules and even to *know* that they exist, although they punish those who break them. No mental hospital ward permits a male psychiatrist to insert his penis into the anus of a male patient, although I doubt whether many people in mental hospitals are aware of such a rule or mention it ever at therapeutic community meetings. Talk about the existence of such a rule would, I believe, be against the rules of mental hospitals, and talk about these latter rules would violate some other set of rules that are never talked about. 'It' may be what some male patients want most although they may be 'treated' if they say so. 'It' never occurs, and no one thinks much about why it does not, because it is unthinkable in a mental hospital to consider the topic as one about which one might think.

At Kingsley Hall no rule prevents the discovery of any secret rules which may be forbidding some sexual acts and permitting others. No rule stops anyone from saying: 'We in the building are behaving *as if* there were a regulation that prohibited all A people from doing *x*, *y*, or *z* with all B people. Why are we?' This is important, since studies of families of 'schizophrenics' show that these families confuse their children by making rules that forbid the awareness of other rules. The parents of 'schizophrenics' punish their children when they disobey the first-order rules of the family, and when they show that they know they exist—a knowledge which violates rules of the second-order.[31]

The rules of 'Kingsley-Hall' force no one to work to earn money if he does not wish to, nor do they oblige anyone not to work. Everyone pays rent money into a communal fund. A person's ability to pay and the solvency of the 'cash-box' determine the amount one pays. The 'community' uses the money in the communal fund to pay for food, heating, electricity, repairs and maintenance of all the rooms in the building, and any other items which they choose to buy. People can, and do, 'turn night into day' and do not get out of bed at all if they do not wish to. A resident who tried to compel another resident to do anything for what he presumed to be the other's good would violate the rules of the group.

If someone wishes to live at Kingsley Hall he must meet some or all of the residents first. Sometimes they invite him to stay for an evening meal or a weekend. The residents ask those people to join the 'community' whom they like or whom they feel would benefit at Kingsley Hall or both. The residents consider it best for a balance to exist between those who are free to deal with ordinary social and economic needs—to shop for food, wash dishes, scrub floors, clean toilets, stoke the furnace, repair broken fuses and pay the bills—and those who cannot or choose not to be, and wish to work upon themselves. The

---

[31] See J. Haley, 'The Family of the Schizophrenic: A Model System,' *Journal of Nervous and Mental Diseases*, 129, 1959, pp. 357–374; and R. D. Laing, 'The Politics of the Family,' *Massey Lectures*, Eighth Series, Canadian Broadcasting Company, 1968.

men who seek the priceless Pearl in the depths of the ocean may drown if no one is topside to monitor their oxygen supply. They need others to look after their physical requirements.

No one who lives at Kingsley Hall sees those who perform work upon the external material world as 'staff,' and those who do not as 'patients.' No caste system forbids people to move freely from one sub-group to another, as it does in mental hospitals. No locus of institutional power subordinates everyone, by an inert sovereign right, to a command-obedience structure that forces those at the 'top' to force those they command to force others, to force others, etc., to limit the freedom of those at the 'bottom' for whose limitation of freedom the institution exists. No organization, no ossified apparatus, imposes upon anyone the need to administrate others: to distribute communal tasks, to allocate responsibilities and to make rules. Each person at Kingsley Hall may choose to assume the obligations of a reciprocal bond with another person, or other people, or the 'group.' He pledges to do so, or dissolves his pledge, by an initiative that originates in his own interior.

Some visitors are curious to know which of the residents had been labelled 'schizophrenic' by hospital psychiatrists before they came to live at Kingsley Hall, and which of the residents had previously worked as 'staff' at mental hospitals as psychiatrists, nurses, or social workers. Their wrong guesses can be amusing. Guests, in staff positions at mental hospitals, sometimes suppose that those who had previously been labelled 'schizophrenic' are really doctors and nurses, and vice versa.

Where is the machinery for decision-making? How

are issues discussed, clarified, classified? How are
agreements reached and implemented? The 'community' answers these questions differently at different
times. Gatherings are most frequent at meals around
the table, or wherever people sit when they eat. People sometimes bring up issues at dinner. An issue
might be that nothing 'important' is being discussed.
Matters of the life and death of the soul are more
'important' than whether anyone shops, cooks, or
cleans, but someone must do these things. Who? But
why should anyone live at Kingsley Hall if 'only' to
concern himself about things like that? People sometimes agree to meet at regular intervals, at set times,
just to share what they have on their minds. But can
a genuine meeting be scheduled? The most common
occasion for a meeting is when some people feel the
need to come together to talk about a specific matter.

When I came to live at Kingsley Hall, several people were meditating together daily from 6 to 7 a.m.
Later, some of us gathered for a couple of hours early
each morning to discuss our dreams of the night before. We ask each other: 'Do different people weave
their dreams out of "day-residents" that derive from
the same events? Do we live out with each other during the day our dreams of the night before? or of the
next night? Can we stop assigning to each other roles
to play in our dream-scripts during the sleep we sleep
when we suppose we are awake?' People symbolized
'Kingsley-Hall' in their dreams as a 'rocket ship in
space,' a 'make-shift camp in an Israeli desert,' a 'children's house,' a 'chalet for skiers on a mountainside,'
a 'Jacob's ladder' and a 'Sinbad's roc.'

Situations which are permitted to unfold at Kingsley Hall would not be allowed to progress so far in other social contexts. Joseph, aged twenty, came to live at Kingsley Hall after three years in mental hospitals. He revealed that 'voices' were 'plotting' against him. 'They were regarding his thoughts as 'bad' and 'they' were talking to each other about the need to condemn and punish him. He had to be careful since they were seeing his belief that they were plotting against him as a 'bad thought.'

He was not sure if he was imagining the voices or if he was overhearing a real plot. If the voices were 'real' they must be using extraordinary means to discover his thoughts—how else could the voices know them? And they must be communicating with each other by unusual means—how else could he hear them and not see them? Maybe they were using 'aerial control.' If so, where was their apparatus? He cut some of the electric wires in the building and disconnected the telephone receiver to see if that would stop the voices. He also broke into other residents' rooms to search for concealed communication apparatus.

One morning he told me that the night before he had experienced 'the most dreadful thing a human being could imagine.' A 'fire' had burned him to ashes and the pain had been unbearable.

In the next few days he began to knock on the doors of girls' rooms in the building late at night to awaken them for a cigarette or to light his cigarette. During the day he would come to their windows and stare at them silently. He would also threaten to set fires and to burn down the building.

People met daily to discuss his behaviour. We invited him to the meetings, and sometimes he came. He always left after a few minutes to dash around the building because he suspected that the visible meeting was a decoy to distract his attention from the 'real' meeting held 'secretly' elsewhere. Was it possible to talk about him without making true in a sense his fantasy that 'voices' were talking about him? Could we dissolve the 'plot' if he saw our efforts to dissolve it as part of the plot? We revealed *our* predicament to him. Did his behaviour serve some purpose for us? We were coming together more often to talk to each other because of him than we had been before. Had he elected himself to be our scapegoat, *for* our sake?

Once, while we met to talk about his behaviour and to decide what our limits of tolerance should be, he put his mattress on the roof and poured methylated spirits on it. He was going to set it on fire, but a resident saw him and stopped him. The roof is made of cement, so no fire he set there could have spread. Still, he had frightened us. He could set a fire that would spread when none of us were awake. He could endanger our life as a 'community' if the neighbours, or the police and fire departments, learned we were allowing a man who had been threatening to set fires to live at large—out of jail or mental hospital.

What did his behaviour mean? Was it worth the nuisance or the risk to us to let him live with us while we tried to find out? What would happen to him if we told him to leave? If we, who wished to understand him and to find a way to live with him, could not, could anyone? We chose to attempt a *modus vivendi* with him a little longer.

Sexual frustration might underlie some of his behaviour. His body had been 'on fire.' He intruded on girls while they slept to ask them to 'light' his 'cigarette.' He felt communication was going on inside other people's rooms from which he was excluded. He looked at girls through their windows. Perhaps his thoughts which the 'voices' were regarding as 'bad' were sexual ones. We confronted him with a sexual translation of his behaviour. Girls told him that he has asked them to light his cigarettes because he lacked enough courage to ask them to make love. Men told him that he had not been able to douse the fire in his body, because he had felt forbidden to masturbate and fuck. His threats to set fires stopped. We revealed to him that he had put our patience to a severe test and that he had approached our threshold of tolerance. We found, by frequently confronting him with our feelings towards him, we could cool the intensity of the situation, though we could not eliminate it.

I am aware of clinical and juridical arguments in favour of imposing clear limits to forbid behaviour of this sort soon after it begins. I am also aware of how much everyone can learn that is new if difficult situations are allowed to unfold. There is no proof that the traditional and customary responses of people to rule-breaking are the most enlightened of all possible ways. Joseph said that he had never realized before coming to Kingsley Hall that people had sent him to mental hospital in the past because his behaviour frightened them. He had been too frightened himself, he said, to be free to see that he had frightened them, and they had not told it to him.

Another resident said to me:
Those who live here see 'Kingsley-Hall' each in his own way. . . . in common to all who live here . . . is a bafflement or refusal as to fulfillment of 'identity' . . . the

problem is for each to discover some inner need—and to find a way to trust it . . . It is in honour of this, that Kingsley Hall is: a place, simply, where some may encounter selves long forgotten or distorted. . . .

Does 'Kingsley-Hall' succeed? An irrelevant question: it does no harm, it does no 'cure'. *It* stands silent, people by real ghosts; so silent that, given time, given luck, they may hear their own hearts beat and elucidate the rhythm.

Anti-Psychiatry:
An Interview with Dr. Joseph Berke

INTERVIEWER: ANDREW ROSSABI

Q.: *Could you tell us a little about yourself?*
BERKE: I'm an American physician. I've been working in London more than five years as a research fellow in Psychiatry and the Social Sciences with the Philadephia Association. This is a mental health charity. Ronald Laing is the Director. The work of the Philadelphia Association has included setting up several communities here where people who had previously been diagnosed as schizophrenic, can live without being treated in the formal medical sense—or in any medical sence, come to that.

Q: *You're specifically interested in schizophrenia?*
BERKE: Well, in the whole range of psychological experience of which schizophrenia itself is a very important part. The term itself is important. I emphasise it's a term rather than a condition; and this is an important part of our work, showing how, in fact, people are invalidated in their own life styles, their life experience, by having this term applied to them.

It could be another term, like 'depressive,' but to take this particular instance of schizophrenia—it doesn't describe their life experience, it's really a label applied to them by certain other people, usually for social reasons.

Q.: *How do you define insanity then?*
BERKE: That would take several months, and the eventual answer would be inadequate. Insanity is really a social rather than personal fact. It's a social and cultural phenomenon. Experiences which are considered 'normal' in a particular culture or subculture may be defined as 'mad' in another cultural setting. Insanity is synonymous with behaviour or experience that is 'unacceptable' within a given cultural framework.

Q: *Could you say something about your association with Dr. Laing?*
BERKE: I've known him personally for over seven years now. He's a brilliant thinker as well as a 'good bloke'. The particular reason why I came over here was that many of his ideas overlapped with the conclusions I was beginning to draw about the way psychiatry operates. I wanted the opportunity to work with him. We both saw that the way people are treated, in the usual medical/psychiatric sense, doesn't alleviate their suffering, but usually perpetuates it; that doctors act as societal trustees in order to maintain a particular form of conventional behaviour and experience; that the kind of treatment that is given is a form of emotional straitjacketing, drugs included. Psychiatrists usually try to get people to for-

get what's bothering them rather than come to terms with it.

Q.: *Surely this is basically a question of time, money, staffing. The establishment psychiatrist has become a kind of bogeyman for the underground, like the policeman—I find this rather a paranoid idea.*
BERKE: I don't think you can be paranoid enough about how psychiatrists function, and how mental hospitals function in their way of dealing with people. One of the most important books in this regard is a study by a sociologist named Erving Goffman, entitled *Asylums.* The book is a study of how a mental hospital functions. Goffman spent several months as a nurse's aide in hospital, which is the proper level for finding out what goes on. The people who run hospitals are essentially nurses and nurse's aides, and only by working on that level can you really find out what goes on in a social and personal sense. Goffman found that instead of helping the person who was admitted as patient, the hospital tended to perpetuate the same kind of 'crazy' family situations and relationships which drove the patient 'mad' in the first place. In other words he showed how and why a mental hospital is a 'maddening' environment.

The important thing is to realise *why* people, especially teenagers, feel that they are going mad, feel that they can't cope, things like that. Usually, it's because of 'crazy' patterns of relationships in their families. We do a lot of work with families, it's an important part of our researches. Often, we find that a person who is labelled insane is the sanest member of his or her family.

Q.: *A kind of scapegoat, in other words?*
BERKE: Yes, that's right. The reason why the
person will be labelled insane is because he will be
trying to escape from the 'crazy' or disturbing relationships—the shared behaviour patterns within the
family. Take a teenager, for instance, who is trying to
assert his own autonomy, rather than going along
with the mores, the rituals of the family. When
such a person is taken to a mental hospital, more
often than not he is probably very frightened, does
not understand what is happening. He is taken to a
very strange place with the idea that people are going
to help him. But sociologically speaking the same
kind of patterns which have invalidated him in the
family are then repeated in the hospital. So the hospital environment often helps to drive people mad—
especially if they feel they are going there to get out
of the binds imposed by the family.

Q.: *You're switching then from one mad environment to another. But what's the alternative? The notion of cure always seems to get lost in all this. How
do you actually treat someone who is suffering?*
BERKE: Usually, two factors are associated with
the type of suffering you're talking about—social
and/or personal invalidation. The first thing to find
out is, what is this person feeling, what is this insanity that the person is worried about. Involved in
this is the question of semantics. A great deal of invalidation comes about because people are seman-
tically invalidating themselves—having to do with the
emotionally loaded word 'schizophrenic' or 'insane' or
things like that. Because insanity is a social and cultural definition, a textbook definition, it doesn't ex-

plain or even express whatever the person is feeling. It's quite possible to read a textbook of psychiatry and feel one is really crazy, because practically everything that is expressed in a textbook of psychiatry is felt by 'normal' people. The point is, there's no such thing as normal people. We're talking about a cross-section of people so the thing to find out is what the insanity is all about, what the experience is all about and to distinguish semantic invalidation from these other forms. Really it's a matter of creating an ambiance whereby people can look at what their suffering is all about, and make it intelligible to themselves. Suffering is intolerable when it's unintelligible. It doesn't disappear when it becomes intelligible but it usually becomes tolerable. It allows one to try to get at the root of what it's all about.

Q.: *A lot of people are trying to find a chemical basis for 'schizophrenia'. Could it be caused by a chemical imbalance in the brain?*
BERKE: No chemical causatory link with a condition called schizophrenia has ever been found. There's no condition called schizophrenia: it's a term of personal and social invalidation. This relates to how the word was coined. Originally, the word was 'dementia praecox', an early invention applied to people whose behaviour seemed to show signs of progessive mental and physical deterioration. They then found out that this deterioration doesn't necessarily occur. You see, there's no such thing as schizophrenia really. It's a hodge-podge term—referring to certain symptoms which doctors can supposedly distinguish in other people during the course of an interview. Laing has told me about a paper written in a German psychi-

atric journal last year by German psychiatrists who
diagnose someone as schizophrenic on the basis of a
feeling they themselves get in themselves—a strange
feeling they call the 'praecox' feeling. In this instance
we can clearly see that the diagnosis of schizophrenia
is made because of the problems the doctor has,
rather than the patient. That's the first point. The
second point is that no physical test has ever been
positively correlated with a particular mental condition.

There exists a pink spot urine test, there exists a
green spot urine test, there exists an orange spot urine
test—all this means is that urine tests of people who
are supposed to be schizophrenic come out with certain results after adding certain chemical reagents
to it. In a mental hospital a few years ago it was
found that the product which was supposed to be associated with schizophrenia had to do with the fact
that the patients were given coffee in the morning.
So, the 'x' spot was a breakdown product of caffeine.
And it goes on and on and on.

The original reason for this situation can be found
in the annals of medical history. Consider the experience and behaviour of people who were considered to
be witches or demons, possessed and things like that.
These people were usually shut away in dismal dun-
geons to protect the public. Now at the beginning of
the 18th century a doctor named Phillipe Pinel came
along and along with him came a lot of other 'do-
gooders'. They tried to stop the inhuman way the
so-called 'crazies' were treated. They said, 'Lo and be-
hold, if we state these unfortunate people are *not*
possessed by demons but have some kind of *sickness*,
like a cold, TB or something like that—then we can

treat them as if they were sick and not as if they were mad.' This is an important difference. Because madness is more often than not, a moral attribution—you're making a statement of morality. A person is *mad* and *bad*; they're very closely associated. Now if you can then say a person isn't just bad, possessed by demons, devils, morally bad, but is *sick,* then one can change the attitude of the general public to the person.

Then the doctors, having *a priori* defined deviant behaviour as a medical condition, had to apply medical techniques in order to understand it. So what did they do? First of all, they dissected the brains of people who died at the mental hospital. They were looking for gross conditions, changes in the brain—these weren't found, either. Next, they tried to study the 'madman's' biochemistry. Nowadays, this approach has become very fashionable. Associations are made to the use of psychedelic drugs because it has been found that the major psychedelic drugs like LSD, or DMT, or mescaline or whatever, are biochemically similar to certain naturally occurring substances in the body such as adrenalin—the reasoning then goes —schizophrenia is due to faulty biochemistry associated with a hyperproduction of psychediliogenic substances. So they began to believe that adrenalin-like substances in the blood cause 'schizophrenia'. Unfortunately this theory has never been substantiated.

In what is usually called schizophrenia, auditory hallucination is a common symptom. People hear things being told to them by somebody else—'Do this.' 'Do that.' 'Don't do that.' Things like that. But an interesting observation is that with psychedelic drugs people *rarely* have auditory hallucinations, most of the experiences of false perception that take place are *visual*. Moreover, people under the influence of psychedelic drugs rarely have hallucinations of any kind. Most of what happens is a form of visual illusion. The difference is quite important. Look at that large wall there. If there was absolutely nothing there, if it was absolutely totally white, and we began to see something there, that would be an hallucination. However, the fact is that on the wall there are various pieces of dirt, kinds of plugs and sockets, and these changes created in *a priori* objects around which the mind can distort, change, make small, make large— these are illusions. Most of the time what happens under psychedelic drugs is that we have strange visual illusions, either from this or from an after-effect like when you look at the window there, close your eyes and you can still see the window—this is called an eidetic image. It's through a distortion of actual real objects on the wall or eidetic images that the illusionary events occur. This is very important because if psychedelic drugs or their biochemical analogues in the blood were causes of 'mental illness', then the people who took such drugs would have hallucinations and they would be *auditory* not visual. In fact it is rare to have hallucinations under LSD. Most of them are illusions, *visual* illusions.

Q.: *Can we switch from chemistry to sex? Wilhelm Reich wrote about the 'schizoid' as a rigid personality unable to find release, true orgasmic flow in sex due to various muscular tensions and armourings. I guess a Reichian would say that the root cause of 'schizophrenia' is sex—in its widest sense—repression as a child, things like that which finally become located in the actual musculature of the body. You, on the other hand, tend to emphasize the family unit, the family background or situation. There's a difference here.*

BERKE: Well, again it has to do with the term schizophrenia which you are using as applied to a kind of condition, a situation of fact. Now I don't use it in that way at all. I never met a 'schizophrenic'. Since I don't choose to attribute certain things to other people by using this word, it really doesn't have much meaning for me. In order really to get anywhere, we have to talk about what *experiences* people have. The point is that the term 'schizoid' is often applied to people who have a kind of disassociation, a break, a split between the soma and the intellect, the body and the mind. This means that most of their feelings, emotions, which really involve both mind and body are split off into a mind component and a body component. This is often what people mean by schizoid. Also the term has to do with a split between the head and the heart, the feelings, the emotions and the intellect. When Reich was using the word orgasm, he wasn't really limiting himself to simply a genital experience, he was really referring to the total emotional, physical, mental experience.

Q.: *Yeah. But I get the impression that for Reich and the Reichians the ideal orgasm involved the total surrender of self—a total commitment to the physical reality of another. Now surely this is something the so-called schizoid is incapable of making: he's absolutely terrified of letting go, going out of control. But it's not much use approaching the individual. That's what impresses me about the importance you attach*

*to family influences, the family situation. But surely
it's more extensive even than the family—you've got
to cure the whole society, change it.*

BERKE: This is an important point. In fact we're
up against a whole society which is systematically
driving its members mad. Individuals might feel that
the problem is in themselves but it isn't. It's a social
problem which is experienced at an individual level.
This is the reason why we shouldn't try to perpetuate the individual suffering, try to trick the individual
people into thinking something is wrong with themselves. In fact it's often very heartening when people
realise that what they're experiencing is shared by a
lot of other people. There's a lot of people who in
the medical sense might be considered schizoid, schizophrenic, whatever it is, who can have great sex, i.e.,
orgasm, but still be unhappy in other areas. Again
this points to the vacuity, the inadequacy of the terms
schizoid, schizophrenic.

Q.: *Sure. Let's invent a more human word. Could
you finally say something about your work with Mary
Barnes? I understand you're writing a book together.
Hers seemed a classic madness, if you'll excuse the
phrase.*

BERKE: Well Mary Barnes is a 45-year-old woman,
English—she had been working in a hospital, experienced nervous breakdowns in the past, and had been
diagnosed as a chronic schizophrenic; extremely regressed in a mental hospital, she had recovered and
then she started feeling mad again—what *she*
thought was going mad. This she experienced as
extreme regression, not wanting to do anything, want-

ing to become a baby again, things like that. She met Laing about six or seven years ago—she'd heard about him through other people—and asked him if she could come to Kingsley Hall, the proposed new 'anti-psychiatric' community. Kingsley Hall opened about 1965 and she was one of the first people to move in.

The point about madness is that it is a term applied to a particular form of experience. In Mary's case the experience was that of a return to an earlier version of herself, a wanting to become a baby again, wanting to return to her roots, almost to the foetus, as a way of dealing with the suffering which she felt as an adult. She wanted to see if she could be reborn again. She had to return almost to the position of a foetus in the womb in order to grow up again. And in fact that was what happened over the past few years at Kingsley Hall. Mary returned to being a baby, she was fed with a bottle, she played with her shit, she was taken care of as a baby, she spent a long time in bed not moving at all and, in doing so, returned to a point which was prior to the time when all the anxiety started. The aim in doing that was to grow up again, without all the anxieties associated with growing up in the first place.

I have had a lot to do with Mary. I was principally responsible for taking care of her immediate needs when I lived at Kingsley Hall between 1965 and 1966, and also afterwards. This very process of assistance was an experience, you might say, a death-rebirth experience for me too. This is the reason why I admire her courage to do what she did—it was a very courageous, very frightening thing to do, especially because adults just don't become babies again.

But Mary's experiences confirmed an idea of
Laing's and other people that an experience of regression, of going back into oneself, can be a very
healing experience. There has been a book written
about this by the Polish psychiatrist, Kazimierz
Dubrowski, entitled *Positive Disintegration*. This is
an important point then and goes back to what we
were saying about mental hospitals. A great deal of
what might be called by a psychiatrist 'regression' is
a person's natural attempt at self-healing. Our work
and what we consider the proper 'work' of the therapist is to help a person along the road of his or her
disintegrative experience—provide the essential services—food, a warm place, a nice atmosphere—and
let the breakdown and recovery happen without interference. Then the return trip—the integrative
phase—will be a very healing experience. The point
of mental hospitals and especially the psychiatrists
and nurses and others who work in them, is that they
stop this healing process from happening because of
their own fears about what's happening. This personal fear of psychiatrists and nurses about themselves makes mental hospitals places where healing
cannot take place. Therefore these places are not hospitals at all. Truthfully they are 'mad houses', i.e.
places where people are driven 'mad', or 'madness' is
perpetuated. What we wanted to do was to create an
asylum in the original sense of the word where healing can happen. Aside from Mary, several other people have had similar kinds of experience at Kingsley
Hall, maybe not as spectacular as she did but just as
useful. Mary and I have written a book together
about this which will be published in 1971. It con-

sists of *her* account of her own experience and her experience with me and *my* account of my own experience and my experience with her. I say my own experience, because it was as much a profound experience for me as for her.

Q.: *Thank you.*

Flection

BY MARY BARNES

FLECTION: the act of bending or the state of being bent. That's how I was at Kingsley Hall, bent back into a womb of rebirth. From this cocoon I emerged, changed to the self I had almost lost. The buried me, entangled in guilt and choked with anger as a plant matted in weed, grew anew, freed from the knots of my past.

That was Kingsley Hall to me, a backward somersault, a breakdown, a purification, a renewal. It was a place of rest, of utter stillness, of terrible turmoil, of the most shattering violence, of panic and of peace, of safety and security and of risk and reckless joy. It was the essence of life. The world, caught, held, contained, in space and time. Five years as five seconds; five seconds as five hundred years.

Kingsley Hall, my 'second' life, my 'second' family, may it ever live within me. My life, within a life. It was a seed, a kernel of the time to come. How can I know what will come. As I write, as I paint, the words, the colours—they emerge, grow, take shape, blend, and part; a sharp line, darkness; light. The canvas, a paper, a life, is full, complete, whole. We are at one with God. Through the half light, the blessed blur of life, we stumble to the God we sense within.

Knowing, yet unknowing. Seeing, yet blind. Striving yet yielding. We reach out, from our own depth to the height of heaven, and in our stretch all life is held, bubbling and breaking with joy, still as deep water, moving as the clouds. Thousands, millions of lives. A word, a colour, alone yet a part. One life seeking to live, expanded consciousness, participation in the 'sight of God'. How would I be in a new place? God knows.

I would let everything 'be'; all the 'Johns' and 'Janets' and 'Peters' and 'Pamelas' I would let 'be'. We should be alone, yet in communion, in communication, with each other. In order to come to the light we have to germinate in the dark.

We must go the way we are made, an oak cannot be bent as a willow. To lay down, to pray, to draw in to the core of one's being, is to 'start a place'. What place? A house, a community, a group of people? You have to wait and see what will happen, and let it happen.

The place that you start is there already, inside the people that will come. It's as white as heaven and black as hell and the background is grey, because that's the mixture we mainly are. How to build heaven on earth, how to save souls. That's what it's all about.

"Don't be too 'spiritual'," says Joe. "No," I replied, "I'll try to express it in psychological terms."

'Dark night of the soul', deep despair, desperate depression; schizophrenia, split mind, tormented with distractions; cut off from God; division of the self; 'to die to the self to live in God'; to get free from the self in the mother to live in God within the self; 'our life as a bird has escaped from the snare', from the bonds, or rather the emotional ties, of the past. From these have I through psychotherapy been released.

Different ages, different terms, the world moves, in the eternal breath of God.

(Of her particular experience at Kingsley Hall Mary Barnes is writing a book with Joe—Dr. Joseph Berke, who guided her through madness.)

Reflection

BY MARY BARNES

RONNIE (Dr. R. D. Laing) told me "What you need is analysis twenty four hours out of the twenty four." I was one of those people who just cannot be healed through spasmodic help, whilst living in an ordinary situation. I just had to be in a special place, a house for madness.

It's the inner state that matters. But it's people less sick than I was, who can get free, whole, through the ordinary course of life. Extreme states help to 'bring it up', to uncover the real self, but to go further in extreme conditions is very rare. How many, in a prison, or physically living with the family they were born into, or in a contemplative convent, reach through to integration, wholeness, sanctity? It's what we are all made for, given time in this life to achieve.

Yet, never, for one moment, do we 'make it' of ourselves. God, through other people, reaches out to us and draws us on. It's a question of suffering but the suffering for many of us means madness before sanity —sanctity—wholeness. We go from false self, to madness, to sanity.

Mother Mary of Jesus early in this century spent two years alone in her cell, in a sense sick, yet not physically ill, before she was able to participate in the life of her community. Many years later she founded thirty-three Carmelite convents in England, Scotland and Wales before she died in 1942.

A convent day school in London is boarding one of their older pupils, because she is in mental distress. But it is rare for an established community to accommodate itself to the needs of such people, and if these people were in psychotherapy as such, with all the tremendous emotional upheaval that entails, it would probably be well nigh impossible to accommodate them within 'so-called' sane living conditions.

A very twisted up person cannot get free without being allowed extremes of behaviour. Regression is a safety valve. Playing, bashing about, screaming, sucking, messing with shit, laying naked, wetting the bed, are all ways of getting the anger into the body, without hurting the body.

Laying in a painful position, being alone for a day, will resolve anger. But resolution through bodily pain, fasting and isolation as all religious orders of all religions through all ages practise, is *not* possible, at least at *first*, for people who are very twisted up, as I was. They have to be allowed, encouraged, to *be* as 'baby' as they feel and emotionally re-grown until they can participate in what might be termed a more 'spiritual' level of development.

Just as one doesn't give a one-year old baby tranquilisers or kneel him down to meditate, so must one *not* have expectations of a person in madness utterly beyond his state. Otherwise, there is danger of just shaking him (a modern way of doing this is electric shocks) or shutting him away in a cupboard (the chronic ward of a mental hospital).

The person must be seen and understood as the baby he is—and allowed to live that way, through it.

He is dying to be loved, to be wanted, to be accepted. He has within himself to emotionally accept, to feel, all the anger, the anguish of the past, to go through periods of deadness when nothing at all can be felt, to be green with envy and hating with jealousy. Still, he must be loved, totally, for what he is, as a baby needs love.

Important as understanding is, it is love and trust that matter most. As a mother knows her baby, so can one 'know' another person. Immediate response of feeling is not in the head. It's the heart, the feeling that counts. Intellect and feeling come together later. Madness is the nursery, not the library. Babies suck and mothers love. Let therapists beware of too much thought and lettered words. (Madness and the understanding of it is more akin to contemplation than intellectual activity, as such.)

As a 'little baby' with eyes tight shut I lay together 'whole' on the floor. Anything more was 'too much'. Too much for my 'wholeness'. (It was better to be 'very baby' and whole than pretending and talking or walking and split.)

Truth wells up from within, and living, growing life brings changing forms and structures to suit the needs on one's being. (After psychotherapists the people I seemed most able to 'meet' in madness, or 'felt' nearest to, were contemplative nuns.)

The fear of coming out of a strait jacketed, stereotyped existence to a consciously unknown, long forgotten life, is very great. Not iron bars or padded cells, nor injections or tablets, but *people*, who love and accept, and know how and when to leave you alone, are what's needed. Given the soil, a plant will grow.

How to let go, lay down, break, be held, be beyond words, float, is a matter of trust. It's trusting God, through another person and no matter if so called 'mistakes' are made, God doesn't 'drop us'. Through every shattering, smashing explosion our life is still there, more whole than before. Our will submitted we are yet free, and every happening is a growing step. When in a mad state one is 'without words', in touch with the 'hidden underneath' of another person. Very sensitive and fragile you respond or withdraw as a snail with a shell. The other person may have no idea what he is hiding, but you pick it up— like a magnet.

Madness is purification. To go through it needs a guide, in the terms of our world today, a psychotherapist. It has to be gone *through*, not round, and only someone else can keep us there. "You're a slippery eel; the more you suffer, the more free you get." So Joe (Dr. Joseph Berke) would tell me.

When of ourselves we would give all, we must take half, and when of ourselves we would take half, we must give all.

Joe taught me a lot about this through food. If in the course of going through madness, the 'baby', regressed state is at times 'leapt above', the baby as it were sensing, seeing, as a 'wise old man', and what might be termed mystical experience is encountered, this should not be 'wallowed in'. It's a drink, a refreshment, a shady tree, a magnificent view, before again going down through the woods.

Going through madness is a matter of right *discipline* and *control*. So *feeling frees* and *serves* us, instead of *binding* and *killing*. A saint feels evil as fire on flesh. Many of us feel much that is not evil as if it was. Something is amiss, we are astray, off track.

The feeling of shame, guilt, that brings us to a dead stillness, makes all giving and receiving of love impossible, is a barrier to all creativity, causes us to feel as ghosts and bury our souls and bodies in 'living death,' and is a *very* great sickness.

When very twisted up so the feelings, the emotions are not true, the impulse of the being is to break down.

To resist, is 'screaming agony' or 'living death'.

To be helped, to make the break, to go *through* madness, *is* salvation.

Afterword:
A Medium With A Message: R. D. Laing

BY BENJAMIN NELSON

I.

IF EVERYONE in our "helter-skelter" days is now talking of Laing, it is because he holds out the promise of helping us build new Paradises out of our old Infernoes. Those divided souls among us to whom—and for whom—he addresses his resonant summons are newly resolved to carry forward long-postponed historic "projects". The wisdom we need is already ours; it was born when our frenzies were born.

Laing's teaching has now replaced the classical poet's maxim with a new one suited to our day. It is not the case that God first makes mad those whom He would destroy; He first makes mad—more exactly, allows dementing societies to make mad—the very ones whom He wishes to be prophets of new annunciations.

There is yet another element in the secret of Laing's appeal today. He strikes a responsive echo among all the "rolling stones" who have had their fill

of the void. Culture—like nature—abhors a vacuum.
It is the very nothingness of our day that Laing makes
into a cosmos. Who will dare say how sturdy a world
so constituted will prove to be?

II.

I do not locate the distinctive features of Laing and
his work where others do. I attach slight significance
to the fact that he is a psychiatrist or that he seems
to aspire to fuse the work of Sartre, Marx, Husserl,
Heidegger, Lukacs, Marcuse—and many—many—
others. What is critical about Laing is the fact that
for our times he is a *medium—a medium with a message*.

In Laing's case, *the politics of experience* is more
than a catch phrase. As such, the phrase is, of course,
not wholly original: before Laing there was already
talk about the "politics of consciousness," the "politics
of ectasy." What is important is that Laing senses that
the hopes of less-alienated communities are destroyed
by the unknowing or deliberate concealment, distortion or pollution of experience. Our available ways
of understanding our existence, our pasts, and our
futures are askew. His work is a warning that if we
are to be helped to understand our fortunes and to
make fruitful use of our options, psychology and
sociology will both need to reconstitute their notions
of existence, experience, and expression.

Politics has both its source and its warrant in experience and expression. If we are to increase the
hopes of creative politics, we have to expand the
chances for making new beginnings out of the chaos
of our divided selves. Politics has a great deal more

in it than GNP growth rates or the appeasment of welfare clients. A polity proves itself by the extent to which it promotes beneficial realizations, fulfillments and equities for its citizens and neighbors.

If Laing is so right on this central point, where does he falter? The answer would seem to be in his disdain of what I have elsewhere called the *"social* reality principle." Laing will not accept the idea that *if we are to do justice to the complex problems and predicaments of complex polycentric societies,* we must resist turning our backs on the lessons to be learned from the histories of the experience of post-Copernican, post-Newtonian, even post-Einsteinian political universes. The worlds in which we need to make our homes are scarcely likely to be helped by persevering in metapolitical myths and mystiques past the point of no return.

III.

As it happens, during the period in which I have been reading Laing, I have been browsing through various diaries and journals of traders, pilgrims, and missionaries who have wandered far from home in the hope of discovering a passage to some fabled land. The writings of Laing remind one of nothing so much as the efforts on the part of explorers in the 15th and 16th centuries once again to find "Cathay" and the "Way Thither." Each of the voyagers of our time offers a new route to the Cape of Good Hope.

Along with the other chapismatics of our day, Laing runs away from the problematical and predicamental aspects of human existence. To suppose that every influence exerted by every individual upon any other individual is lethal, is to be trapped in nightmare. Unhappily, as is true of the other pneumatics of our time, Laing's supposition is that of a one-person universe—a universe in which only the Transcendental Self has reality. Despite the continuous talk about the I and the Thou, the Other has only so much right as the Transcendental Self allows. When two or more persons are in the world, it proves that there is at least the prospect of conflict, competition, and dominance as well as fusion. Until Laing soaks himself more fully than he has so far done into the knotted realities of concerted effort, he will resist making due acknowledgment to the "*social* reality" principles. His rhetoric may for a moment have more appeal than that of other leaders of contemporary circles of "Great Awakeners," but he will not offer us a clue as to how we must fend to ford our way through the present chaos.

Laing and other contemporary spokesmen—Ginsberg, Norman O. Brown, Marcuse, Leary—are witnesses to deep fissures in our received structures of conscience and consciousness. If we are to understand the prophets of our time and the movements which speak in their names, we need to see them as spokesmen and symbols of a new "Great Awakening," one whose outcome cannot now be clearly foreseen. One thing, though, is sure. We need to see them against wider horizons than we are offered by the contemporary historians of politics, psychiatry, or even religion. Evidently so far as both the "West" and "East" are concerned, we are at a time of new conflicts and new fusions.

Laing puts me in mind of the itinerants who appear in the remarkable studies on the conflicts of faith and ways of life in the Hellenistic and Roman worlds, where all seeking to be reborn from the death of this life looked for "the widest illumination from converging lights." *The Politics of Experience* becomes especially interesting when read again along with Sir Samuel Dill's immortal studies of Roman society from the frantic time of Nero to the feckless days of Gregory of Tours; Pierre de Labriolle's wonderful chapters on the pagan polemics against Christianity; Sir James Frazier's pages in the *Golden Bough* on the deaths and rebirths of Tammuz and Dionysus.

February 1971

NOTES ON CONTRIBUTORS

MARY BARNES lived at Kingsley Hall for several years beginning in 1965, and worked with R. D. Laing and Joseph Berke especially during that time. Her paintings have been exhibited at several recent shows in London . . . JOSEPH BERKE is a practising analyst who wrote with Mary Barnes the volume *Mary Barnes: Two Accounts of a Journey Through Madness* (Harcourt, Brace & World, spring 1971) . . . ROBERT COLES is a therapist at Harvard University's Department of Mental Health Services. His most recent volume is the biography of Erik Erikson, a National Book Award nominee . . . LESLIE H. FARBER is chairman of the Association of Existential Psychiatry & Psychoanalysis and author of the volume *The Ways of the Will* . . . EDGAR Z. FRIEDENBERG is currently professor of Education at Dalhousie University in Canada and author of *The Vanishing Adolescent* and *Coming of Age in America* . . . JAN B. GORDON teaches English at SUNY, Buffalo and has published essays in many magazines . . . THEODORE LIDZ is former chairman of the Department of Psychiatry at Yale and author of several books including *The Family and Human Adaptation* and *The Person* . . . KENNETH LUX is a clinical psychologist at the Albany Medical Center . . . BENJAMIN NELSON is Professor of Sociology in The Graduate

Faculty at the New School for Social Research. He
has served as a General Editor for the Harper Torch-
book Series . . . SUZANNE OSTERWEIL is a free-
lance artist who lives in New York City. Her drawings
and woodcuts appear regularly in SALMAGUNDI
. . . MORTON SCHATZMAN is a young psychotherapist who has worked at Kingsley Hall . . .
PETER SEDGWICK worked for ten years as a psychologist in Liverpool, at Rivermead Hospital, Oxford,
and at Grendon Psychiatric Prison. He is on leave at
present from the Department of Politics, York, England, teaching Sociology at Queens College in New
York. He has translated and edited two major works
by Victor Serge, and published articles on Marcuse,
Deutscher, Orwell, and others. The essay he wrote for
this issue is a chapter in a book on Laing he is writing
which will be published in England by Pluto Press
. . . MIRIAM SIEGLER, HUMPHRY OSMOND,
and HARRIET MANN work at the Bureau of Research in Neurology and Psychiatry, New Jersey Neuro-
Psychiatric Institute, Princeton, New Jersey. Dr.
Osmond is Director of the Institute.